Values in Education

Social Capital Formation in Asia and the Pacific

Values in Education

Social Capital Formation in Asia and the Pacific

Edited by John D. Montgomery

Contributors:

Kai-ming Cheng

William K. Cummings

Nathan Glazer

Ruth Hayhoe

John M. Heffron

Alex Inkeles

Wing-On Lee

John D. Montgomery

Library of Congress Cataloging-in-Publication Data

Values in education: social capital formation in Asia and the Pacific
/ edited by John D. Montgomery : contributors, Kai-ming Cheng . . .
[et. al.].
    p.   cm.
Papers presented at a conference in Hong Kong, January 1997.
"Soka University of America, Pacific Basin Research Center."
Includes bibliographical references and index.
ISBN 1-884186-07-6 (hardcover : alk. paper)
1. Education—Social aspects—Asia—Congresses. 2. Education—
Social aspects—Pacific Area—Congresses. 3. Values—Asia—
Congresses. 4. Values—Pacific Area—Congresses. 5. Social
values—Asia—Congresses. 6. Social values—Pacific Area—
Congresses. I. Montgomery, John Dickey, 1920– . II. Cheng,
Kai-ming. III. Pacific Basin Research Center.
LC191.8A78V35   1997
306.43′2′095—dc21   97-41370
                                                                            CIP

Hollis Publishing Company, 95 Runnells Bridge Road, Hollis, NH 03049

Printed in the United States of America

♾The paper used in the book complies with the Permanent Paper Standard issued by the
National Information Standards Organization (Z39.48-1984).

10 9 8 7 6 5 4 3 2 1

In celebration of

Tsunesaburo Makiguchi (1871–1944)

Activist, philosopher, and martyr of
Values in Education

PREFACE

These papers mark the first phase of a five-year project on social capital formation, initiated by the Pacific Basin Research Center of Soka University of America at a conference in Hong Kong in January, 1997. For purposes of this research, we have defined "social capital" to include communal resources generated by individuals and groups engaged in some form of collaboration; it is the cumulative capacity of social groups to cooperate and work together for a common good.

The most immediate and obvious source of social capital is the formal and informal education that links generations and peoples. This definition permits us to undertake three analytical tasks: (1) to conduct empirical examinations of how values influence and respond to education; (2) to observe how institutions affect values, both in the formal and informal arenas; and (3) to consider how societies "invest" in order to develop that capacity and to evaluate how they use and consume it. Essays in this book address the first two tasks as they relate to education. The third task is a project for the future.

Social capital creates or reinforces the mutual trust that binds people together, whether by exchanging information or by generating and respecting social norms that enable participation in collective decisions and actions. It is found not only in humanity's political environment and its educational systems, but also in social groups such as industrial organizations, peace movements, organized ethnic accommodations, nongovernmental welfare activities, ecumenical movements, and the arts as well as in the leisure and entertainment activities that bring people together.

The Hong Kong papers incorporated in this book are suggestive of more extensive research to come. The first chapter, by Heffron, summarizes and appraises the historical antecedents of some current philosophical interpretations of values relating to education and development. Montgomery's chapter follows, with its exploration of Asian values and its query as to whether, and how, they are "different" in such fundamental issues as the practice of human rights and their influence on education policies. In the next chapter, Glazer presents comparative cultural and historical evidence identifying core values in the Pacific Rim as potential elements that favor economic growth and political democracy. Inkeles follows, offering some empirical measurement of values arising in the context of social changes that attend modernization. Hayhoe takes the analysis one step further, documenting some of the processes by which formal and non-formal education actually communicates values. Next Lee tackles the difficult problem of identifying, and even measuring, the impact of changing values on individuals and society. Cummings shows how values have infused the Japanese educational system and its diffusion throughout East Asia. The concluding chapter by Cheng invites us to consider the extent to which values can be "engineered."

The Pacific Basin Research Center was created in 1991 by the newly established Soka University of America, located near Los Angeles, California. The university began its graduate program in 1994, specializing in linguistics and English as a second language. Soka's undergraduate program will open in 2001. The PBRC produced its first book, *Great Policies: Strategic Innovations in Asia and the Pacific Basin,* in 1995. Another volume, *Human Rights: Positive Policies in Asia and the Pacific,* is to appear in 1998. This book defines plans for a third wave of research on social capital formation in Asia and the Pacific.

The Pacific Basin Research Center acknowledges gratefully the collaboration of the Comparative Education Research Centre of the University of Hong Kong in mounting the original conference; of Michael Loo who contributed his editorial expertise; and of Lynn Akin whose skill at the computer console translated these papers into their present form.

In dedicating this volume to the memory of Tsunesaburo Makiguchi (1871–1944), the Center also acknowledges the generous support of Soka University of America and its founder, Daisaku Ikeda. Makiguchi coined the term "soka" in 1930 to convey the importance of humane values and their educational role in the school, home, and surrounding community. He died at the hands of the Japanese military government in 1944, a martyr to these convictions.

John D. Montgomery
Editor

Soka University of America

Soka University of America is an independent, co-educational institution located in Calabasas, California, with another campus under development in Aliso Viejo, a community adjacent to the seaside communities of Orange County, California. Current University programs include a master's degree in second- and foreign-language education; English-language classes for Japanese students; and the Pacific Basin Research Center. The Aliso Viejo campus, scheduled to open in the fall of the year 2001, will combine Asia-Pacific and Western perspectives in a four-year liberal arts program leading to the baccalaureate degree. "Soka" is a Japanese expression meaning to create value.

The emblem of Soka University of America portrays the nib of a pen flanked by the wings of a ho-o, a legendary bird of China and Japan. The pen represents wisdom and the wings symbolize the ability to put knowledge and wisdom into the service of humanity.

The Pacific Basin Research Center, Soka University of America

The Pacific Basin Research Center (PBRC) was inaugurated in 1991 and awards grants and fellowships to researchers studying public policy interactions in the Pacific Rim. The research has concentrated on international security, economic and social development, educational and cultural activities, environmental protection and human rights issues. Upon completion of a three-year cycle of studies of human rights, PBRC will publish a volume of essays representing the work of its postdoctoral fellows. The Hong Kong workshop is the foundation stone for a new five-year project on social capital formation in Asia and the Pacific Basin. The PBRC is directed by John D. Montgomery, Ford Foundation Professor of International Studies, Emeritus, Harvard University.

The Pacific Basin Research Center's logo contains two ideographs for "so" and "ka," meaning to create value. Situated over the Pacific Ocean, the graphic suggests a confluence of Asian and American cultures.

Values in Education *was developed under the sponsorship of the Pacific Basin Research Center, Soka University of America.*

John M. Heffron is University Professor of History and Director of Educational Research Programs, Pacific Basin Research Center, at Soka University of America. He is the author of "Toward a Cybernetic Pedagogy: The Cognitive Revolution in the Classroom, 1948–Present," *Educational Theory*, Fall 1995, and "Elitism and Democracy: The Lincoln School of Teachers College" in Susan F. Semel, ed., *Schools of Tomorrow, Schools of Today: What Happened to Progressive Education?* (Peter Lang, forthcoming).

1. DEFINING VALUES

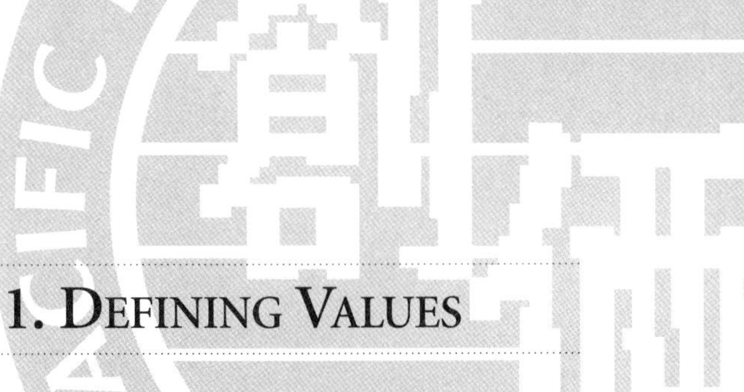

John M. Heffron

"My thesis is, then: we can, in principle, have a descriptive, naturalistic science of human values: that the age-old mutually exclusive contrast between 'what is' and 'what ought to be' is in part a false one; that we can study the highest values or goals of human beings as we study the values of ants or horses or oak trees or, for that matter, of Martians."
—Abraham Maslow

There is a central paradox in the definition of values, one with important implications for the study of the genesis, evolution, and implementation of these important human artifacts. The paradox is a commonsense one. It seems only obvious that the meaning people attach to their actions should be reflected in the values they espouse. One common technique for assessing behavior is simply to ask a random sample of publics what they believe about a particular object, such as "the health care system in the United States," or the statement "honesty is the best policy," or the principle of "one man, one vote." It is almost axiomatic in conducting such a survey that a limited population contains fewer extraneous sources of variation which can affect the object under study than a broad population affords. The leap from special universe to general is always a risky one, but the risks can be reduced considerably through the use of small sample populations and narrowly defined indicators. Yet when we ask ourselves, as we must, about the validity or generality of those findings—our measure of the degree to which a particular response obtains for all the members of our population—we enter a realm, in the words of Heinrich Rickert, "beyond subject and object," where the validity of the values in question holds independent of people(s) and structures (Oakes 1988: 98; Rickert 1910–11). In spite of their ethereal quality, such values are said to be in a limited sense universal and transcendent.

The problem of defining values and that of measuring them are intimately connected, if in fact the real problem for understanding values in the broader context is to determine their validity. "A right definition," it has been said, "gives a right choice of indices," and nothing could be truer than for the study of values, those indeterminate things that, in John Dewey's words, are "as unstable as the forms of clouds" (Dewey 1958: 396) and that when linked to quantifiable attitudes, preferences, or beliefs remove us paradoxically to a world beyond "subject and object." These dangers of ascription—the tendency to assign meaning to abstract categories which may not have anything to do with the way people actually behave or that submerge troublesome individual variations in larger and larger sample groups—make both the definition and study of values an extremely sensitive one. How much more so when instead of following from it the choice of indices and level of analysis drives the definitional process, as the following examples illustrate.

In one well-known study, the personality traits associated with modernity are found to be uniform across a representative sample of six developing countries. These traits include an openness to new experience, belief in the individual as the locus of authority, engagement in civic affairs, respect for education and achievement, and faith in science and technological progress. Such "syndromes" point to "the actual psychic unity of mankind in a structural sense and the potential psychic unity of mankind in the factual sense" (Inkeles and Sasaki 1996: 573). Modernity (or the researchers' definition of modernity) becomes a self-fulfilling prophecy when syndromes that show up in survey materials *loaded toward those syndromes* point to the actual and potential unity of humankind around values associated with modernity.

Another study identifies seven basic "value types" generalized at the cultural rather than the individual level of analysis, where one may perceive "a near-universal set of psychological dynamics" but fail to discover the shared norms that "prescribe" those dynamics. Those norms reside in the organizational structure and value preferences of societal institutions. "They are expressed in the goals of these institutions and in their modes of operation," not in the behavior of individual agents, aggregate or otherwise (Schwartz and Ros 1995: 93). The meaning and significance people derive from these institutions is an expression of their power to create and uphold certain defining values. For the authors of this one study those values included conservatism, intellectual autonomy, affective autonomy, hierarchy, egalitarianism, harmony, and mastery—"contrasting dichotomies," in Ferdinand Tonnie's trenchant phrase, by which complex societies order their value priorities. Whereas Inkeles and Sasaki would universalize individual values at the psychic level, Schwartz and Ros err on the cultural side, universalizing institutional norms while relegating their pschodynamics to a subordinate, almost dependent, status.

The search for larger and larger agglomerations of these and other core institutional values has reached something of a peak in globalization studies. The Commission on Global Governance, an independent group of 28 world leaders, began its work of forging a transnational "good neighbor" policy by identifying a set of putative core values which unite people of every culture and creed. The new global community was in the first place a "universal moral community" governed by a respect for life, liberty, justice and equality, mutual respect, caring, and integrity. These values descended from even more general principles enshrined in the United Nations Charter and calling for recognition of "the inherent dignity and equal and inalienable rights of all members of the human family (Commission on Global Governance 1995: 49). What it takes to be a global citizen, as well as what it takes to be a modern one, is part of this larger search for more inclusive conceptualizations and for a more comprehensive typology of human values that has been one of the preoccupation's of comparative sociology for the past 30 years. This chapter attempts to unravel this larger history, locating its origins in the debate over positivism and its subsequent reincarnation, in theories of social embeddedness and institutionalism, in the scientific study of values, and in qualitative educational research, especially in developing countries.

To restate our original paradox (the absence of particulars in universal statements of value designed to explain them) as a question: How do we get to measures of validity from the values of people and things that (theoretically anyway) don't exist? To pose it as a research problem: For any finite number of cultural and institutional values, tests of validity, insofar as they can demonstrate universal acceptance, become post hoc explanations of the very phenomena they presume to test for, understand,

and validate. Axiomatic claims for the dominance of certain values deny the irreducibility of universal values to axiomatic claims of any kind—a logical presupposition of all values analysis. On the other hand, without the search for such claims, it seems we must abandon tests of validity altogether—an equally unacceptable alternative, since it would mean that values exist only in the particular, never as a general case of the structural beliefs and metaphors of whole societies, cultures, and institutions.

And yet it is not enough to simply establish forward and backward linkages between social and economic institutions and certain axiomatic values, when the values and institutions in question share so little, if any, prior legitimacy. On a more pragmatic level, it might be better to begin by asking, as William James did, what difference it makes that we hold one set of values and beliefs instead of another. "If no practical difference whatever can be traced, then the alternatives mean practically the same thing, and all dispute is idle" (James 1928: 45) Any real choice, James was saying, must acknowledge the existence of rival claimants for selection. There is no selection without rejection, and this applies equally to our interests and biases. According to rational choice theory, a "rational" human being cannot prefer two equal and opposite outcomes. He cannot prefer to be both shorter and longer, fatter and skinnier, wealthier and poorer. Much less does he make a rational decision when the choice is between states of the world that "mean practically the same thing."

Choices, when they force themselves upon us, are always complete in the sense that they represent an absolute distinction between two equally plausible alternatives. Otherwise, they are not choices. And if they are not choices, according to this view, they are value-neutral. They may reflect transient tastes and preferences (perhaps even a preference for inaction), but they will not reflect enduring and self-sufficient values. "From any environment," writes the dean of choice theory, Kenneth J. Arrow, "there will be a given choice alternative, and in the absence of a deadlock no place for the historically given alternative to be chosen by default" (Arrow 1967: 10). In this sense, our choices and the values they uphold are self-reinforcing, at least for so long as they stand unopposed by new and different choices. Even when new values supersede older ones they never come to lie evenly on those below, but show a familiar pattern of twists and outcroppings in their new topography. Values in any given society remain stable and they change in just such indirect and irregular proportions, falling more often along a continuum of apposite effects than into polar and autonomous categories (Materialist/Postmaterialist, Modern/Traditional, Gemeinschaft/Gesellschaft, Collectivist/ Individualist, etc.). The message to researchers is that they need to pay as much attention to the information people exclude or only partially accept as to what they include when they make complex moral choices (Sen 1984).

Value preferences are not simple rational choices between competing, equally plausible, alternatives. They also reflect embedded social considerations, structural and institutional restraints and opportunities (Ramsay 1996). On this account, decision making is a dynamic process involving extensive public dialogue, negotiation, and debate. Values are neither "given" preferences (as in traditional social choice theory) nor the maximizing, ego-centered behavior of *Homo economicus* (as in traditional public choice theory) (Hirschman 1977; Sen 1987, 1995; Anderson 1993). As artifacts of culture, as the social facts of existence, they need to be seen as part of a process of "becoming and interacting, not the static one of being and determining" (Billig 1994: 673). According to the philosopher John Dewey, individual and social values were for this very reason "fugitive and precarious." He often spoke of the "undeniable insecurity," the incessant "appearance and disappearance" of values in actual experience. When we begin to understand their diverse and contradictory qualities, values nevertheless cease to be a simple datum of experience. They become problems. As problems, wrote Dewey, they imply "intelligent inquiry into the conditions and consequences of a value-object." (Dewey 1958: 396, 398–99; Westbrook 1991).

Policymakers are attracted to research on values (even when it fails to meet strict empirical standards) for a number of reasons. Values, like all conceptual schemes, are ways of organizing the world, framing it, reducing it to manageable proportions and understanding it. They provide a picture of the world that is economical and logical, comprehensive, and psychologically satisfying. When a conceptual scheme finally leads to results that are incompatible with observation, when, for example, "The Mandate From Heaven," once a unique Chinese prescription for democratic control, is no longer able to prevent ineffectual public officials from remaining in power, belief must be surrendered and a new theory adopted. After this the process begins again. But these occasions are rare, and how many people are able to adopt new views which on examination are *absolutely* incompatible with the old? Belief systems become that much harder to change when they become entangled in some larger fabric of thought, when physical theories of the universe get entangled, for example, in local religious and cultural systems. Overthrowing the former then means overthrowing the entire social, religious, and political system; and how many people, no matter how discrepant their observations, are willing to do that? To upset everything? Researchers who study human development appreciate perhaps more than anyone else how slowly, invisibly, and with what profoundly disruptive effects values change, especially when those values represent the core assumptions and defining metaphors of an entire society (Block 1981; Costa and McCrae 1980). Indeed it often takes an entire generation to die out before fundamental value changes can occur, an unlikely event, however, since this would mean in effect abolishing education and most other forms of social reproduction (Inglehart 1981).

For purposes of discussion, let me propose three separate but related lines of inquiry concerning values and their functioning in formal and informal education. These will be large framing questions that try to get us out of the "clinical-idiosyncratic mode of analysis"—the tendency to focus on incommensurable personal and cultural differences—and to substitute "an explicit, standardized analytic scheme," one that tries to steer clear of the post hoc fallacy while contributing to the discussion some discrete and identifiable variables for empirical research (Inkeles 1997: 44). For each of our research questions we will want to determine: (1) the history and background of the problem; (2) the different pathways to resolution, focusing on the contributions of economics and political sociology; (3) the potential influence on the selection and analysis of data; and (4) the lessons for a comprehensive, comparative methodology.

THE PROBLEM OF BELIEF: ARE VALUES EMPTY OF PROPOSITIONAL CONTENT?

The question of the objective existence of values is one of the oldest unresolved debates in the history of the social sciences. In the present century it began as a debate against logical positivism, pitting John Dewey against A. J. Ayer in the late 1930s and Thomas Kuhn against Karl Popper in the 1960s and early 1970s (Dewey 1939; Ayer 1936; Kuhn 1962; Popper 1957, 1959, 1963; Lakatos and Musgrave 1970). While it is not possible here to revisit these debates in their entirety, the theoretical issues they raise are important for a proper understanding of what it means to study values, and to try to do so empirically with all the latest quantitative as well as qualitative research methods at our command.

The question we want to ask here is not whether values can be measured. We can measure anything we define well enough, anything we can establish a sample population and indicators for; and certainly as much has been said and done before for values. What we need to establish is that value expressions (e.g., "My family is the most important thing in my life"; or, from the Japanese "Peace Constitution," "All people shall have the right to receive an equal education correspondent to their ability") have a propositional content. Are they statements *in and of themselves* of empirical fact, rather than simply expressions of emotion? Are they verifiable in the same way that a chair or a table or the fact that I am breathing is verifiable? In Popperian terms, are they falsifiable? Can we submit them to a "crucial experiment" designed to falsify them, predicating our confidence in their validity on whether they pass our test?

Of course, for Popper as well as for Kuhn, most beliefs end up failing this test, so that what enters the domain of normal science is very restrictive, an elite club of our most impregnable theories. But how impregnable are human values—those subjective entities that even an idealist like Dewey had to admit were as shifting as "the forms of clouds"? Even when the values of a society comprise all-powerful conceptual schemes, social paradigms as implacable as any scientific paradigm, they are not nearly as inelastic as their more rational counterparts. They are often able to tolerate higher levels of cognitive dissonance than the normal scientific tradition, which tends to repress awkward anomalies. The elasticity of our social values paradoxically makes them resistant to change, even as they become more inclusive in the process.

Recent changes in the Chinese value system are a good case in point. The rise of nationalistic antitraditionalism from the Cultural Revolution to the present has entailed a denaturing of traditional Confucian values with their emphasis on the ethical-religious dimensions of self and community. The new nationalism has produced a "flat cultureless culture" of frankly commercial, expansionist, and utilitarian values (Cohen 1991: 130). At the same time, to the ongoing frustration of Chinese officials, the typical identifiers of "being Chinese" continue to remain the country's traditional social and religious practices, mediated but not entirely corrupted by the introduction of Western-style goods and services. Some writers even detect the emergence of a "Third Epoch of Confucian

Humanism," rising on the crest, not the ashes, of an invigorated, culture-free market socialism (Tu 1991). China is not alone in this commensurability of divergences. The cultures of Korea, Taiwan, Japan, Singapore, and Hong Kong have exhibited similar patterns of value change and stability that make them, from a strictly empirical point of view, harder not easier to study. The statement from 1970 that "as science grows, the power of empirical evidence diminishes" remains a warning to social scientists who, lured by the convergence of physical theory and probabilistic statistics, imagine themselves on the verge of a new science of society, one in which human actions can be explained and predicted in just the same way as natural events (Lakatos and Musgrave 1970: 105).

There is another, more extreme, position on this subject; it comes out of the same rationalist tradition social scientists have been so anxious to embrace. A. J. Ayer and Karl Popper are probably its two most representative spokesmen. Statements of ethical value, Ayer argued, are not in any sense statements of empirical fact, but rather simply "expressions and excitants of feeling." Because they do not involve "any assertions," and hence cannot be judged scientifically to be true or false, they are "pseudo-concepts and therefore unanalyzable" (Ayer 1946: 102–112). In his widely read and discussed anti-Marxist volumes *The Poverty of Historicism* (1957) and *The Open Society and Its Enemies* (1945), Popper railed against "subjectivist" interpretations of physics, "relativism" in any form, the "myth of the framework," or any attempt to "sociologize" knowledge. In these and subsequent works Popper set out to establish a demarcation criterion between "scientific" and "metaphysical" propositions. The latter were a species of "methodological psychologism," the doctrine that all social problems could be reduced to problems of psychology, to the mental states and affects of the "human factor." For Popper and other so-called objectivists, the human factor is "*the* ultimately uncertain and wayward element in social life and in all social institutions." Attempts to better understand and bring it under control, using scientific methods, were not only doomed to failure but also politically "suicidal" (Popper 1961: 158–159).

Around the same time, another philosopher of science, basing his conclusions on a careful study of the major scientific revolutions of the past from Copernicus to the discovery of the atom, enshrined the human factor and social values in general at the heart of the scientific enterprise. Since its publication in 1962, Thomas Kuhn's *The Structure of Scientific Revolutions* has become a classic, a routine point of reference for discussion and debate throughout our culture generally. His major thesis—that knowledge is a collective creation, founded not only upon autonomous individual reason, but upon the evaluations we make together in social situations—gave a patina of scientific respectability once again to custom and precedent in human affairs, including the conduct of science. Even scientific inferences must be seen as instances of customary behavior, not merely as the isolated discoveries of a lone genius. Kuhn's work, although not perhaps as far off from Popper's as many have supposed, has had a liberating effect on the social sciences. It laid bare the defects of rationalism in an idiom agreeable to those who for the most part accepted it. Without denying a role to either verifiability or falsifiability, and without relaxing the entrance requirements of normal science, Kuhn established a central place for values in a world of hard facts and numbers. He gave researchers the confidence that values are propositionally valid, that they may be captured in axiomatic form and isolated from pseudovalues (pleasures, interests, compulsions, and benefits added), and that they are thus comparable.

The definition of values that began to appear in the sociological literature after 1962 fairly bristled with the new justificationist rhetoric. Values were defined as plans, blueprints, generalized ends that guided behavior toward uniformity in what were otherwise diverse, often highly dissimilar situations (as in the comparison between advanced, developing, and undeveloped economies). Empirical studies of values were made to answer to familiar scientific criteria of repeatability, articulation, specification, and control (Fallding 1965; Hook 1967; Williams 1971). Cross-national survey instruments and computer-modeling programs that could take into account period, cohort, and life-cycle effects made the study of culture, once the exclusive preserve of anthropologists, a more open and democratic affair in which scores of social scientists in all the disciplines were now free to participate. The definition of culture itself changed from the theoretical diffusiveness of Clyde Kluckhohn's generation and the semiotic interpretivism of Clifford Geertz to a much different understanding of culture as a dynamic system of "external adaptation and internal integration" in response to fundamental economic, social, and political changes (Kluckhohn 1959; Geertz 1973; Barnes 1986; Inglehart 1990).

Structure came to matter in a more specific, functional sense as researchers, following the theoretical work of Merton and Parsons, began to study actualized values within exogenous systems, using a standard taxonomy of values rather than relying, as in the past, on the subjective testimony of local informants (Merton 1968; Parsons 1949). Endogenous values became important only as they affected the system's capacity to respond to exogenous influences. Otherwise they were noncontroversial, a species of what Parsons called "affective neutrality." The elaboration of values as functional categories (Parsons' pattern variables: affectivity vs. affective neutrality; diffuseness vs. specificity; particularism vs. universalism; ascription vs. achievement; collectivity vs. self) permitted researchers to study larger, wholesale shifts in values, showing, for example, how education contributes to the transition of individuals from less developed pattern variables (such as particularism and ascription) to more modern ones (such as universalism and an achievement orientation) (McClelland 1961; Inkeles and Smith 1974; Fagerlind and Saha 1983; Inglehart 1990).

There is no simple yes or no answer to the question of whether values are "empty of propositional content"—not a felicitous phrase but one that captures nicely the extremism surrounding the question. If we cannot be too quick to ignore the subjective basis of values in the human personality, we also cannot be too quick to label all models that are empirically grounded as incapable of telling us anything. What would a research design look like that tried to move beyond the distinction, pervasive in the social sciences, between conceptual and empirical reality? That tried to avoid "ideal types," "before-and-after" models, and time-series analyses that Max Weber worried would roll out "with the necessity of a law"? Is there a third level between objective and subjective indicators, one that does a better job of making sense of the mutual interdependence of ideal and real-world values?

THE PROBLEM OF STRUCTURE: DO VALUES CONFORM TO A STANDARD TAXONOMY?

The definition of values as "preferences," as choices between equally plausible alternatives, suggests that it is possible to rank-order them from the least to the most desired. Economists call this ranking after Bentham "utility," where the utility assigned to a preferable situation is greater than the utility assigned to a less preferable one. Economists tend to pay attention, however, to choices among quantifiable options (for example, the relative quantities of food and shelter sought, the number of hours worked per week, or the votes distributed among specific propositions) while holding constant the other factors that affect behavior (psychological attitudes, peer group pressures, personal experiences and general cultural conditions). This *ceteris paribus* assumption is involved in all economic analyses of utility-maximizing choices, where utility refers to an overall feeling of satisfaction or welfare. Recently some economists have begun to question this assumption, among them Amartya Sen and Elizabeth Anderson, suggesting that not all utility or rational choice is a function simply of maximizing one's economic self-interest. As Anderson writes: "When rational choice is represented in terms of the maximization of value or preference satisfaction, and when intrinsic value and rational preferences are defined independent of expressive norms and contexts, we are tempted to think that the optimizing behavior of consumers in the marketplace sets the standards of rationality for all social life" (Anderson 1993: 218). An individual may make a perfectly rational choice to sacrifice some of his or her welfare for the sake of another or to seek certain nonmarket goods and aspirations, like trust and friendship, for example. Sen argues that when individual preferences take into account altruistic social considerations they reflect "values" in general and not simply "preferences." Moreover, the results of social interaction often produce unintended value formations for which it may be difficult to find a simple economic measure.

This is particularly true of education, which is not simply a teaching and learning activity but plays a social function as well. In so-called Third World countries, for example, educational outreach to child-age mothers has led to a value formation that, over and above reducing family size, puts a premium today on basic education for women, democracy, and free public information (Sen 1995: 17). These and other externalities may be expected when policies directed at people's well-being produce, sometimes unexpectedly, new modes of individual freedom and agency.

Still, the need for some classificatory scheme of values, however potentially reductionist, is difficult to ignore. If the social sciences have taught us anything over the last century, it is that we live in stratified societies, stratified by class, race, ethnicity, gender, occupation, family status, religion, and education. As a matter of pure economy, relatively few value dimensions constitute the organizing principles for hundreds of specific beliefs and attitudes. The former may be termed the core values of a society; the latter its subordinate or instrumental values. The problem for an empirical classification of values is to identify those penultimate generalities that people judge to be intrinsically satisfying and that anchor all the other *desiderata* that affect their lives. Harold Fallding writes:

> The ordering of ends into a hierarchy means that a person will
> desire not only one thing, but everything he believes its attainment
> depends upon. Yet it would still be realistic to say that he values only
> one thing, if his other desires include only the things he believes are
> necessary for it and are made instrumental to the autonomous end.
> There is a world of divergence between two persons who desire the
> same things, if an end which is instrumental to one is self-sufficient
> to another. . . .Thus values are organizing ends, organizing precisely
> because many other satisfactions and actions are subordinate to
> them (Fallding 1965: 225).

A rank-ordering of these organizing ends and of the instrumental satisfactions leading up to them is one way of beginning to come to terms
with the enormous range and complexity of human values.

Let me offer as a point of discussion three separate but related rank-
ordering models, one from the policy sciences, one from sociology, and one
from anthropology. Certainly one of the most durable and well-traveled is
the Lasswell Value Dictionary (LVD), consisting of the following eight
terms: Power, Enlightenment, Wealth, Well-Being, Skill, Affection,
Respect, and Rectitude. This list has been employed to study political
behavior, development performance, jurisprudence, educational policy,
and most recently "positive" human rights (Namenwirth and Lasswell
1970; Lasswell, Lerner, and Montgomery 1976; Lasswell and McDougal
1992; Cummings 1996a). This basic scheme is defined in chapter 2.
As applied to education, these values would suggest the following normative principles:

1. *Power.*   Education should increase the political capacity of individual citizens to effect change not only in their own lives but in the lives of
others. Power is inherently unequal. "The division of society into elites and
masses is universal," according to Lasswell, and even in a democracy, "a few
exercise a relatively great weight of power, and the many exercise comparatively little" (Lasswell and Kaplan 1950: 219). Education in itself does not
necessarily reduce uneven relations of power.

2. *Enlightenment.*   Education should create the desire and capacity
for further learning. It should aid the student in the process of creating
value and in pursuing "the good." Teacher and student work together for
the full development of the individual's inherent potential.

3. *Wealth.*   Education should raise capital-generating and income-earning potential through basic education, commercial science courses, job training, career counseling, and professional development.

4. *Well-Being.*   Education should improve the health prospects of all people by introducing them to the fundamentals of health and hygiene, including the physical, emotional, and psychological sources of wellness.

5. *Skill.*   Education should improve the quality of the work force through job training and apprenticeship programs, vocational education, and basic math and science education.

6. *Affection.*   Education should reaffirm family and community values through civics courses, community service requirements, and regular parent-teacher conferences. Affection implies loyalty and commitment. "You can love an individual," wrote Josiah Royce, the author of the best philosophical defense of loyalty in this century, "but you can be loyal only to a tie that binds you and others into some sort of unity, and loyal to individuals only through the tie" (McDermott 1969: 862).

7. *Respect.*   Education should raise the level of tolerance of diversity through multicultural learning and teaching, mainstreaming and "inclusion," and school desegregation policy.

8. *Rectitude.*   Education should provide a moral standard of right and wrong either through religious instruction or through more cognitive approaches such as values clarification (Kohlberg 1975).

Of course, the magnitude and direction of these values may vary considerably from one region, one country, one educational system, even one school and classroom to the next. Equilibrating effects have to be distinguished from disequilibrating ones as the effort to maximize one or all these values may lead to either conflict or consensus. Achieving, for example, as much power as possible may run directly counter to such other values as affection, respect, and rectitude. Maximizing these latter values may, on the other hand, inhibit the value of power or wealth. While the Lasswellian values describe a fairly consistent and acceptable set of goods, they cannot all be maximized, at least not without jeopardizing what is characteristic and discrete about each of them. For all social choices there are always tradeoffs. The important question is what direction these tradeoffs take. For some individuals or for some policies they may involve a complete reordering of preferences or directions; for others only a partial and temporary reordering; and for still others no real reordering at all, but merely changes of "face" value. A more neutral, "value-free" rendering of these concepts would have to treat them as more or less discrete independent variables—a difficult thing to do considering how loaded these terms are in the first place.

There is one other matter left unresolved by LVD, at least as it applies to education. It is not at all clear what role this schema can be expected to play in informal education, where the institutional supports for their implementation are often weak or missing. Recent studies of the social capital invested in civic associations and groups, including random organizations such as the street, the neighborhood café, and the beauty shop, suggest that the survival of nonformal institutions is a key to the vibrancy not only of democratic institutions but of their ability to sustain and purchase the "preferred outcomes" necessary for their survival (Putnam 1993; McGinn 1996; Oldenburg 1989; Lasch 1995). In the absence of vibrant, informal civic associations for the education of the young, where they can learn the civic arts of sociability, conviviality, and disciplined political conversation, people lose their ability to distinguish between credible social commitments and the idiosyncratic personal preferences, tastes, and "lifestyle questions" that are the fashion of the day.

Figure 1-1 depicts Abraham Maslow's famous hierarchy of needs, a useful complement to the Lasswellian inventory for several reasons. It satisfies certain basic requirements for differentiating regnant from subordinate values; it attempts to rank-order the former; and it points to a productive new line of inquiry, the emergence of a postmaterialist value system and its implications for the quality of modern life. Ronald Inglehart and Alex Inkeles have put this concept, first introduced in the 1960s by the futurist Alvin Toffler, to the empirical test in *Culture Shift in Advanced Industrial Society* (1990) and *National Character* (1997). By *postmaterialist,* Toffler means a society in which most material needs of the people have been satisfied (via technology). And as Maslow points out (in a theory now well accepted by social scientists as well as by sales managers), when an individual is satisfied in his (material) needs for physical and psychological security, he then yearns for greater acceptance, followed by more esteem, and then self-actualization. Whether this final stage of development is a spiritual one or only the highest form of individual self-aggrandizement begs the question. Postmaterialists are not just idealistic products of affluence; they know they have a responsibility for meeting their own physiological and security needs through employment but they also expect that employment to provide "a purpose and meaning

Figure 1-1. Maslow's hierarchy of needs.

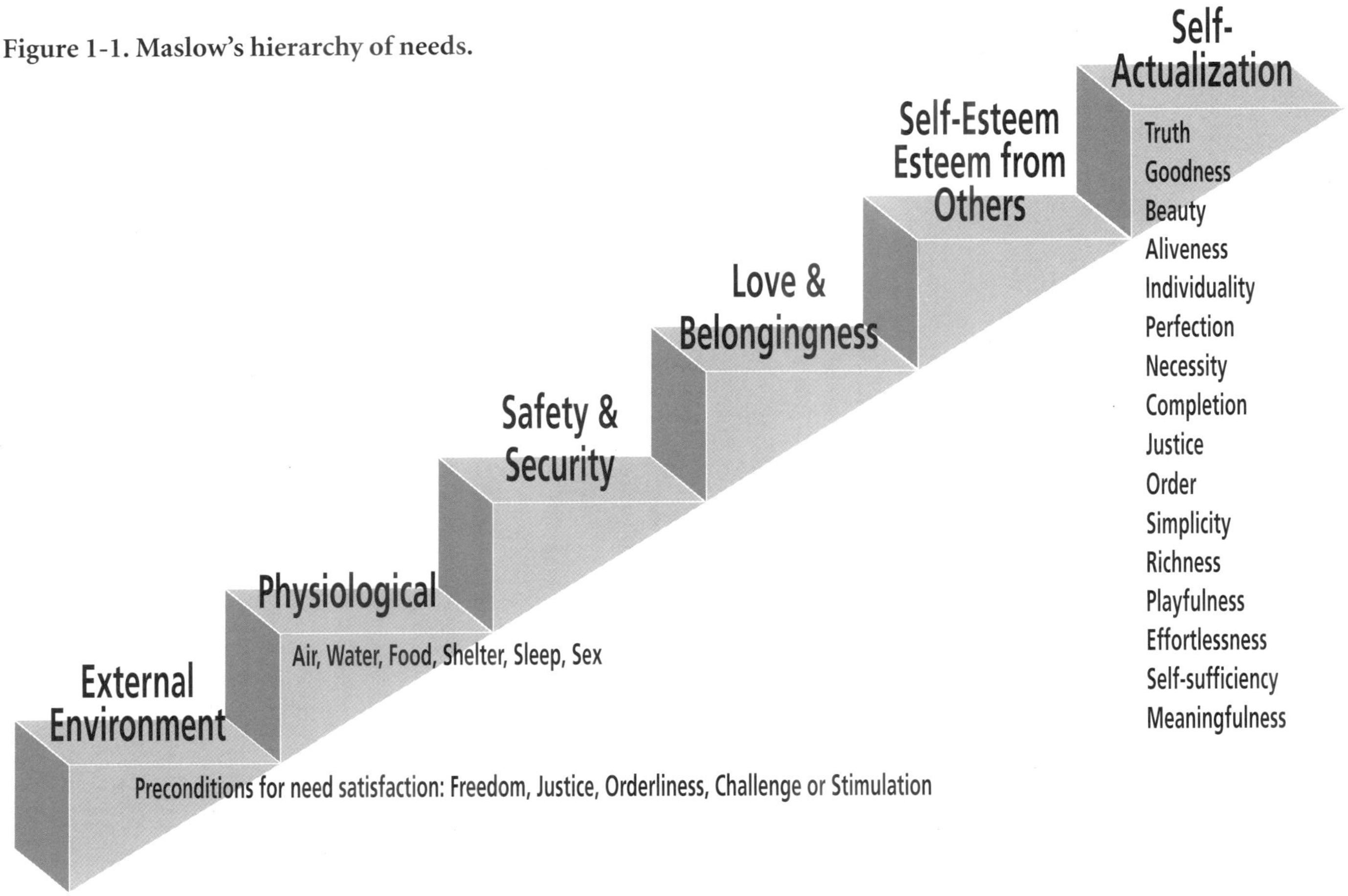

to life" and/or enable them to "build a better society" (Inglehart 1981).

For the sociologists, Helen and Robert S. Lynd, whose study of the values of a small boom town made headlines across the United States when it came out in 1929, the anthropological approach seemed a good compromise between traditional religious ideals and the new scientific sociology. Like religion, it considered values and beliefs to be crucial, but like scientific sociology it regarded no single value system as normative. Like the debate over postmaterialism, the Lynds' study of consumer values produced a number of unexpected, almost counterintuitive results. Because it seemed to show that the people of Muncie, Indiana, took genuine satisfaction in their new role as consumers (of popular magazines, radio, movies, health and wellness), the study in effect stood Maslow's hierarchy of needs on its head (Lynd 1929). What were once luxuries (balloon tires, fingernail polish, a second bathroom) became necessities in a consumer culture that could deliver new satisfactions with a speed and efficiency that made the nonmarket values of the past (justice, community, loyalty, fidelity) seem quaint and old-fashioned. In a chapter of *Middletown* entitled "Why Do They Work So Hard?", the Lynds offered a view from the editorial pages of the local press: "The first duty of a citizen is to produce" but not at the expense of an even higher duty, "The American citizen's first importance to his country is no longer that of a citizen but that of consumer. Consumption is a new necessity" (Lynd & Lynd 1929: 88). It is unclear where either Lasswell or Maslow and the postmaterialists would place the social cost of unbridled consumption, a prevailing sense of spiritual emptiness and dessication, not fulfillment.

The Lynds developed a classificatory scheme of six "main-trunk activities" to test the impact of industrialization (controlling for urbanization) on Muncie residents: Getting a Living, Making a Home, Training the Young, Using Leisure, Engaging in Religious Practices, and Engaging in Community Activities. Their most distressing finding, according to John Dewey, concerned the debasement of religion and the rise in its place of a schizophrenic therapeutic culture. "The glorification of religion as the final seal of approval on pecuniary success, and supplying the active motive to more energetic struggle for such success, and the adoption by the churches of the latest devices of the movies and the advertiser, approach too close to the obscene." In Dewey's reading, the city of Middletown was a "house divided against itself," preaching idealism and practicing materialism (Lasch 1991: 424–425).

The Lynds were never able to rank-order their indicators or to imagine them falling into any kind of teleological order like Maslow's for precisely the reason that the general orientations no longer expressed a coherent world view. The transition from the old order to the new, as *Middletown* seemed to show, was not a gradual, piecemeal process with one stage clearly leaving behind the other; it was an untidy, comprehensive one in which everything was related to everything else. Older values were not so much displaced in the transition as upended with all the other newer values to produce the hybridized reality of Muncie in the 1920s and '30s. The Lynds' work offers a cautionary note (or perhaps a footnote) to the use of absolute categories for understanding and accounting for the full range and complexity of values. If they are right, we will have to attack the problem—the contested, temporal, and emergent nature of values and their representation—from multiple directions and using a variety of analytical tools. Rather than settling upon any one single taxonomy, we will have to begin to identify the generic qualities that make for robust analysis, qualities like uniformity, flexibility, utility, and historical accuracy.

VALUES AND THE POLICY PROCESS: HUMAN-CAPITAL DEEPENING IN ASIA AND THE PACIFIC

All values are expressive of both ends and means. They function as accomplished results of a system, but they also constitute its plans, its ends-in-view, perhaps even its contingencies. As plans, values have a vital role to play in the policy process. The failure to take them into consideration—not as adjuncts to a process that is primarily a technical one, but as directive means themselves—has plagued education projects, especially in developing areas, time and time again in country after country (Oxenham 1989; Havelock and Huberman 1977; Hanson 1986; Cheng 1997).

Hofstede (1980) has identified organizational values that depending on their manifestation can turn reform efforts into either a blessing or a curse. *Power distance* describes the degree to which power is distributed evenly in an organization, and can affect such intangibles as trust, loyalty, and respect. *Uncertainty avoidance* is the level of tolerance people have for the contingencies of life, for the element of unpredictability, not only in events but in people and institutions. A low tolerance for legitimate conflict and confrontation may trigger an exaggerated need for consensus, conformity, and regulation. Exaggerated fears of the last of these may lead to more pathological forms of conflict and competition, including war and violence. *Individualism-collectivism* describes the continuum along which most human behavior and values lie in a society. People are either more or less committed to community and self, economic dependence and independence, national sovereignty and local self-government. *Role differentiation* refers to the extent to which the major functions of a society are differentiated by race, class, gender, and ethnicity. A well-ordered society, according to the functionalist perspective, neither has too many people at one end of the spectrum nor too many at the other but resembles a bell curve, with the majority of people and their worth to society falling somewhere in the middle. These tend to be meritocratic societies governed by norms of independence ("You have no one to blame but yourself"), achievement ("Good intentions don't win the race"), universalism ("If I make an exception for you, I will have to make it for everyone"), and specificity ("The exception proves the rule").

Hofstede's four value orientations—power distance, uncertainty avoidance, individualism-collectivism, and role differentiation—have a profound affect on the policy-making process. Setting management strategies that are sensitive to the cultural values not only of the men and women who manage and implement policy but of those who are served by it is a principle of effective planning (Rondinelli, Middleton, and Verspoor 1990). Policymakers must be willing to adapt their plans, however enlightened, when they run up against local conditions and expectations that dictate otherwise. Kai-ming Cheng reports a study of female school enrollments in an ethnic minority area in China, where the local custom of teaching girls embroidery skills superseded the more "abstract" value of universal schooling. Embroidery, not the high cost of schooling, sexual discrimination, or irrelevance (all treatable causes), was the decisive factor in keeping girls out of school. "If social conditions and cultural expectations are not changed in these Miao villages, there does not seem to be an easy way to improve girls' attendance. The cultural issue that has to be given attention in order to make compulsory education possible is much greater than the problem of compulsory education itself" (Cheng 1997: 78). In these and comparable cases, the immediate social context determines the rationality and ultimate workability of national policies. Clearly, changing local customs and traditions to make way for modernization is a much more complex problem than the advantages available to people—universal education, occupational mobility, political enfranchisement—would imply.

Recent studies nevertheless leave little doubt that human-resource development has played a major role in the remarkable postwar economic development of the Asia-Pacific Rim (Ogawa, Jones, and Williamson 1993). Human-capital formation, in terms of the "value added" to productivity gains in the region, has resulted from a powerful combination of reduced fertility, high economic growth performance, an expanding international labor market fueled by the growing presence of women in the market, and more equal income distribution than in other developing areas. These changes and the savings they have effected are the cause and consequence of an enormous rise in spending on education at both government and household levels that began as early as the late nineteenth century. Economists have long recognized that some personal qualities are more conducive to planned economic development than others, but could not have predicted, I think, the enormous role that cultural factors have played in the development of Asia and the Pacific, where per capita educational investments are some of the highest in the world. What makes the influence of these cultural factors ironic is their relative *isolation* from the economic determinants of "human capital" theory—the idea that nations develop when the skills and knowledge of the labor force increase, primarily through schooling.

Human-capital theory, as an attempt to understand the role of education in development, has run into a number of difficult empirical problems from the beginning. First, researchers were presented with the problem of defining which components of educational expenditure were investment and which were consumption. The same dilemma shows up in other social expenditures such as public health and welfare and commercial science and technology policy. Then there was the enormous practical problem of measuring the total value of educational investments by an individual or a society. This problem of course increased as the definition of what constitutes an educational agency was expanded to include family, church, and community sources of socialization. The results of early empirical work offered a kind of intuitive support for the claims of human-capital theorists but provided little in the way of rigorous empirical evidence. Researchers did in fact find positive correlation's between per capita GNP and school enrollment levels in cross-national studies, but the statistical relationships were not particularly strong, and there was no way of telling whether increased school enrollments were a cause or a consequence of prosperity (Bowen 1968; Maynes 1985). Economic development may have as much to do with levels of planning and state activism (in a number of different fields, including but not limited to education), with openness to international trade and flows of technology, or with the domestic political forces shaping development strategies as with education per se (Haggard 1990).

Only in the last one hundred years or so, not until the beginning really of the second industrial revolution, has mass public education been considered a "resource" for economic and national development. The link between education and modernization was only dimly understood by the eighteenth- and nineteenth-century mercantilists, who for the most part viewed mass education more as a threat than as a safeguard of the status quo. The industrial working classes of Western Europe, as E. P. Thompson and others have shown, demanded free public education not in a bid for access to skill development or vocational education but in order to take their rightful place among the cultivated classes. Unionization, democratization, and the spread of enlightenment values of reason, liberty, and equality went hand in hand with demands for a basic education that included not only functional but cultural and critical literacy as well. To understand the critical perspective on literacy—its emphasis on political empowerment, social action, and collective strug-gle—is to begin to understand something of the fear and dread with which most elites viewed education in colonial and early national peri-ods. It is important to understand that the story of development (eco-nomic, social, and political) in the Asia-Pacific Rim is not simply one of the imposition of Western models of development on a hapless and docile native population. Schools throughout the world are foci not only of political socialization designed to instill loyalty, patriotism, and confor-mity to national goals; they are also sites of resistance and re-fashioning with externalities and "value-added" that cannot always be captured in rate-of-return percentages.

The contemporary educational picture, one could argue, is particu-larly clouded in the Asia-Pacific Rim where traditional Latin, Euro-American, and Asian cultures must contend not only with their own internal forces of change but with new external exigencies, including con-siderable economic pressures, that sometimes downgrade the importance of the content of education or the quality of teaching. Converted to a pol-icy format, the questions for the Pacific Basin Research Center (PBRC) are the fundamental ones of values change and stability. What values are changing? What values are latent in the existing educational systems? How do the reformers in a country develop a following, and how do they get something new on the statute books or planning papers? To what extent does the "reform" that follows embody the new values, and how do they conflict with the old? In the end, what really happens to education in the curricula and classrooms? In the process of trying to answer these and similar questions for other sectors of society, PBRC hopes to identify and track values in the region associated with traditional conceptions of civic culture and development: life satisfaction, interpersonal trust, absence of support for revolutionary change, support for the current social order, and levels of political discussion.

REFERENCES

Anderson, Elizabeth. 1993. *Value in Ethics and Economics.* Cambridge, MA: Harvard University Press.

Arrow, Kenneth J. 1967. "Public and Private Values," In *Human Values and Economic Policy,* ed. Sidney Hook. New York: New York University Press.

Ayer, A. J. 1939. *Language, Truth and Logic.* 2nd ed. New York: Dover.

Barnes, Samuel H. 1986. *Politics and Culture.* Ann Arbor: Institute for Social Research.

Billig, Michael S. 1994. "The Death and Rebirth of Entrepreneurism on Negros Island, Philippines: A Critique of Cultural Theories of Enterprise." *Journal of Economic Issues* 28:659–678.

Block, Jack. 1981. "Some Enduring and Consequential Structures of Personality." In *Further Explorations in Personality,* ed. A. I. Rabin et al. New York: Wiley-Interscience.

Bowen, W. G. 1968. "Assessing the Economic Contribution of Education." In *Economics of Education. Vol. 1,* ed. M. Blaug. New York: Pergamon.

Cheng, K. M. 1997. "Qualitative Research and Educational Policy-Making: Approaching the Reality in Developing Countries." In *Qualitative Educational Research in Developing Counties: Current Perspectives,* ed. M. Crossley and G. Vulliamy. New York: Garland.

Cohen, Myron L. 1991. "Being Chinese: The Peripheralization of Traditional Identity." *Daedalus* 120:113–134.

Coleman, James S. 1966. *Equality of Educational Opportunity.* Washington, D.C.: Government Printing Office.

Commission on Global Governance. 1995. *Our Global Neighborhood.* Oxford: Oxford University Press.

Costa, Paul T., Jr., and Robert R. McCrae. 1980. "Still Stable After All These Years." In *Life-Span Development and Behavior,* ed., Paul B. Bates and Orville G. Brim, Jr. Vol. 3. New York: Academic Press.

Dewey, John. 1939. *Theory of Valuation.* Chicago: University of Chicago Press.

———. 1958. *Experience and Nature.* New York: Dover.

Fagerlind, I., and L. J. Saha. 1983. *Education and National Development: A Comparative Perspective.* Oxford: Pergamon Press.

Fallding, Harold. 1965. "A Proposal for the Empirical Study of Values." *American Sociological Review* 30:223–233.

Freire, Paulo, and Donaldo Macedo. 1987. *Literacy: Reading the Word and the World.* South Hadley, MA: Bergin and Garvey.

Geertz, Clifford. 1973. *The Interpretation of Cultures.* New York: Basic Books,

Haggard, Stephan. 1990. *Pathways from the Periphery: The Politics of Growth in the Newly Industrializing Countries.* Ithaca, NY: Cornell University Press.

Hanson, E. Mark. 1986. *Educational Reforms and Administrative Development: The Cases of Columbia and Venezuela.* Stanford, CA: Hoover Institution Press.

Havelock, R. G., and A. M. Huberman. 1977. *Solving Educational Problems: The Theory and Reality of Innovation in Developing Countries.* Paris: UNESCO.

Hirschman, Albert O. 1977. *The Passions and the Interests: Political Arguments for Capitalism Before Its Triumph.* Princeton, NJ: Princeton University Press.

Hofstede, Greet. 1980. "Motivation, Leaders, and Organization: Do American Theories Apply Abroad." *Organizational Dynamics* (Summer): 42–62.

Inglehart, Ronald. 1981. "Postmaterialism in an Environment of Insecurity." *American Political Science Review* 75:880–900.

———. 1990. *Culture Shift in Advanced Industrial Society.* Princeton: Princeton University Press.

Inkeles, Alex. 1997. *National Character: A Psycho-Social Perspective.* New Brunswick, NJ: Transaction.

Inkeles, Alex, and Masamichi Sasaki, eds. 1996. *Comparing Nations and Cultures: Readings in a Cross-Disciplinary Perspective.* Englewood Cliffs, NJ: Prentice Hall.

Inkeles, Alex, and D. H. Smith. 1974. *Becoming Modern.* Cambridge, MA: Harvard University Press.

James, William. 1928. *Pragmatism: A New Name for Some Old Ways of Thinking.* New York: Longmans, Green.

Kluckhohn, Clyde. 1959. *Mirror for Man: A Survey of Human Behavior and Social Attitudes.* New York: McGraw-Hill.

Kohlberg, Lawrence. 1975. "The Cognitive-Developmental Approach to Moral Education." *Phi Delta Kappan* 56:670–677.

Kuhn, Thomas S. 1962. *The Structure of Scientific Revolutions.* Chicago: University of Chicago Press.

Lakatos, Imre, and Alan Musgrave, eds. 1970. *Criticism and the Growth of Knowledge.* Cambridge, MA: Cambridge University Press.

Lasch, Christopher. 1991. *The True and Only Heaven: Progress and Its Critics.* New York: W. W. Norton.

———. 1995. *The Revolt of the Elites and the Betrayal of Democracy.* New York: W. W. Norton,

Lasswell, Harold D., Daniel Lerner, and John D. Montgomery, eds. 1976. *Values and Development: Appraising Asian Experience.* Cambridge, MA: MIT Press.

Lasswell, Harold D., and Myres S. McDougal. 1992. *Jurisprudence for a Free Society: Studies in Law, Science and Policy.* New Haven: Martinus Nijhoff.

Lasswell, Harold D., and Abraham Kaplan. 1950. *Power and Society.* New Haven: Yale University Press.

Lynd, Robert S., and Helen Merrill Lynd. 1929. *Middletown: A Study in Modern American Culture.* New York: Harcourt, Brace & World.

Maslow, Abraham, 1968. *Toward a Psychology of Being.* 2nd ed. New York; Van Nostrand Reinhold.

Maynes, Mary Jo. 1985. *Schooling in Western Europe: A Social History.* New York; SUNY Press.

McClelland, David. 1961. *The Achieving Society.* Princeton: Van Nostrand.

McDermott, John L. ed. 1969. *The Basic Writings of Josiah Royce.* Chicago: University of Chicago Press.

McGinn, Noel F. 1996. "Education, Democratization, and Globalization: A Challenge for Comparative Education." *Comparative Education Review* 40: 341–357.

Merton, Robert. 1968. *Social Theory and Social Structure.* New York: Free Press.

Namenwirth, J. Zvi, and Harold D. Lasswell. 1970. *The Changing Language of American Values: A Computer Study of Selected Party Platforms.* Comparative Politics Series 1:1–69.

National Assessment of Educational Progress. 1985. *The Reading Report Card: Progress Toward Excellence in Our Schools.* Princeton, NJ: Educational Testing Service.

Oakes, Guy. 1988. *Concept Formation in the Cultural Sciences.* Cambridge, MA: MIT Press.

Ogawa. Naohiro, Gavin W. Jones, and Jeffrey G. Williamson. 1993. *Human Resources in Development along the Asia-Pacific Rim.* New York: Oxford.

Oldenburg, Ray. 1989. *The Great Good Place: Cafes, Coffee Shops, Community Centers, Beauty Parlors, General Stores, Bars, Hangouts and How They Get You Through the Day.* New York: Paragon House.

Parsons, Talcott. 1949. *The Structure of Social Action.* Glencoe, NY: Free Press.

Popper, Karl. 1957, 1961. *The Poverty of Historicism.* New York: Harper & Row.

———. 1959. *The Logic of Scientific Discovery.* New York: Basic Books.

———. 1963. *Conjectures and Refutations: The Growth of Scientific Knowledge.* New York: Harper & Row.

Putnam, Robert D. 1993. *Making Democracy Work: Civic Traditions in Modern Italy.* Princeton: Princeton University Press.

Ramsay, Meredith. 1996. "The Local Community: Maker of Culture and Wealth." *Journal of Urban Affairs* 18:95–118.

Rickert, Heinrich. 1910–11. "Vom Begriff der Philosophie." *Logos* 1:1–34.

Rondinelli, Dennis A., John Middleton, and Adriaan M. Verspoor, eds. 1990. *Planning Education Reforms in Developing Countries: The Contingency Approach.* Durham: Duke University Press.

Schwartz, Shalom H. and Maria Ros. 1995. "Values in the West: A Theoretical and Empirical Challenge to the Individualism Collectivism Cultural Dimension." *World Psychology* 1:91–122.

Sen, Amartya. 1984. *Resources, Values and Development.* Oxford: Basil Blackwell.

———. 1987. *On Ethics and Economics.* Oxford. Basil Blackwell

———. 1995. "Rationality and Social Choice." *American Economic Review* 85:1–24.

Torney, Judith V., A. N. Oppenheim, and Russel F. Farnen. 1975. *Civic Education in Ten Countries.* New York: John Wiley.

Tu Wei-ming. 1991. "Cultural China: The Periphery as Center." *Daedalus* 120:1–32.

Westbrook, Robert B. 1991. *John Dewey and American Democracy.* Ithaca: Cornell University Press.

Williams, Robin M., Jr. 1971. "Change and Stability in Values and Values Systems," In *Stability and Social Change,* ed. Bernard Barber and Alex Inkeles. Boston: Little, Brown.

John D. Montgomery, Director of Soka University of America's Pacific Basin Research Center, is Ford Foundation Professor of International Studies, Emeritus, at Harvard, where he has been since 1963. He has also served as dean of the faculty of Babson College, head of academic instruction of the National Institute of Administration in Viet Nam, and consultant to the U.S. Agency for International Development, the World Bank, the Asian Development Bank, and a number of governments, universities, and research organizations. His first major book is *Forced to Be Free: The Artificial Revolution in Germany and Japan* (1957); he is also author of *The Politics of Foreign Aid: American Experience in Southeast Asia* (1962). His most recent books are *Great Policies: Strategic Innovations in Asia and the Pacific Basin* (Dennis A. Rondinelli, co-editor, 1995), *Aftermath: Tarnished Outcomes of American Foreign Policy* (1986), and *Bureaucrats and People: Grassroots Participation in Third World Development* (1988).

2. Are Asian Values Different?

John D. Montgomery

On the whole we must conclude that Asian governments are more reluctant to commit themselves to human rights in the international arena and in their constitutions than they are through the policies they practice at home. The practices are better than the principles. . . . Their hesitance to accept the implications of a political order and civil society as defined in declarations, protocols, and other agreements is perhaps attributable to nationalistic resistance to new forms of "cultural imperialism."

Westerners who dabble in Asian affairs tend to recoil at hearing the familiar theme: "But Asian values are different!" They encounter this refrain as often as they suggest new, supposedly universal, norms in the region. But how different are these values? Are they proof against change? This book explores several answers to those questions as they relate to education, especially when interpreted as a means of generating and protecting human rights and forming new social capital. For values cannot be ignored: they play a central role in determining the temper and quality of the common life, though they can be observed only indirectly, and thus leave abundant scope for speculation as well as description.[1]

A few bold strokes will render the questions approachable empirically. A few simplifying definitions will help. "Asia" we can define geographically, and we include the Pacific Basin in our cognitive map so that we can introduce the Americas for comparative purposes, taking regionalism as a cultural concept.[2] The term "values" is more troublesome, since it has been used to describe aspirations that range from getting to work on time to accepting the moral obligations we recognize as elements of social capital. We suggest thinking of "values" as categories of human preferences, which rise in political valence as their moral content increases. There are several major taxonomies of values, ranging from Lasswell's universalistic policy sciences canon, which we follow in this chapter, to the pragmatic pyramid of Abraham Maslow, along with many other useful interpretations, some of which are used in this book as well.[3] "Rights" we define as legally or politically recognized claims placed by individuals and groups in pursuit of their values.

"Social capital" is the most obscure of all these terms, since it is sometimes perceived as the mutual trust that binds people together, including the exchanging of information and social norms, sometimes as the mere act of participating in collective decisions and actions.[4] This chapter will define it as the cumulative capacity of social groups to cooperate and work together for a common good. It is partly a product of education, formal and nonformal. It includes familiar qualities such as the solidarity that churches and public service institutions create, and a sense of social and political efficacy, as well as loyalties to nongovernmental organizations such as corporations engaged in the pursuit of common values, all of which may be generated, strengthened, or weakened by formal and informal educational programs. Social capital is not a static dimension of social organization, since it incorporates changing sets of attitudes and behaviors as they respond to challenges and issues of the moment. Its dynamic features include myths and techniques; it is influenced by education and socialization, by regulatory interventions designed to produce common responses, and by the influence of subsidies and penalties or fees levied by governments and other organizations. This definition invites us to examine the values that inform social action; to study the institutions that affect these arenas; to consider how social groups "invest" in developing that capacity, and to evaluate how they use and consume it.[5] Essays in this book address the first two tasks; the others are projects for the future.[6]

SEEKING INTERNATIONAL STANDARDS

To describe Asian values as "different" invites the question "from what?" From those of another region? If so, perhaps it is the other region that is different, and Asia that is the baseline. From some international standard? If such a standard exists, can it serve as a template against which to compare all regions? This chapter will start by considering whether we can identify the values that the international community instructs us to consider universal: those that underlie the rights proclaimed in the three important documents that make up the International Bill of Rights: the Universal Declaration of Human Rights (1948); the International Covenant on Economic, Social and Cultural Rights (1966); and the International Covenant on Civil and Political Rights, with its two Optional Protocols (1966).[7] The venture begins as we dissect these enumerated rights to find their ultimate sources in a code of values, after which we can locate the relative standing of Asian values in the tabernacle of international law.

One of the most useful, and best used, definitions of values is that developed in the "policy sciences" canon, mentioned in chapter 1, which classifies human values according to eight arenas of preference that represent possible aspirations of individuals and groups. In varying degrees, people are said to seek to advance the quality of their lives by pursuing gains in Power, Enlightenment, Wealth, Well-being, Skill, Affection, Respect, and Rectitude. For those who are plagued with poor memories, policy scientists have adopted a mnemonic device[8] for recalling these eight values: the pronounceable but quirky term PEWBSARD. Each of these categories of preference can be used to describe aspirations[9] that society agrees individuals may pursue as "rights." Thus, Power would include (among other aspirations) the right to exercise some influence in the decisions of groups and organizations that affect one's life; Enlightenment, to gain and exchange information about the nature of one's surroundings; Wealth, to retain the fruits of one's labor; Well-Being, to enjoy the positive attributes of one's physical or psychological nature; Skill, to develop one's talents for creative, recreational, or aesthetic purposes; Affection, to associate with relatives, friends, colleagues, and others with whom one shares values; Respect, to participate in the social order without discrimination on grounds of ascriptive characteristics; and Rectitude, to observe one's moral standards freely and to award and receive just recognition of one's lawful rights. Each value is implicitly recognized in the international documents, and collectively they represent authoritative recognition on the basis of which rights become legitimate. Each value is a significant element in the educational processes of most Asian societies, explicitly or otherwise.

The Universal Declaration of Human Rights is generally regarded as the progenitor of the major postwar documents on the subject. Its 30 articles set forth at least 28 distinct rights, involving all eight of the PEWBSARD values (see Table 2-1, next page).

Table 2-1. Values Defined in Major Human Rights Agreements

Values*	Universal Declaration of Human Rights	International Covenant on Economic, Social, and Cultural Rights	International Covenant on Civil and Political Rights	Vienna Declaration of 1993	Total by Column	Percentage by Column
P	7	1	6	5	19	19
E	3	1	1	3	8	8
W	2	2	1	4	9	9
B	1	5	0	0	6	6
S	2	2	0	1	5	5
A	6	3	4	6	19	19
R	2	1	5	6	14	14
D	5	0	8	3	16	17
Totals	28	15	25	28	96	—

*Power (e.g., rights to security of person and political participation); Enlightenment (the right to education and free speech); Wealth (prosperity rights); Well-Being (health and environment); Skill (right to work and enjoy its fruits); Affection (family and community rights); Respect (right to equal treatment); Rectitude (religious rights and freedom of conscience).

The rights it mentions most frequently are those of life and security of person (Power values, cited in Arts. 3, 12, and 14) and the right of access to effective legal remedies for violations (a Rectitude value, cited in Arts. 8 and 11a and 11b), along with that of freedom of thought and religion (Enlightenment values, in Arts. 18, 19, and 26) and that of assembly, association, and community (Affection values, Arts. 19, 20, and 23), each of which is listed three times. There are two references each to the right not to be discriminated against, i.e., the right to equal treatment (Respect values, cited in Arts. 2 and 7), to recognition as a person before the law (Respect values, as in Arts. 6 and 10), not to be arrested or imprisoned unjustly (Power values, Arts. 9 and 13), to family relations (Affection values, appearing in Arts. 16 and 26), and to "social security," or a basic standard of living (Well-Being values, Arts. 22 and 25). There is one reference each to the following rights: not to be tortured (Power, Art. 5), not to be enslaved (Power, Art. 4), to work for pay (Skill, Art. 23), to nationality (Power, Art. 15), to property (Wealth, Art. 17), to political participation (Power, Art. 21) to leisure (Well-Being, Art. 24), to cultural life (Skill, Art. 27), and even to the international order (Power, Art. 28). Counting the number of references does not, of course, indicate which rights are fundamental and which derivative, or how readily they may be enforced (it is hard to imagine, for example, how some of them, like social security and the right to an international order, would take the form of justifiable or politically sustainable claims). But the mere iteration conveys some sense of the importance of issues described in the document, especially as they reflect what is in the minds of those who drafted and ratified it.[10] They are intended to be universal, i.e., above regional differences.

Taken together, all of the documents in the International Bill of Rights give Power first place, including both negative and positive elements—antislavery (Art. 4), antitorture and (5), antiarrest (9), as well as personal security (13), freedom of movement (13), participation in government (21), and the right of asylum (14). Affection or loyalty rights come next along with guarantees of nationality (15), family (16), assembly and association (20), unions (23), and community (29). The relatively low threshold of concern for property rights is surprising in that it undermines the myth that international human rights derive from Western values, which presumably give it a high priority. The explanation that the Declarations were drafted in international conferences representing nation-states rather than people may seem to challenge the claim that they represent individual human rights at all, at least in the Western mode. It suggests, if anything, a non-Western concern for nonmaterial values. The Declaration also offers a surprisingly low appreciation of well-being values such as health. Even so, it is more positive than negative: among the 28 rights it mentions are 23 positive assurances and 5 negative injunctions, a proportion that may be a surprise to those accustomed to monitoring human rights in terms of violations rather than affirmations. Some of these rights are hard to interpret, like that of the "will of the people" in Art. 21, and the right to an international order and a just society in Arts. 28 and 29 (Freeman 1995: 23–40).

Before turning to the relevance of these values to Asian education we consider the extent to which these governments have reaffirmed them as they have ratified other international agreements.

AFFIRMING THE STANDARD

There are only 35 Asian governments among the 189 countries that have participated in these agreements. All have had repeated opportunities to vote their convictions, since there are now 25 major human rights instruments that are listed in the United Nations Chart of Ratification as at 31 December 1994.[11] No nation has ratified all of them. The Asians have shown a greater disparity of response than have other regions;[12] Europe comes closest to unanimity, and it is the contrast between them that suggests the cleavage between "East" and "West." Among Asian countries, the Philippines is champion supporter, having ratified or signed 20 of these instruments; Australia comes next at 19, New Zealand 17, India 16, and Seychelles 15. Among "Western" countries, the U.S. has signed or ratified 13, Britain 17, and France 19. At Asia's other extreme, Brunei Darussalam has a score of 0 and the Federated States of Asia, Micronesia, and Marshall Islands, Nauru, and Vanuatu, 1 each. In between are Nepal (14), Sri Lanka (13), Korea (12), China (9), Japan (8), North Korea (5), Indonesia (5), Malaysia (4), Thailand (3), Singapore (3), and Bhutan (3).

Perhaps these signatures and ratifications are as much the result of momentary impulses or incidental influences as of moral convictions or national character. But however they are to be explained, they represent a standing, formal commitment and they therefore suggest at least one means of comparing the regions. Being "Westernized" certainly does not account for the Asian choices: the Philippines may be more so than Nepal, and South Korea more than its northern counterpart, but it is far from clear that Sri Lanka ranks above Singapore on any such scale. The

interpretation may well be that participation in international conferences rather than national character explains these commitments; otherwise it is hard to explain why Cambodia, at 11, outranks Thailand,
whose commitment is apparently equal to Bhutan's. But whether these
commitments are carried out in educational systems and social behavior
is an empirical question.

REGIONAL COMPARISONS

For a somewhat deeper insight into Asia's commitments to these values,
we can desegregate the national votes by issue and compare the results
across regions. We then find that the 35 Asian countries have offered
much greater support to the protection of special disadvantaged groups
(children, racial minorities, and women) than they have to economic,
social, and cultural agreements, and still less to civil and political rights.
At the bottom of the list of issues is that of monitoring and implementation, where Asia's commitment is shaky. These findings help us identify
the profile of values likely to appear in Asia's formal and nonformal education systems. By way of comparison, the 30 Latin American countries
also rank disadvantaged groups first in priority of concern, but they give
very high acceptance to the other rights, about which Asians seem
ambivalent. Latins have even accepted the implementing agreements, and
in all categories the Americas give much greater support than does Asia.
Neither region comes very close to the degree of European commitment,
but the differences are manifest (see Table 2-2).

Table 2-2. Asian, Latin American, and European Human Rights Commitments

International Agreement	35 Asian Coutries (%)	30 Latin American Countries (%)	15 European Council Member Countries (%)
Economic, Social Cultural	40	80	100
Civil and Political	37	83	86
Implementing Protocol	17	63	80
Rights of Child	83	100	100
Racial Discrimination	60	83	100
Women	57	100	93

Apart from the special needs of disadvantaged groups, these documents identify general statements of rights that apply to all persons. Here, too, the Asian responses were more muted than European or Latin American affirmations. Asian votes for civil and political rights not only lagged further behind those for such special cases as the rights of the child and the condemnation of racial discrimination, as compared with Latin America, but also they scorned the implementing protocol so important to Europeans, without which human rights declarations have no real force even in the anorexic body of international law. The votes seem to confirm the assertion that Asia's support to human rights of individuals ranks below its concern for communities or groups. These votes suggest the possibility that education in Asian countries will emphasize communal over private values, and display less concern over political values except for those that promote solidarity.

Human "wrongs"—abuses and violations—also define a society's approach to values. They are the reverse side of the coin, a mirror image of the formal ratification of international agreements. Freedom House has ranked all countries in terms of these violations from the best (score of 1) to the worst (score of 8, for the most violations). The basis for the rankings is not consistent across countries and over time and have been justifiably challenged on methodological ground (Goldstein 1992: 48), but the comparisons are suggestive nevertheless. Asia's diversity shows in these rankings as well as in the record of international agreements. Over the period from 1973–1996 these scores ranged from Australia and New Zealand (1 each) and Japan (1) at the top down to Vietnam (6.8), Burma, (6.64) and China (6.5). On the whole, countries with the highest commitment to international agreements also had the lowest incidence of human rights violations, India (2.79) being a good example of commitment matching behavior; island nations like Micronesia and Marshall Islands (1 each), Nauru (1.92), and Vanuatu (2.5) had few ratifications, but also few violations. There is not much formal human rights activity there, or much need for it. In between are some anomalies: Nepal ratified 14 agreements, but had a violation score of 4.1; Sri Lanka ratified 13 but violated with a score of 3.3; Korea had scores of 12 and 4.1; South Indonesia rated 5 and 5.3; Malaysia ratified only four but had a decent score of 3.75; Thailand ratified only three and had a less impressive score of 3.8. China, an outlier, ratified nine agreements but had an inconsistent score of 6.5. "Negative values," which suggest toleration of abusive treatment of individuals, are too unstructured to dominate educational content. Affirmations are predictably a greater influence on classroom curricula than violations.

Observing the record over time shows trends that the averages conceal. No country among the 32 listed in Asia went from "best" to "worst" in terms of reported violations or from "worst" to "best," but there were some notable variations. The Philippines, starting with a dismal 5 in 1973, jumped to 2.5 the next year, and stayed there until sinking to 4.5. Bangladesh suffered even more extreme fluctuations, starting at 3 but pushing the extreme of 5.5 in 1984–5 before settling to 2s and 3s after 1992. India has been deteriorating, holding at 2.5 until descending to 4 in the years after 1994. Indonesia, too, has declined in observance of human rights, starting unimpressively, holding a steady 5 in 1973–84, falling to 6.5 in 1994–96. At the bottom were Brunei, Burma, and China.

While abuses of human rights do not provide a powerful tool for analyzing Asian values, it is noteworthy that the contrast with Latin America's performance reinforces the findings of our comparison of affirmative human rights in the two regions. The 29 countries of dictator-ridden Latin America actually did better, with an average score of 3.46 over the same period, nearly a full point above Asia (4.3). Here, too, some countries fluctuated wildly (Cuba, Haiti, Nicaragua, and Peru have poor records, Guatemala and Colombia have deteriorated, and Argentina, Brazil, Chile, Ecuador, Honduras, Panama, and Paraguay have made the greatest improvement).

Latin America's values are converging toward the European norm faster than are Asia's. The current trends show greater improvement in Latin America than in Asia. These numbers even in their raw form tend to confirm the fact that Asia's human rights commitment and observance are below those of Latin America. But they do not in themselves suggest a uniqueness in Asian values as measured by the human rights metric.[13]

Nor do the specific cases of human rights violations reported by Amnesty International (Report 1996) identify Asia's uniqueness. The three types of abuses most frequently encountered in Asia and Latin America were torture, including flogging, suppression of political opposition, and unlawful arrest. As the other evidence would suggest, the Asians were more abusive than the Latins on average, according to the annual reports: serious physical abuses were reported in six of the 26 Latin American countries in the list, as compared with 15 of the 22 Asian countries. Only one of the Asian countries was wholly abuse-free, as compared with five in Latin America. The "difference" is not one in which Asians can take pride, whatever other values they espouse.

CONSTITUTIONAL COMPARISONS

This conclusion is supported by a comparison between constitutional guarantees of human rights in the two regions. Constitutional guarantees of due process may be the best formal indicator of national commitments to civil rights; indeed, due process is arguably a minimum requirement for protection of all rights. Among the world's 132 constitutions that were in effect in 1970, nearly all made some reference to such guarantees. The Inkeles-Hooper analysis defines these guarantees as follows: (1) a general provision acknowledging the concept, along with specific requirements such as (2) the use of a warrant in case of arrest, (3) the specification of limits of time for formal charges, (4) the documentation of arrest action, and (5) the requirement of habeas corpus; plus guarantees of (6) the right to trial, (7) the timing of the trial, (8) the right to counsel, (9) the right to a jury, and (10) the right to appeal. Other rights in this sample included (11) hearings regarding the confiscation of property, (12) provision for compensation, (13) the right to petition, and (14) the right to a response to one's petition (Inkeles and Hooper 1993: 41–51).

In comparing the two regions, we find that an average of 4.83 of the 14 due process rights were guaranteed in the 24 Asian constitutions in effect, as contrasted with 7.79 in those of the 24 Latin American states. Some of this difference may be accounted for by the dates of adoption: recent constitutions offer *fewer* such guarantees than early ones. Thus there appears to be a deterioration in the universal acceptance of these fundamental rights in the constitutions of new nations, and it is perhaps no surprise that Asian countries, relative newcomers to the scene, are less supportive than Latin Americans. Among the constitutions in effect between 1870 and 1970, the average year of origin in Asia was 1948, as compared with 1893 in Latin America. The Asian shortfalls might there-fore be dismissed as a function of the general deterioration of constitu-tionalism as the guarantor of due process, rather than of a cultural difference; but whatever the cause, once more it becomes apparent that Asian values produce less formal allegiance to human rights in national constitutions than do those of Latin American countries. Constitutional protections of human rights conform to the same pattern as the commit-ment through international agreement. One should expect a similar con-trast in educational values of the two regions.

HUMAN RIGHTS PROGRAMS

The effect of value preferences on actual human rights policies is perhaps the best predictor of how Asia's values will appear in its educational systems. National behavior in support of these values offers a more important guarantee of human rights than national agreements or even constitutional clauses. The detailed annual reports of adverse behavior (Report 1996) that we have consulted describe random events or egregious circumstances, but they do not reveal much about general policies or about average lives or values in those countries. Scholars would be hard pressed to justify their use as national indicators (Spirer and Spirer 1993) in spite of their political usefulness as a basis for determining diplomatic and economic punishments and rewards. Similar studies of positive policies, those that advance social values, and especially those that affect the public at large, are needed to tell us what society really expects its education to represent.

In its current effort to discover how positive human rights policies affect basic values, the Pacific Basin Research Center has developed a series of case studies of programs that are intended to offer support to individual and collective values.[14] The cases drawn from the Pacific Basin are summarized in the Appendix to this chapter.

We examined 16 of these cases in detail, drawn from seven different countries, all representing programs that were designed to advance or protect clearly defined rights. Ten of these programs served individual values, six of which protected political and legal rights; four, property rights; four, rights to work and to enjoy the fruits of labor; three, educational rights; and three, the right to health services. None involved security of person, and only two protected family or community rights as such. Of the six that advanced collective or group rights, two served family values, two served those of a traditional community and two actually weakened them, and three protected other groups such as women and lower castes. If these examples should turn out to be typical, the actions of these seven Asian governments could be said to lean more to individual rights than to those of a community, and the rights involved would resemble the balance sought by the International Declaration of Human Rights more than those of the special groups whose pleading attracted such favorable responses in Asia and Latin America. Policies of this sort are better indicators of what Asians expect of education than formal commitments through agreements and constitutions.

These experiences suggest a much more positive view of human rights values than do the official positions that Asian governments have taken in their commitments to international human rights agreements. What these governments are doing is more important than what they are saying. These 16 programs followed conventional uses of government resources. Like their Western counterparts, they resemble other social services, both in Asia and elsewhere. Ten relied on legal procedures and administrative organizations, and five on the provision of education and training opportunities: human rights in Asia do not display any special uniqueness in the administration of government programs relating to them. On the whole, positive human rights policies do not make unusual demands on the financial resources of a country, but they underscore the extent to which human values are served by public programs like education.

SOURCES OF ASIAN RIGHTS

These cases also give us an opportunity to consider whether human rights as practiced in Asia have emerged from a distinct regional course of history. In the cases we have studied, the origins of rights trace back to social developments more than to international sources, though reinforcement from abroad surely have strengthened the claims of internal groups. We found at least four sources for these demands, based on the legitimate claims of individuals or communities to be free to pursue their own moral values within the constraints of civil society:

(1) Religious teachings and cultural traditions, which arise out of presumed relationships between "God" and "man" or out of long-established patterns of human behavior. Most societies associate such rights with duties (even privileged classes observe some degree of "noblesse oblige"), but few would regard them as universal if they apply only to one group or community. Examples are the claims of Coorg lineage group rights to land use and caste privileges and obligations in India.

(2) Perceptions of human nature, which make it "self-evident" that individuals have identifiable moral aspirations, and in turn society associates them with duties toward others. These perceptions find expression in constitutional bills of rights and international declarations as well as other formal legal acts. Because of their "natural" origin they are usually presented as "universal." Examples include women's rights laws in Japan

and China; the generation of opportunities to work in Japan; and traditional kinship rights in India.

(3) Demands created by policies that were adopted in response to changes in civic society. Often these policies generate new benefits and expectations, some of which become "entitlements." Since the "civic society" is constantly revising its political relationships, dissatisfied groups seek to improve their status by asserting their rights. Responses usually take the form of expanded protections of rights hitherto assumed but not stated. Examples in our research: "ethnic rights" to affirmative action in India and presumptive claims to benefits of technological innovations in Bangladesh.

(4) Responses to external influences such as international conventions and conditions of diplomatic or commercial transactions. Examples considered in PBRC's review include the Chinese government's support to legal aid and the abortive introduction of instruments for political participation through elections in Cambodia. The genesis of human rights in Asia when they emerge in the practice of governance is not unique to the region.

CONCLUSION

The state of human rights in Asia, while not "unique," is "different" enough to permit some speculations about the influences of values on most educational systems in the region: predictably the balance would favor loyalties to the family and the community more than respect for individual claims,[15] when compared with Latin America and Europe; there would be more attention to duties than to rights; insofar as the educational curricula included references to public policies, those that serve family and community obligations would rank higher than those that protect individual claims; evidence about human rights violations anywhere would receive less attention than in European or even in Latin American schools; encouragement to "social capital forming" activities in Asia would be expected to emphasize religious and ethnic traditions more than economic activities; and constitutional studies would focus on nationalistic or security concerns rather than on due process.

These expectations are, of course, extremely generalized, but on the whole we must conclude that Asian governments are more reluctant to commit themselves to human rights in the international arena and in their constitutions than they are through the policies they practice at home. The practices are better than the principles. Thus one should not expect the educational systems to seem as callous as the reluctant formal commitments of these governments to Western-style human rights. Their hesitance to accept the implications of a political order and civil society as defined in the declarations, protocols, and other agreements is perhaps attributable to nationalistic resistance to new forms of "cultural imperialism," or perhaps to the political ambitions of political leaders to whom a stout independent stance is preferable to a passive meekness that swims along with the diplomatic tide. At home, however, the governments respond to the same pressures that politics provide in most states, especially from groups whose status is perceived as the result of neglect or oppression. When such groups are in league with international movements, their political claims are significantly enhanced. Hence women's groups, ethnic minorities, and labor unions can call for, and receive, support for their rights-based demands. These demands may also be expected to appear in changing school curricula and in the building of social capital; thus the internal dynamic is enriched by political activism and participation. In this sense, human rights are political more than legal, and national as much as international in their origins and expression. And so are educational systems.

APPENDIX
____

CASES STUDIED BY THE PACIFIC BASIN RESEARCH CENTER

1. Rights involving work

   - Bangladesh's technological innovations have affected property, political, and community rights of poor and rich, rural and urban, industrial and agricultural populations, but the least privileged have derived the greatest share of benefits.

   - Employment-generating projects implemented by nongovernmental organizations in Indonesia succeeded not only in creating work opportunities, but also significantly provided social empowerment opportunities for the rural poor.

   - Cultural factors in Japan, including existing business practices, continue to restrain the effectiveness of legal protections that accord women equal opportunity in the workplace. In recent years, however, there has been a modest increase in the number of complaints and a few court cases regarding discriminatory treatment. Laws designed to protect the employment rights of women in Japan have had little effect on right-to-work behavior in the public or private sector as yet, however.

   - Policies intended to alleviate mandatory retirement practices in Japan have actually diminished older workers' personal claims to human dignity.

   - Japanese vocational high schools have had greater success with job placement than their U.S. counterparts because the employers have participated more directly in recruiting students and have taken more seriously the teachers' student recommendations and grades. The decentralized, largely volunteer-based U.S. programs reached a racially diverse group of mainly low-income youth, however, and enhanced their ethnic pride and political efficacy.

2. Legal rights

   - National Human Rights Commissions in India and elsewhere have been able to transcend their lack of political and enforcement authority by using their prestige and skill to advance human rights causes.

   - Chinese government policies of promoting gender equality are increasingly expressed in terms of legal rights and implemented through legal means. Where political and bureaucratic commitment is strong and local women's associations are active, this legal-rights model has shown potential for improving women's status in selected fields. But there are also clear limits to this approach, stemming from the nature of the Chinese legal system, weak rights-consciousness among Chinese women, and structural features of Chinese society and the Chinese economy.

- Biographical studies of "untouchables" who have benefited from affirmative-action programs in India have shown that legalized access to opportunities for self-advancement have significantly advanced the careers of these disadvantaged persons.

3. Property rights

- Community-based forestry projects posed conflicts over property and environmental rights as they provided employment and other economic opportunities for rural villagers.
- Private investments in industrial development have been more effective than public policies in discouraging "premature urbanization" in China.

4. Health and welfare rights

- Public health policies in both the authoritarian and the democratic regimes in the Philippines have benefited the nation as a whole, but ideological differences between the two services have influenced the direction as well as the emphasis provided in different programs and consequently the access of different populations to these theoretically value-neutral, standardized benefits.
- Efforts to improve sanitation for slum dwellers in Bangkok, Thailand, failed to reach the least privileged groups in the community, especially those with limited education.

5. Political liberty and security of person

- In seeking to find family members who had been forcibly removed from their homes by security forces in Central America, new groups, including many under female leadership with no experience in political action, formulated a politics of social resistance and moral regeneration, later expanding their activities to include demands for justice, as well as welfare and women's and labor rights.

- There is a significant difference between U.S. and Japanese efforts to advance human rights in China because of different priorities in the two nations. Given China's own priorities, foreign pressure on the human rights situation have had only marginal effects, but the U.S. influence on China's basic human rights is even more limited than Japan's.

6. Indigenous rights

- Schools established in India by the Tibetan government-in-exile to protect the cultural heritage soon resembled those the Chinese introduced in Occupied Tibet itself in that neither is primarily devoted to protecting the tradition of the people because of limitations imposed by the political environment.
- More effective organization at different levels among indigenous Andean populations, supported mainly by NGOs, has led to the accumulation of greater capacity to assert their political, property, and other rights.

REFERENCES

Acharya, Amita. 1995. *Human Rights in Southeast Asia: Dilemmas for Foreign Policy*. Toronto: University of Toronto-York University Joint Centre for Asia Pacific Studies, Eastern Asia Policy Papers 11.

Addams, Jane. 1902. *Democracy and Social Ethic*. New York: Macmillan.

Amnesty International. *Report 1996*. New York: Amnesty International USA.

Brown, L. David, and Darcy Ashman. 1996. "Participation, Social Capital and Intersectoral Problem-Solving: African and Asian Cases." *World Development* 24: 9, 1467–79.

Cobb, Roger. 1973. "The Beliefs Systems Perspective: An Assessment of a Framework." *Journal of Politics,* 35, (February).

Coleman, James S. 1988. "Social Capital in the Creation of Human Capital." *American Journal of Sociology* 94 Supplement S95–S120.

Dobyns, Henry F., Paul L. Doughty, and Harold D. Lasswell, eds. 1971. *Peasants, Power and Applied Social Change: Vicos as a Model*. Beverly Hills and London: Sage.

Emmerson, Donald. 1996. "Do Asian Values Exist?" Conference Report on "Cultural Sources of Human Rights in East Asia." *Human Rights Dialogue* 5, (June): 3.

Flora, Cornelia Butler. 1995. "Social Capital and Sustainability: Agriculture and Communities in the Plains and Corn Belt." Journal Paper No. J 16309, Iowa Agriculture and Home Economic Experiment Station, Project No. 3281, 1995, reprinted in *Sustainable Agriculture Newsletter,* (fall).

Freedom House. 1997. *Annual Survey of Freedom Country Scores, 1972–73 to 1995–96*. New York: Freedom House.

Freeman, Michael. 1995. "Are There Collective Human Rights?" *Political Studies,* Special Issue, Politics and Human Rights, 43:23–40.

Goldstein, Robert Justin. 1992. "The Limitations of Using Quantitative Data in Studying Human Rights Abuses" In *Human Rights and Statistics: Getting the Record Straight,* eds. Richard P. Claude and Thomas B. Jabine. Philadelphia, University of Pennsylvania Press.

Holsti, Ole. 1962 "The Belief System and National Images: A Case Study." *Journal of Conflict Resolution* 6: 3, (September).

Inkeles, Alex, and Jon C. Hooper. 1993. "A Century of Procedural Due Process Guarantees in Constitutions Worldwide: Testing the World Polity and Convergence Models." *La Revue Tocqueville, The Tocqueville Review* 14: 2, 41–51.

Kaplan, A. "Content Analysis and the Theory of Signs," *Philosophy of Science* 10. 230–247.

Lasswell, Harold D., and Allan R. Holmberg. 1969. "Toward a General Theory of Directed Value Accumulation and Institutional Development." In *Political and Administrative Development,* ed. Ralph Braibanti. Durham, NC: Duke University Press, 354–399.

Lasswell, Harold D. 1946. "Describing the Contents of Communications." In *Propaganda, Communication, and Public Opinion,* ed. B. L. Smith, H. D. Lasswell, and R. D. Casey. Princeton: University Press.

Lasswell, Harold D., Daniel Lerner, and John D. Montgomery. 1976. *Values and Development, Appraising Asian Experience.* Cambridge, MA: the MIT Press.

Lasswell, Harold D., Nathan Leites, et al. 1949. *Language of Politics.* New York: Stewart.

Loury, Glenn C. 1995. "The Social Capital Deficit." *The New Democrat,* May/June.

McDougal, Myres S., Harold D. Lasswell, and Lung-chu Che. 1980. *Human Rights and World Public Order.* New Haven: Yale University Press.

Nussbaum, Martha, and Amartya Sen, eds. 1993. *The Quality of Life.* Oxford: Clarendon Press.

Putnam, Robert D. 1993. *Making Democracy Work: Civic Traditions in Modern Italy.* Princeton, NJ, Princeton University Press.

———. 1993. "The Prosperous Community, Social Capital and Public Life," *The American Prospect* 13, Spring.

Spirer, Herbert F., and Louise Spirer. 1993. *Data Analysis for Monitoring Human Rights.* Washington: American Association for the Advancement of Science.

United Nations. 1995. *Human Rights, Status of International Instruments: Chart of Ratifications as at 31 December 1994.* New York and Geneva: United Nations, ST/HR/5, Sales No. E87.XIV.2.

N athan Glazer is Professor of Education and Sociology Emeritus, at Harvard University and co-editor of the quarterly journal of public policy, *The Public Interest.* At Harvard since 1968, he was previously a professor of sociology at the University of California, Berkeley. He writes mostly on American racial and ethnic issues, urban problems, and social policy. His recent books include *The Limits of Social Policy,* and *We Are All Multiculturalists Now* (both published by Harvard University Press), and *Conflicting Images: India and the United States,* co-edited with Sulochana Raghavan Glazer. He lived and studied in Japan in 1961–62, and has traveled and lectured often in Japan, India, and elsewhere in Asia. He published "Social and Cultural Factors in Japanese Economic Growth" (in *Asia's New Giant,* edited by Hugh Patrick and Henry Rosovsky) in 1976. He is also a contributing editor of *The New Republic,* for which he writes regularly.

3. Diffusion of Values and the Pacific Rim

Nathan Glazer

When we speak of "Asian values" we seem to have something in mind that extends beyond the specific tradition of Confucianism, something that needed no great tradition, great books, or classic philosophers to codify. That is the role that family, whether extended or nuclear, plays in almost all societies that have not reached the level of industrialization, urbanization, and state welfare provision typical of the economically developed countries of Western Europe and North America. . . . When we say Asian values today, when state Confucianism no longer exists, we are thinking of . . . pretty much what American politicians have in mind when they extol "family values" and mourn their demise.

When the "diffusion of values in the Pacific Rim" was first proposed as a topic for a conference and research, the somewhat flippant question immediately presented itself: Was the assumption to be that "we" considered it desirable that "our" values (those of the eastern shore of the rim, that is, the United States and Canada) diffuse to them, or that their values diffuse to us? (Mexico and Central and Latin America are also on "our" side of the Pacific, as Australia and New Zealand are on "theirs," but they do not enter into the discussion, which contrasts rather the Anglo-American nations on the Eastern Rim, with Japan, China, and the smaller nations of East Asia on the Western Rim of the Pacific Ocean.)

This question presented itself because both possibilities, and both directions for diffusion, have figured significantly in the relationship between the two sides of the Pacific Rim. During the first half of the half-century since the end of World War II, during which the United States has militarily and politically dominated the Pacific Rim, it was taken for granted, at least on this side of the rim (and by many on the other side, too), that, yes, it would be desirable for our values to diffuse to them. The unquestioned assumption of the time, at least in the United States, was that our values served as the basis for our solid and long-standing democracy, and for our economically prosperous and innovative society; their values—whatever they might be—had supported no such desirable results. They had either served as the basis of, or at least did not prevent, the long-standing economic backwardness and political and military disorder of China and the aggressive militarism of Japan. What could we learn from them? We had also just defeated Japan in war. One doesn't expect to learn from one's defeated enemy. We were on the contrary busily engaged in trying to impose our values on occupied Japan.

In China, 50 years ago, the traditional values seemed to have been suddenly replaced wholesale by the new values propagated by a victorious—and it appeared hardly Chinese—totalitarian Communism. Whatever these values might in time contribute to China's achieving wealth and prosperity (and of course we were doubtful about that, and expected democratic India to do better), they were fundamentally the expression of a society that radically suppressed all dissent, maintained and expanded powerful military forces, and was seen as—as it indeed was—a potential threat to its neighbors. We hoped they would not be diffused, and we devoted much treasure and many lives in the next few decades to preventing that.

We thought no better of Japanese values. We insisted that the emperor be replaced as the near-divine apex of a hierarchical society and reduced to a figurehead, and that democratic institutions, as we understood them, should be established throughout the society. "Democratic" to us meant "American," so we insisted for example that the control of education be decentralized, and that local and independent school districts should be run by elected school boards, just as in the United States. (Was centralized French education then less democratic than ours? No matter, we believed Japanese values should be changed, and introducing American institutions, it was hoped, would change them.) We also required that the land be divided, unions be recognized, and the economy be policed against trusts and cartels, just as the economy of the United States was.

So during the brief "American century," which may be dated from the victory of the United States in World War II to the economic crises of the early 1970s, we took it for granted that our values were better than theirs, our institutions were better than theirs, and one had to be of heterodox opinion indeed to suggest otherwise. But since the 1970s and the many challenges to the overwhelming predominance of the United States in world affairs—militarily (note Vietnam), economically (note the loss of manufacturing predominance in many spheres), and to some extent even culturally and politically (though there American predominance is least threatened)—we have seen first a questioning and then almost a reversal of our views of our values and theirs. Their values may not be so bad after all; at least they seem not to be contradictory to rapid economic development, as we once believed, are certainly concordant with it, and indeed may even be better for initiating and sustaining rapid economic development than ours. We are more doubtful about their relationship to democracy.

We have simultaneously become more doubtful about the relationship between our own values and our democracy and economic health than we were in the 1950s and 1960s. Our values, most American believe, have changed radically. The American family is weaker, much more subject to divorce and breakup than in the past, out-of-wedlock childbirth has climbed sharply, crime and juvenile delinquency have gone up markedly, school achievement leaves us dissatisfied, and we believe ourselves to be more self-centered and hedonistic than we were. Our democracy is still strong, but it is undoubtedly weakened by the fact that Americans in general think much less well about the institutions that maintain American democracy in the 1990s—Congress, the presidency, the courts—than they did 30 years ago. Our economy is also strong at the moment, but we have gone through some serious scares in the last few decades, and our fears are aroused by the remarkable economic performance of first Japan, then the little tigers, and now China. The prevalent view is that our values are not as good as they were, from the point of view of maintaining an ordered democracy and continued economic achievement, a viewpoint that sustains such phenomena as William Bennett's *The Book of Virtues.*

Such a change in our self-image must have consequences on how we view the values of others. Values once thought to hamper economic achievement no longer appear to do so. As a result hard-nosed economists now join sociologists, anthropologists, and political scientists in recognizing values as important features identifying a society and differentiating it from others. Even the relative newness and weakness of democracy in many countries of the Western Pacific Rim, and its absence in others, leads us to ponder whether we censure these deficiencies too harshly. Perhaps, we question ourselves, "their" values—those of the other side of the Pacific Rim—may in time sustain a different kind of democracy, less individualistic and rights-oriented, more socially concerned and duty-oriented, and one not worse than ours. It is something we would never have considered 30 years ago, but as our democracy goes through scandal after scandal and struggles with deep moral conflicts that divide Americans sharply, it is a thought that cannot be dismissed out of hand.

ARE THERE "ASIAN" VALUES?

We may divide the last 50 years of close engagement with East Asia into two periods of roughly equal duration, one in which most informed opinion took it for granted that it would be better for them and their world if our values diffused to them, and one in which we have at the least doubts about the matter and have pondered the ways in which some of their values may be better than ours.

This is an initial and far too crude formulation of the issue. There are many questions that must be cleared out of the way before we can even make sense of talking about their values and ours. The first of course, is what are their values, and what are ours? The second is, can we speak of "their values" when there are so many and such diverse societies on the other, western, side of the Pacific Rim? Can we even speak sensibly of "our values" when we have undergone a huge transformation in our society? Culture wars rage, racial divides persist and deepen, mass immigration brings representatives of every culture—including prominently those of East Asia—into ever more significant roles in American life, multicultural disputes rend the common fabric of our education, our once-vaunted common school. And the most difficult question of all—what is, after all, the relationship between economic effectiveness and values? Economies can be understood as the result of the application of the factors of capital, labor, technology, and of wise polices suited to situation and time. Is more necessary? Most economists think not. And yet, as human capital looms ever larger as an explanation of economic effectiveness, as the role of education becomes ever more important in explanations of economic growth, it would appear we do have some reason to take values seriously. Do not values play a key role in education?

Attention to all these initial empirical and methodological questions is indeed necessary before we can speak sensibly of the diffusion of values. These questions have been engaged steadily over the past 50 years, and have become the coin of much sociological and social-psychological research.[1] We have seen fashions in this research come and go. We used to speak about "national character," a term widely used in World War II and after, but which in time fell into disuse and disrespect because of its odor of national arrogance. The comparative study of values has come to substitute for the study of national character, but it does very much the same thing. The main bases for this research have been ethnographic inquiry (particularly for the countries on the other side of the Pacific Rim—ethnography is generally something employed for the "other"), public opinion polls often designed specifically to get at values, and less extensive but more intensive social psychological investigations using ingenious tests such as eliciting responses to moral dilemmas. Despite the difficulties in drawing conclusions from such research, we do find some striking differences among nations in how people order certain values and goods.[2] Yes, there are differences between their values and ours, at least as determined by the tools available to us.

While human beings everywhere desire security, prosperity, respect, freedom, and a variety of other goods, they do not necessarily order them in the same manner. Nor are the differences simply random ones. They seem to aggregate into complexes characterizing a nation, a society, a culture. With more or less confidence we can characterize the individuals in a society and its overall patterns as bearing some large distinctive characteristics, for example, whether they emphasize "individualism" or some alternative transcending the individual and his interests—family, clan, company, or nation. Quite typically, in speaking of the nations of the Western Rim of the Pacific in contrast to those of the Eastern Rim, we do contrast individualism, seen as distinctively American, with various kinds of collectivism, seen as more typical of the Asian nations. These are sticky contrasts, yet so many informed persons make them, whether journalists with long residence in these countries or social scientists who have studied them, and they are so visible in some research, that we must assume there are good grounds for considering them real instead of simply expressions of bias and prejudice.

There are of course great differences among the nations of the Western Rim whose rapid economic growth has brought to prominence these questions about their values and ours. Japan, Korea, Taiwan, Hong Kong, Singapore, the big dragon and the little ones, differ in many respects. Koreans, for example,[3] are outraged by being taken for Japanese, and the various countries populated by the Chinese differ sharply on the basis of their very different political histories. As Malaysia, Thailand, and Indonesia have joined the countries of the Western Rim in achieving rapid economic growth—the Philippines and Vietnam may soon be joining the club—the diversity becomes even greater. What sense then is there in speaking of "their" values as contrasted with "ours"?

There is one major reason why social scientists believe we have not created a meaningless omnium gatherum of the countries of the Western Rim in speaking generally of their values in contrast to ours. It is that there is indeed a common great cultural tradition which plays a dominant role in the history of most of the countries of the Western Rim. It finds expression in many small traditions, the ordinary expectations and practices of common life, and principally in the texture of family life. That great tradition is Confucianism. It is supplemented throughout the area by the world religion of Buddhism, which appears to be less influential on economic growth than Confucianism.

Admittedly when we reach Thailand, Malaysia, and Indonesia we are well outside the specific influence of Confucianism and the Confucian world ethic, and have to begin to take account of Islam, if we think of the great cultural and religious traditions. Yet some scholars, noting the very important role of Chinese émigrés and their descendants in the economic life of these countries would argue we are not yet quite beyond the sphere of Confucianism and its influence.[4] With the Philippines, we are even further outside this tradition. What sense then, as these countries join those who are achieving rapid economic growth, in speaking of Confucianism as the common source of the values that support this development? Clearly our theoretical inquiries trail behind the empirical developments they try to explain. If the non-Confucian countries of the Western Rim continue in the pattern of rapid economic growth, and if further they are joined by the countries of the Indian subcontinent, we will have other hypotheses in the field of values and their historical background to consider when we try to understand the differences among nations.

But there is no arguing with the fact that it is the nations that share to a substantial degree a background in Confucianism, a doctrine which emphasizes the significance of orderly hierarchical relations in family life, in education, in relation to rulers, that first surprised us by demonstrating rapid economic growth. Had Japan remained unique as an industrializing and economically developing nation there might have been no need to refer to Confucianism. While Confucianism was among the Chinese (and Korean) influences that have shaped Japanese culture, Buddhism was more significant, as was native Shintoism. But as the little dragons joined in, and then China itself, the common Confucian background, in some form or another, attracted the attention of scholars as diverse as Peter Berger and Roderick MacFarquhar. Herman Kahn was perhaps the first to note it in his remarkable book, *The Emerging Japanese Superstate.*[5] It is this complex of values which has been investigated most thoroughly as the source of the values that have supported this development.[6]

For one example of this concordance of values among the diverse countries on the western side of the Pacific and its difference from ours, consider the research of Harold Stevenson and his colleagues contrasting classrooms and parental attitudes in Japan and Taiwan with classrooms and attitudes in the United States. This research was conducted in Sendai in Japan, Taipei in Taiwan, and Minneapolis in the United States. There seems to be little difference between Japan and Taiwan, and both differ greatly from the United States. Larger classes on the other side of the Pacific Rim nevertheless produce better results. Children are more responsive to the authority of the teacher, are more committed to working hard, are readier to assume it is their own responsibility if they do not succeed. Their parents expect more from them, and even though the children do better than American children, academically, their parents are less satisfied. On the American side, parental satisfaction with modest results is certainly consistent with so many criticisms of our current values, their slackness, their falling away from any idea of rigor, their adoption of immediate pleasure for long-term satisfactions, their minimization of responsibility to family or state.[7]

It is true Taiwan was under Japanese rule for the first half of this century (as was Korea), but anyone with knowledge of the two societies knows they are quite different, and it is not because of Taiwan's old connection with Japan that we find these similarities among them, and these differences from the United States. We would find the same in Korean schools, and in mainland Chinese schools, in Hong Kong schools, in Singapore schools. Some common base of values, whether to be found in Confucianism or elsewhere, seems to be working its effects in all these societies, different as they are, in many characteristics. We are justified in considering there is some basis of commonality in the cultures of East Asia, and substantial differences from what we find in the United States, whether those differences are explained by Confucian values or something else.

HOW VALUES MATTER

Even if we can make distinctions among nations, and for certain purposes can combine nations as various as Japan, Taiwan, and Korea, what is the basis for our assumption that these divergent values matter in important ways? Our initial question is based on the assumption that some values are better for some purposes than others, in particular for economic development and for political democracy.

The debate among social scientists on these matters has been shaped overwhelmingly by the work of Max Weber. Since Weber and his monumental researches on the relations between the ethic or ethics of various religious orientations and economic development, the question has been pursued again and again: Just what was the relationship between the Protestant ethic, specific to Western Europe in the sixteenth and seventeenth centuries, and the rise of capitalism? And if we find capitalism rising in Japan, the little dragons, China, what does that do to Weber's thesis?

The literature in support of, or in opposition to, or inspired by Weber's thesis is enormous. But in the first half-century after the publication of Weber's seminal essay *The Protestant Ethic and the Spirit of Capitalism* in 1904–05, the debate around Weber's thesis was confined to analyzing it in the context of the unquestioned reality that capitalism had indeed developed in the West, along with the other forms of rationalization of different spheres of life (law, government, the sciences, the arts, etc.) that Weber emphasized as the distinctive contribution of Northwestern Europe. The East hardly entered into the discussion, even though as early as 1905, with Japan showing amazing economic development as demonstrated by its victory over Russia, the question could have been asked. And what explains Japan? Certainly not the Protestant ethic in the specific Calvinist form that Weber postulated as the spirit of capitalism. Perhaps there was discussion before World War II of Japan's rise and its significance for Weber's thesis, but I have seen no references to such literature, even in writing by East Asians about the East Asian countries.

Weber did expand his researches into important comparative studies of ancient China, India, and Judaism, but these did not enter much into the initial argument over his thesis. Critics have proposed as alternative or supplement to these a Jewish ethic, or a secular ethic, or even a Catholic ethic, all discussed within the confines of European civilization; but no one has paid much attention to other forms of economic development, perhaps indeed other capitalisms elsewhere. Weber's research on ancient China, Hinduism, and Judaism did not much engage his epigones and critics until well after World War II. Weber had little to say about the relationship between values and political democracy, but social scientists since, such as Seymour Martin Lipset, Samuel Huntington, Gabriel Almond, Sidney Verba, and Alex Inkeles have had a great deal to say. We will reserve the discussion of the relations between values and democracy for a later section.

Weber's work, as well as the debate around it, is directly relevant to our initial paradox: Until the 1970s or so we believed that everyone needs our values for economic development and political democracy, while after that time we have been in considerable doubt about the matter, as the rapid economic rise of the countries of the Western Rim began to lead us to consider whether we might not be better off with some of their values instead. Weber stands at the beginning of any serious contemporary discussion of the relationship between values and economic development; the problem is that, according to Weber, the Confucian ethic which dominates East Asia is exactly what we would expect to hamper economic growth, rather than contribute to it. Confucianism places the scholar at the top of the social hierarchy and alongside him the government bureaucrat supporting the emperor, who is ideally a scholar in another manifestation. And so we have the great examination system of Imperial China which lasted for two thousand years and which was imitated in Korea. Confucianism emphasizes a chain of loyalties beginning with filial piety and extending upwards to subservience to government. Japan did not adopt the examination system, but there we find the same chain of unquestioned loyalty based on feudalism. None of this seems to be ideal for capitalism, which we see as innovative, individualistic, indeed destructive of past traditions and forms.

The individualism fostered by various traditions in the West—from the Hebrew Bible, to Christianity, to science, to its Weberian apogee in

Calvinist Protestantism—is simply not important in the East. And yet Weber argues that it is the most extreme form of individualism—the quest for evidence of personal salvation by way of material success in this world—that is the source of capitalism and Western rationalism. How do the eminently Asian values epitomized in Confucianism connect to the result we see, where the most successful economies of the past few decades have been Japan, the little dragons, and now China released from the chains of Communist economic ideology?

The problem was put sharply by *The Economist* in an article on the role of cultural values in economic development: Nowadays, what seems important about the tradition is its encouragement of hard work, savings, and investment for the future, plus its emphasis on cooperation toward a single end. All these features have been adduced to explain why the tradition has helped Asian growth. To Max Weber, however, the same tradition seemed entirely different. He argued that the Confucian insistence on obedience to parental authority discouraged competition and innovation and hence inhibited economic success.[8]

Eastern and Western social scientists have come together many times to explore this paradox. Was Weber simply wrong? Was he mistaken about what supported the rise of rational capitalism in the West, or what hindered its rise in the East? Or are there simply many routes to economic development, of which the West exploited one and the East another?

WEBER'S THESIS TODAY

One problem in the discussion of Weber's thesis has been its complexity. It is quite typical for even the best informed to get it wrong, according to the keepers of the true flame. Thus in one important conference in Singapore dealing with the relations of values to the economic success of East Asia, Roderick MacFarquhar, among the first to raise the possibility that it is indeed Confucian values that underlies the rise of the Western Rim, points out, sensibly enough:

> There is no difference between the entrepreneurial dynamism of certain Indian merchants and the Chinese merchants in Southeast Asia. I am not so sure that a religion which preaches rejection of the world necessarily implies one cannot have entrepreneurial spirit. In fact Hinduism is essentially about individuals. The individual has to seek his rebirth. It is up to the individual to decide whether or not in this life he performs acts which force him to a worse rebirth in the next life.[9]

This seems to make sense to me. The exemplar of Weber's Protestant ethic seeks his individual salvation. Is not what the individual seeks in Hinduism an equivalent?

But Wolfgang Schluchter, who has played the central role in the reexamination of the Weberian thesis as it applies to the East, corrects him:

> The spirit of pursuing monetary gain, the greatest possible monetary gain, has existed in all civilized countries. An entrepreneurial spirit of this kind is based on the pursuit of happiness, an unleashing of the natural impulse to acquisition. But this is not the kind of entrepreneurial spirit Weber had in mind. He talked about the spirit of rational capitalism. Its distinctive feature is the idea that making money is to be regarded as a moral duty, as a calling, and this implies the rational tempering of the natural impulse to acquisition. Strictly speaking, those endowed with this spirit do not pursue utilitarian end [sic] in economic activities, but are dedicated to a cause that calls for methodical life conduct, for inner-worldly asceticism in one's occupation.[9]

Weber was indeed quite severe on China's possibility of parallelling Western development. He fully understood China's achievement in various fields, such as technology, but to him all this was empirical rather than rational:

> Practical rationalism, the intrinsic attitude of bureaucracy to life, free of all competition, could work itself out fully [in China]. There was no rational science, no rational practice of art, no rational theology, jurisprudence, medicine, natural science or technology; there was neither divine nor human authority which could contest the bureaucracy. Only an ethic congruent with bureaucracy could be created. . .[10]

But in all fairness to Weber, one should point out he was writing of a China descending into warlordism and poverty, and he did make a distinction, as Gary G. Hamilton and Kao Cheng-she point out, "between the independent development of capitalism and its subsequent diffusion." He wrote at the end of his study of China:

> The Chinese in all probability would be quite capable, probably more capable than the Japanese, of assimilating capitalism which has technically and economically been fully developed in the modern

culture area. It is obviously not a question of deeming the Chinese "naturally ungifted" for the demands of capitalism. But compared to the Occident, the varied conditions which externally favoured the origin of capitalism in China did not suffice to create it.[11]

This gets Weber off the hook (except for his odd expectation that Japan, even after it had demonstrated its economic and military prowess, would be less capable of assimilating capitalism than China), but the fact is that this concession still does not help us understand how the predominant values contributed to economic development. From Weber's point of view, and the point of view of the contemporary Chinese reformers of his day, Confucianism and Chinese institutions generally not only stood in the way of originating capitalism but stood in the way of fostering it or any other important element of modernity:

> Ironically, from the beginning of this century, especially since the New Cultural Movement of May Fourth in 1919, most intellectuals have held the view that the root of China's backwardness lay in her cultural traditions, especially Confucian values. Not surprisingly, they vigorously attacked all aspects of Confucianism, particularly the Confucian value system. Their anti-traditionalism was total and uncompromising.[12]

At a time of national humiliation, the reformers were thinking of national power of course as well as economic power, but the latter was essential to the former. Sun Yat-sen thought the same way: "the Chinese, he said, lacked any national cohesion; they were 'a sheet of loose sand.' This condition he attributed to an excess of individualism and to a loyalty centred on the family rather than the nation."[13] Individualism can take many forms: Sun Yat-sen was clearly thinking of the commitment to family as standing in the way of the national cohesion he sought.

The commitments that modernist reformers and Sun Yat-sen thought of as standing in the way of developing economic strength and national power are what we today believe contributed to the economic rise of East Asia. We can call it, as others have, "post-Confucianism" or "vulgar Confucianism" or "popular Confucianism."

The essential point is that the chain of loyalties of classical Confucianism, and the attendant virtues it exalts, has been broken when it comes to loyalties above the family level, and of institutions that are family-like in their character, such as the family firm or quasi-family firm.

But loyalty at that lower level has remained firm. It has survived the elimination of emperor worship in Japan, the crushing imposition of a Communist antifamily value system in China, Japanese rule and the disasters of war in Korea, the unbridled free market of Hong Kong, and the economic development under strict state guidance of Singapore. If one thinks of their values and ours today, we cannot but be impressed by the low figures for divorce or children born out of wedlock in these countries, the high rate of savings, the emphasis on hard work primarily for ensuring the family future, the strong support of children's education and the insistence that they too work hard for the sake of the family, and the low crime rates. Not all these effects are to be found uniformly in East Asia, but taking the countries of the Western Rim as a whole, they stand in marked contrast to the United States on these measures of social stability.

SURVIVALS OF CONFUCIANISM

Weber wrote about state and imperial Confucianism, the great tradition that did work itself down, in doctrine and practice, to the relations between parent and child, brother and brother. That tradition does not survive intact anywhere, though it continues to be studied by scholars who try to reformulate it and adapt it. The little traditions that derive from it however survive everywhere, as current empirical research demonstrates. A few examples follows.

In Korea, only a tiny fraction of the population gives its religion as Confucian, though there remain in Korea a substantial number of Confucian institutions and scholars, perhaps more than in any other East Asian country. Yet when one examines convictions and practice, as has been done by the Korea Gallup survey, to determine whether respondents adhere to Confucian beliefs ("filial piety, the three cardinal virtues and five ethics, veneration of the ancient sages and wise men, inviolability of tradition," etc.), and to Confucian practices ("ancestral memorial ceremonies, filial piety, seniority deference," etc.) one finds that most Koreans can be described as Confucian. "Statistically 90 per cent of Catholics and 76.4 per cent of Protestants in Korea can be said to be Confucian according to their convictions and practices. In the case of Buddhists, the figure was as high as 100 per cent."[14] "All men are Confucians," in Korea at any rate, asserts Koh Byong-ik.

In a detailed study of the role of Confucianism in one Korean city, it was reported that "the city council awards special prizes to filial sons and virtuous women on the recommendation of the local Confucian society. Although the women's liberation movement criticizes the awards as contributing to the perpetuation of sexual inequality, it is done in all counties of the nation."[15]

A major corporation founded by the descendant of a leading Confucian scholar of the area favors local people and relatives for employment. "Workers easily adopt pseudo-kinship terminology for use among themselves. Seniors always emphasize Confucian ethics with regard to the relations between senior and junior, between father and son, and between brothers." Giant corporations such as Samsung and Hyundai "fill the presidencies of their member companies with the sons and nephews of their respective founders."[16]

In Hong Kong, where of course there has never been any official Confucianism (as there was in Korea when it was an independent kingdom), a 1982 survey, with two-thirds of the sample under the age of 35, showed that "57 percent maintained they were Chinese because they preserve values like filial piety, frugality, and respect for teachers." A survey of university students showed they perceived a number of areas of difference between themselves and Westerners: "The first is in family life where the Chinese will endorse filial piety, and have reservations about voicing opinions different from their parents."[17] Business enterprises depend on family for recruitment.[18]

Taiwan shows similar patterns. Hwang Kwang-kuo reports on research using Kohlberg's "moral stages" research. In Kohlberg's own research in the 1960s, boys in the United States and Taiwan were similar at age 10 in their moral evaluations. "By the age of 16, the situation has changed. Compared with the U.S. group at age 16, their Chinese counterparts in Taiwan use more of the "good boy" types of thinking of stage 3, display less of the contractual-legalistic orientation of stage 5, and less of the conscience-or-principle orientation of stage 6." I will not describe these stages of moral development in any detail, but the highest, or sixth stage, bears some similarity to Weber's "Protestant ethic." It is a stage of autonomous moral judgment. We can argue whether it is indeed the "highest"—the point here however is only to demonstrate the difference.

This research was replicated in the early 1980s: "[T]he authority and social-order maintaining orientation of stage 4 becomes the predominant type of moral reasoning for Chinese after the age of 17. In other words, Chinese youths tend to identify with the norms of the society or group to which they belong. They have strong concern for the good of society as a whole and tend to make moral judgments from a perspective which is believed to be shared by other "typical" members of the group. Their needs, values, or judgments are subordinated to those of the group; usually they show respect for authority and emphasise the importance of maintaining social order for its own sake."

Behavior follows suit: "The majority of Taiwanese parents are living with at least one of the married sons. Couples who do not live with the husband's parents usually remain linked to them by visits or financial support."[19]

CONFUCIANISM OR "FAMILY VALUES"?

Are we really speaking of Confucianism when we report findings such as those in the previous segment? Many more could be reported, showing a consistent bent in the countries of the Western Rim toward what has been called post or vulgar or popular Confucianism. In none of these countries does any official Confucianism prevail, in government or in education. Are we speaking of more than a strong family ethic, perhaps not very different from that which prevailed in the United States until recent decades, and that still prevails among new immigrants, indeed the same family ethic that has been the almost uniform brick and mortar of all traditional societies before Westernization, modernization, urbanization, industrialization, mass communication, and their corrosive influences?

When we speak of "Asian values" we seem to have something in mind that extends beyond the specific tradition of Confucianism, something that needed no great tradition, great books, or classic philosophers to codify. This is the role that family, whether extended or nuclear, plays in almost all societies that have not reached the level of industrialization, urbanization, and state welfare provision typical of the economically developed countries of Western Europe and North America. In other words, when we say "Asian values" today, when state Confucianism no longer exists, we are thinking of (and one must excuse the banality of the expression) pretty much what American politicians have in mind when they extol "family values" and mourn their demise.

The family is universal. Some particular degree of closeness and responsibility binding family members in given relationships is also near universal. Mothers are expected to rear children; fathers are expected to help; brothers and sisters have certain relationships and responsibilities they are expected to maintain. And so on. Admittedly the definition of who is to be included in family may differ—in one society, the father's relatives, but not the mother's, in another, vice versa, more or less of the relatives outside the nuclear family, etc. The nuclear family remains the basis of society, a basis that becomes markedly reduced in advanced modern society, where various functions are taken over by extrafamilial institutions. We still count on the family, for the most part, to raise, socialize, and in some measure educate the children who will form part of the society. But we also have developed in advanced Western societies substitutes in abundance, either because they were essential owing to the initial weakening of the family under the strains and stresses of urbanization and industrialization, or because these varied substitutes have themselves undermined the family; that of course is a subject of permanent dispute between liberals and conservatives.

Clearly for economic effectiveness these family bonds are important. Children are spurred on to work harder in school and to achieve, not only for the honor of the family but because they are expected eventually to support—financially and socially—aged parents. Businesses generally find the most dependable employees in family or quasi-family members, in people from the same village or town, and the most dependable subordinates and successors in children and nephews and in-laws. Superiors demand respect and deference, and inferiors give it. This is the way the world has run for millennia. And this is what the social scientists exploring the role of Asian values in the countries of the Western Pacific Rim report.

But this cannot be the key ingredient, helpful as it is, in economic success and achievement. If it were, we would be at a loss to explain why the Indian subcontinent lags behind, for example. There is no problem there about weakness of family ties. Indeed, Indians viewing American movies have as their first response, where is the family? In Indian movies, the hero has a family, the heroine has a family, even the villain has a family. In American movies, each person stands as an individual, devoid of familial and kinship ties. No problem with family values in India. Yet some other features have hampered Indian economic development. I suspect our interpretation of what these features are will all be after the fact, as is the case with so much in our efforts to understand the differences among nations. To quote *The Economist* again: "In countries as various as Japan, India, Ghana and South Korea, notions of cultural determination of economic performance have been proved routinely wrong (in 1945, India and Ghana were expected to do best of the four—partly because of their supposed cultural inheritance)."[20] *The Economist* does not say whose expectation that was. But it need not have been any minor social scientist—recall Max Weber's expectations concerning the suitability of China and Japan for capitalist development.

Why familism sometimes contributes to economic success, as in the Western Pacific Rim, and sometimes fails to, as in Africa, will lead us to think of the differences among societies and cultures as to what family connection means. Some report that in Africa, family connection means not that family members will assist the entrepreneur by providing willing and loyal employees but will move in on him and insist that they have a right to be supported, which will eat up his profits and preventing productive reinvestment. Family connection and closeness also mean nepotism, as the researchers from the Western Pacific Rim report (probably least in Japan), but nepotism, in government and business, also can undermine economic effectiveness.

John Wong, writing on Singapore, makes the excellent point that economists will not take seriously the argument that ascribes great importance in East Asian economic development to Confucian values until "it is expressed in a testable hypothesis. It is not enough to argue in general terms that the Confucian ethos is conducive to increased personal savings and hence higher capital formation. It must also be demonstrated forcefully and specifically whether such savings have been productively invested in business or industry or have been squandered on noneconomic spending, such as the fulfillment of social obligations, which is after all also a part of the Confucian social system. It must also be shown how Confucian values have actually resulted in effective manpower development in terms of promoting the upgrading of skills and not in encouraging merely intellectual self-cultivation or self-serving literary pursuits. A typical Confucian gentleman in the past would have shown open disdain for menial labor."[21] One is reminded of explanations of Jewish intellectual and economic achievement by resorting to the Rabbinic tradition of learning. One has to be more specific: what one learns is not, at first glance, conducive to either economic development or the winning of Nobel prizes in science.

The family features described by social scientists that are a central part of the great tradition of Confucianism, and that still survive in various popular forms, are as yet too crude to serve as instruments to help us understand how values have contributed to the extraordinary rise of the Western Pacific. This leads us back to many of the other factors that are necessary ingredients in economic success. We do seem to find elements beyond the economic factors of production and political stability that we think have contributed to economic success on the Western Pacific Rim. After the fact, we have decided that the absence of material resources is not as important as we once thought it was for economic development and that human and social capital are more important than we thought they were.

In describing Asian values, we seem to be referring to features that are found in all traditional societies. These elements seem to be particularly helpful, in combination with other factors, in spurring on economic development once it gets started—family loyalties, the commitment to aid family members, the investment in children's education, saving for family advancement, all come into play. Curiously, it is just these values that some claim have been undermined by economic development in the West—"destructive effects of capitalism on bourgeois values," according to Joseph Schumpeter, or "the cultural contradictions of capitalism," in the view of Daniel Bell.

With rapid economic development well under way, we see a rising concern in the countries of the Western Pacific Rim that the traditional values that they long took for granted are being undermined by Westernization. It is then that "Confucian values" come into their own, and leaders wonder how they can shore up these guiding principles, as Singapore tried to do for a while. None of the states of Eastern Asia thought Asian or Confucian or traditional values would be helpful in getting them started on the road to economic development. At this point they worry about losing values that seem, in retrospect, to have been important in spurring their surprising takeoffs, and now are threatened by Westernization.

Singapore has been perhaps most self-conscious about the matter, and indeed for a few years tried to introduce into its schools the study of "Confucian values."[22] This course of study was not very popular, and did not stand up well against the growing strength of Christianity and the revival of Buddhism (which were perhaps in themselves responses to rapid economic growth and modernization?). In 1988, the First Deputy

Prime Minister "brought up the idea of a national ideology, arguing that Singapore, as an open society constantly exposed to western ideas and values, needed to formalize a set of core values." Four core values were identified: "community over self, upholding the family as the basic building block of society, resolving major issues through consensus, instead of contention, and stressing racial and religious tolerance and harmony." They obviously include Confucian elements but are expected to be acceptable to all the elements of the Singapore population, Chinese, Malay and Indian, and all the religions.[23]

ASIAN VALUES AND DEMOCRACY

The Western Rim of the Pacific has apparently needed no assistance from the economically more advanced Eastern Rim when it comes to the values that were helpful in getting onto the path of rapid economic development; its own values served well enough. When it comes to political democracy, however, matters are different. The specific elements of political democracy were originated and first clearly formulated in the West— the rule of law, independent judiciaries, constitutions, equal rights, political equality, parliamentarian government—and were exported to Asia, as they were to all parts of the world. They are now considered almost everywhere the necessary characteristics of modern political states, even if many regimes fall short of implementing them. The formal institutions of political democracy were adopted in scores of new and old non-European states, but democracy as an everyday reality has progressed slowly. It has become well established in Japan (though some Western observers remain skeptical as to democracy's health and strength in that nation), but a strong authoritarianism that brooked no political opposition has dominated South Korea and Taiwan for most of their postwar history, Hong Kong was a non-self-governing colony, and China remains under Communist rule, which of course does not allow political opposition. Most interestingly, the leader of Singapore is formulating a version of democracy which to Western eyes falls considerably short of what democracy should be.

Here the Eastern Rim, which in the postwar period imposed its values and institutions on Japan as clearly the best, has good reason for believing the Western Rim still has something to learn, and that it would be well for the values that support political democracy to continue to move westward across the Pacific. We have already referred to Singapore's effort to place the teaching of Confucian values in its schools and then to formulate a "national ideology" that placed community and family over self. One reason for this development was to maintain the conditions that have fostered Singapore's remarkable economic growth. Looking at these developments from the perspective of the Eastern Rim, however, one strongly suspects that another reason to emphasize community and to downplay individualism is to maintain the control of the dominant party.

Clearly a number of elements come together to explain this concern with the threat of "Westernization" in Singapore. We see the same in Malaysia, and similar concerns in other East Asian countries. One element is, as in Singapore, the desire to maintain the values that support economic achievement.

Another is to protect the society against the social and cultural changes—in family structure, in sexual behavior, and in education—that have so transformed the advanced Western democracies in the last few decades and which no Asian leader would want to see at home. Hardly any Western leaders wanted to see them either, it could be pointed out; they were rather simply helpless in the grip of these changes, which are promoted by mass media, mass entertainment industries, mass education, all abetted by competitive open markets and rapid economic growth.

It is a third element that arouses suspicion: that is, that one motivation behind the emphasis on "Asian values" and the demand that they be protected against "Westernization" is to maintain the existing power and authority of the ruling elite and to prevent effective political competition and opposition. This is scarcely a valid reason for the attack on the West: As Amartya Sen effectively argues, what is at stake here is not Western power, which is gone, or Western influence, but the rights of Asians.[24] Whatever the history of the formulation and the defense and justification of these rights, they are now almost universally accepted as the due of every human being, in international instruments adopted by the overwhelming majority of the nations of the world.[25]

How effective Asian leaders will be in preventing the progress of democratic values and practices in the countries of the Western Rim of the Pacific remains to be seen. Clearly democracy was no necessary precondition for economic rise. The social changes and affluence of economic development, however, may well be a force, if not a necessary precondition, pushing for more democracy.[26] It is hard to believe that societies in which the great mass of the populace is educated to a high standard, in which the middle class grows rapidly, in which the professional classes increase in size and influence, in which the mass media, new and old, give access to developments around the world, will long accept authoritarian rule without protest.

Here is another issue in the relationship between wealth and values on which we cannot pronounce with any confidence as social scientists. Certain values, as we have seen, may well be necessary—along with other things—in making possible rapid economic growth. Once that growth has taken hold, these values may be undermined by the society and civilization that growth brings into being, but economic growth may also foster other values, such as those that support democracy. Students of the relationship between wealth and democracy lend some credence to this thesis but whatever the state of the evidence, here is one set of values and practices that the Eastern Rim, even while it is shaken in its self-confidence and arrogance by the economic rise of the Western Rim, can advocate without embarrassment.

lex Inkeles is currently Senior Fellow of the Hoover Institution and Professor of Sociology, Emeritus, at Stanford University. He previously was Professor of Sociology at Harvard University. Author of some 150 articles in sociology and social psychology, his work focuses on comparative studies of nations, societies, and cultures. Most recent fruits of this effort are *National Character: A Psychosocial Perspective,* issued by Transaction Publishers in 1997, and *One World Emerging? Convergence and Divergence in Industrial Societies,* which Westview Press will publish in 1998. Among his honors he counts election to the National Academy of Sciences, the American Academy of Arts and Sciences, and the American Philosophical Society.

4. Continuity and Change in Popular Values on the Pacific Rim[1]

Alex Inkeles

The Pacific Rim is being inundated by a flood of forces exposing it to industrialization, modernization, and globalization. Occupational systems are transformed, mass communication of all kinds washes over every shore and reaches every distant corner. . . . In the process, many fundamental values are challenged and reformulated, basic human relationships are redefined and reordered.

In the deepest part of the Brazilian rain forest, near the city of Manaus, two great streams come together, and they respond to their joining in a distinctive way. One branch, already dubbed the Amazon, arrives a muddy, sand colored, churning river. The other, seeming to flow equally strongly, is by contrast more nearly brown, close to the color of tobacco, noticeably clear and even translucent.[2] At the point where the two rivers come together, they do not immediately blend but rather run side by side within common banks for several miles, so sharply delineated at their common margin that one could easily imagine there was a great glass wall separating the two. But gradually the swirling and eddying of the river becomes manifest. The two streams begin to run together at the edges and then gradually to blend into a new more uniform consistency. A few miles further on, the Amazon has become one uniform stream, once again a predominantly muddy sand color. Perhaps a scientific test of the waters might identify individual elements which had been carried into the mixture of the two great tributaries. But certainly to most observers it would seem that the predominant character of the new river more reflected the original Amazon than it did the stream which had recently joined it.

Just so in Asia, and especially on the Pacific Rim, we see the confluence of two great streams of culture, operating, however, under the vast and powerful stimuli of industrialization, urbanization, modernization, and globalization. As in my geographical account, these two streams—Asian and Western—do manage for a period to run side by side, preserving remarkably intact their distinctive identities. But as more time passes, and as they increasingly become entangled with each other, a vast blending ensues. Both great sources contribute in very significant ways to the new melded stream. But I believe the nature of the forces at work insures that one of the streams will come to predominate, and that the emergent new river will more reflect the long-standing properties of the one rather than the other.

The river metaphor, and the model it suggests of modernization as a dominant force in the contemporary world, certainly have imperfections and surely can operate only within certain parameters. While acknowledging these limitations, I still think the metaphor and the model capture the essence of the great transformation many societies and cultures on the Pacific Rim are experiencing.

A Pause to Consider Certain Conceptual Issues

If we are to make a case for change, we need some agreement as to the character of the entities whose change we purport to document, and some common standards to enable us to judge whether or not change has occurred.

One great strand in the web of change girdling the Pacific Rim may be broadly characterized as organizational or structural. An example might be the development of a modern system of law and of the supporting institutions and professions—courts, barristers and solicitors, and wardens and prisons—under British rule in Hong Kong. We count as at the same level of importance the development of the political structure on Taiwan, with its various elements such as a system of legislative bodies, an effective administrative apparatus, and ultimately a collection of free-standing and competitive political parties. Along similar lines, varying by place and time, a whole panoply of institutional change and innovation in social structure, especially in the economic and political spheres, has spread over the Pacific Rim. Profound changes have been introduced in education, in the occupational structure, in urbanization, and in transportation and communication. These changes may be thought of as the main force producing the shifts in attitude and behavior that I have taken as the focus of my investigation. I note here in passing how aware I am of this process of structural transformation, and commit myself, as I come to my conclusions, to return to those structures and their influence. Apart from structural change, there are at least two great realms of human response which may be seen as proper foci of our attention. Those realms may be thought of as broadly divided into the cognitive and the behavioral. As manifestations of the cognitive, I have in mind attitudes and values, images of the good life, personal aspirations, and ideas about interpersonal relations both formal and intimate. Such mental sets and ways of thinking about the world are properly separated from, and understood to stand in a problematic relationship to, actual behavior. Thus people may affirm the virtue of charity but give very little to private welfare organizations, and they may stress the moral obligation for filial piety without necessarily providing for the suitable maintenance of their aged parents.

A Methodological Excursus

As we get closer to our subject matter, a number of challenges, or perhaps cautions, are likely to confront us, stemming in part from differences in style characteristic of different investigators, but also arising from experience—sometimes bitter—in the actual pursuit of the issue at hand.

If we take seriously the idea that we are looking for evidence of *continuity* and *change* in attitude, value and behavior, we must acknowledge that the form in which most data will be available to us does not provide a compelling basis for judging the relative stability over time of popular sentiments in the Pacific Rim countries. Unfortunately, a large number of the most interesting questions have been asked only once. We are thus usually left with an *absolute* datum taken at a single point is time, rather than having the preferable *relative* fact for several points in time. To get around this limitation, we must perform a particular intellectual exercise. We do this by evaluating the single observation we have for the current situation against the condition *assumed* to have existed at a prior time. That assumption, in turn, is based on historical and cultural analysis.

Consider, for example, the possibility that current research finds some 75 percent of young women in an Asian population say they expect to select their own mate rather than have their parents make the selection. If everything we know about that population based on historical and cultural analyses suggests that in earlier times it was standard for parents to select spouses for their children, then we may reasonably *assume* that our current information reflects a substantial change in norms, and probably in behavior. But we cannot know for certain that there actually was such a change, because our reading of the historical and cultural record, and the assumptions based on it, may simply have been in error.

Considering the considerable risk of being misled by such possibly unwarranted assumptions, we should seek wherever possible to build our case on measures applied at more than one point in time.[3] Even having data for two points in time can put us at risk of premature closure. For example, we may be tempted to make a good deal of a shift of 10 percentage points in the popularity of a given attitude, neglecting the fact that with the kind of sample used in the study one must assume a margin of error of at least 6 percent.

Lack of measures over time will surely tempt us to substitute what is often assumed to be reasonably equivalent, namely the analysis of age groups within the *same sample.* A steady progression of attitude change as one moves across the age range within a national sample may certainly indicate real *cohort* or *generational* change, but, alas, it may also reflect merely the influence of aging. Use of this kind of evidence should therefore always be closely scrutinized to ascertain how far it is reasonable to assume the observed shifts across age groups are unlikely to be an artifact of the mere process of aging.[4] Much less ambiguity attends this issue when, as in the studies by Martin Whyte, different *generations* within the *same families* constitute the sample.[5]

Ideally, therefore, we should have measures for the same or broadly comparable populations over multiple points in time. As we have noted, there are some studies which meet this demanding criterion, and insofar as they confirm the impressions from other sources they greatly strengthen our confidence in the conclusions we can draw. In general, however, we must accept a lesser standard of rigor in the quality of the available data. That fact, in turn, requires us to acknowledge the tentativeness of our conclusions, at least as concerns any single trend or tendency.

The General versus the Specific

There is a great and at times seemingly unresolvable tension between those who stress the distinctiveness, indeed even the uniqueness, of the change process in a particular setting and culture, and those who believe in and seek to find commonalities across nations and cultures. I cannot resolve this tension, and candor requires that I acknowledge that I am one of those who have a disposition to search for the general. Fairness of course obliges me to be ready, as I think I have been, to acknowledge the many instances which my locally rooted colleagues may be able to offer showing how, in their particular microcosm, the presumably general forces I deal with operated differently from the way they operated elsewhere, thus challenging the validity of some too sweeping generalization. While gladly accepting this caution, I hold to the view that it is, nevertheless, intellectually appropriate to search for the more general and to insist, as well, that exceptions, within certain limits, do not invalidate generalizations so long as those are stated in less than absolute or universal terms. Generalizations, however basically sound, cannot in themselves, deny the validity of seeming exceptions, but neither should exceptions, even if well documented, be assumed to disprove the validity of generalizations which have been properly stated with clear limits.

A comparable tension, encouraging a similar type of challenge and caution, involves generalizing across the elements within a single broadly defined realm of human activity such as the system of kinship and marriage. Evidence that a considerable number of the elements of such a system have changed, indeed changed profoundly, does not constitute proof that all elements of the given realm have changed in equal degree, or even have changed at all. As we shall see, there are communities in which the virtually universal selection by parents of their children's mates is almost totally replaced by individual choice, yet in those same communities commitment to the support of aged parents remains virtually undiminished. Global images of change sweeping across each and every aspect of some complex system of human relations may easily fail to differentiate and discriminate between those elements of a system which change, and those which persist in the face of seemingly general change. There is a parallel here with the analysis of cultures. Change in most aspects of a social subsystem, such as that regulating marriage and family life, cannot be taken as proof of change in all aspects of that subsystem. But it is equally true that well-documented exceptions to a general pattern of change across some broad range of the elements of a sociocultural system, however notable, do not in themselves prove that a generalization, properly circumscribed, is in error. They only prove that it has limits, limits we are happy to acknowledge. Indeed, in locating the limits of our generalizations, and in seeking to explain the exceptions, we find some of the most interesting and challenging tasks for the student of social change.

THE EVIDENCE FOR CONTINUITY AND CHANGE

I present evidence to illustrate four processes, which I designate:

1. The strengthening of tradition.
2. The persistence of tradition.
3. The adaptation of tradition.
4. The abandonment of tradition and the substitution of new attitudes and values.

I cannot at this point claim to have done an exhaustive survey, nor indeed, one which is rigorously systematic in its search for evidence. Rather, I have searched for studies which meet high standards with regard to sampling, design, and data analysis. One consequence of this selection procedure has been to limit the number of nations represented in my survey. As of this writing I have found the kind of data I consider relevant to my purpose only for Hong Kong, Taiwan, Mainland China, and Japan, with some modest representation of East Pakistan and India as well. Obviously adequate representation of the Pacific Rim as a whole will require that in time I find comparable data for other nations such as Singapore, Indonesia, Malaysia, and the Philippines. At the same time, in deciding which issues to discuss I have cast my net rather wide, since evidence on many issues of theoretical and practical importance is not truly abundant. Taken all together, however, there is a considerable weight of available evidence. That evidence, as I read it, is notable in its consistency across populations and study topic. And it has satisfied me that the peoples of the Pacific Rim have been and are undergoing a remarkable reorientation and transformation of values and life styles that in depth, scope, speed, and intensity closely match the extraordinary economic development which over the last decades has been enjoyed by those same populations.

The Strengthening of Tradition

In a world in which various kinds of religious fundamentalism are burgeoning on every hand as a response to the perceived threats of modernization and Westernization, it seems appropriate to inquire whether or not the nations on the Pacific Rim may be experiencing some of the same tendencies. Indeed, Lau and Kuan envisioned the possibility of an "erosion of modern elements by traditional concerns" and "a reinvigoration of traditional forms" (Lau and Kuan 1988: 3). I see very little evidence that the Pacific Rim is anywhere generating the kind of intense reassertion of tradition that is evident in so many parts of the Muslim world, but there certainly are indications that some Asian populations are in some ways reinvigorating traditions that had been slipping under the impact of forces for change. In some cases, the pattern seems to be one in which some externally forced process of change, such as was imposed by the cultural revolution in China, is now lifted, permitting the expression of value commitments which never fully died out. At least, this is the interpretation I put on the data from Baoding where the now adult offspring are more likely than their own elderly parents, who lived through the Maoist era, *to disagree* with the modern idea that obligations to children or careers should come ahead of obligations to parents.[6]

A widespread and deep-seated element of many Asian cultures is *ancestor worship*. Yet it is also something one might well expect to be eroded by the acids of the modernizing experience. It is therefore notable that in Taiwan there seems to have been a resurgence of commitment to this ancient tradition. Between 1963 and 1991, the proportion of Taiwanese who claimed to have attended an ancestor-worship ceremony increased from 39 percent to 75 percent (Marsh 1996: T. 7-2). Something similar, although less dramatic may have occurred in Shanghai (Chu and Ju 1993). These developments can perhaps be explained as exemplifying a principle I first enunciated in my research on individual modernity in six developing countries. Contrary to popular expectation, we noted that the more modern individuals claimed to fulfill the practice requirements of their religion not less but rather more often than the nominally more "traditional" individuals in our samples. We explained this outcome as follows: To fulfill the practice obligations of one's religion requires that one be reasonably integrated and functioning effectively in one's environment. In addition, such practices often require a financial commitment. Both of these conditions were more likely to be met by individuals who had more fully joined the modern economy, hence the greater participation in religious practice of the more modern. Following this logic we might argue that on the Pacific Rim as well, the more people increased their incomes and sought the outward signs of social respectability, the more they might be expected to participate in religious practices and rituals which earlier they felt they had neither the free energy nor the discretionary income to expend on.[7]

One additional example of the strengthening of tradition comes to us from the long-term studies of the Japanese national character mounted by Professor Hayashi and his collaborators every five years from 1953 on. In their assessment of *giri-ninjo,* which they identified as a key element of Japanese culture, they asked their national samples to select two values out of a set of four to which the respondents felt most committed. One of the set of four was *filial piety.*[8] Contrary to expectation, the preference for this value actually rose year by year. In 1963, the first year this question was asked, filial piety was selected by 61 percent of the respondents, but by 1983 it rose in popularity to be selected as one of the two most important values by 73 percent of those interviewed, and it held its rank as number one value in the subsequent surveys through 1993.

Clearly, there is some evidence that on the Pacific Rim, much as in other parts of the world, the response to the forces of modernization may be an actual recommitment to, and strengthening of, some traditional values and behaviors. At the same time it must be acknowledged that in this region of the world such reaffirmations seem modest in number.

The Persistence of Tradition

If we expected traditions to be reaffirmed and strengthened beyond the historical norm, then we may have set too high a requirement. Perhaps it should be notable enough if traditions can persist at roughly the level of commitment they experienced before the countries of the Pacific Rim were washed over by the tides of industrialization and the modernization of their economies. To assess this outcome we especially searched for evidence collected over time. We find that despite changes in the economy and the opening of society to Western influences, many traditions managed to hold steady in their support from the populations on the Rim.

We begin with an item about which we believe those who know the Pacific Rim are least likely to take exception. Everyone in the world is by now aware of the reputation of those of Chinese origin for hard work, steadfastness of effort, and readiness to sacrifice and save. These are characteristics shared by many of the peoples on the Pacific Rim. But one can easily imagine that some forty years of Chinese socialism might have deeply eroded these tendencies in a population so long organized in communal enterprises and encouraged to become totally dependent on their *danwei,* or local production unit, at close hand, and on the Communist state, at greater remove. But this seems not to have happened. In Shanghai around 1990 the population was asked to rate some 18 basic values. The score for each value was given as the percent affirming a value minus those who were contrary. At the top of the list stood the value "diligence and frugality," with a score of +86, indicating, given the scoring system, that virtually everyone was for this value and exceedingly few denied its relevance for themselves. Further supporting the claim that in the population of China the old value of hard work persisted despite more than forty years of Communism, the same survey showed that 72 percent of the people of Shanghai considered that failure in life was due to "not working hard enough" even though the question wording offered them the alternative of blaming such an outcome on "fate" (Chu and Ju 1993: 260).

Filial piety   We turn next to a topic already introduced, namely *filial piety,* but we excuse the repetition because this sentiment is so often cited as distinctive to some many of the cultures of Asia. Our evidence comes from Baoding, on the mainland, and we have the advantage that both the elders and their adult children in the same family were asked the same question. Surely, if there was a movement across generations this would be the ideal design for identifying a value shift. Instead, across the generations, there was a remarkable consistency with which the value of filial piety was affirmed, with approximately 95 percent of both the elders and their adult children stressing the absolute importance of commitment to this value.

Supporting evidence comes from a survey of the people of Hong Kong. In this case we have neither a generational nor an over-time survey to assess stability, but since a strikingly large proportion of 88 percent of the respondents agreed with the idea that "government should punish the unfilial," it seems reasonable to interpret the result as evidence of the persistence of a traditional value. There seems every reason to accept Martin Whyte's conclusion that "filial obligations are robustly intact, with little sign that parents and children are separated by a 'generation gap' when it comes to these attitudes" (Whyte 1996: 8).

Dominant opinion in Japan   Turning next to Japan, we may assess the persistence of traditional views by examining the stability over time of a set of so-called "dominant opinions." In the Japanese national character research, a view of the world was defined as a "dominant opinion" if 75 percent or more of the population held the view in question. Because they win such high consensus, these orientations might be broadly interpreted as defining the essential elements of the national culture, ethos, or belief system.

It is notable that despite the many economic and social changes Japan experienced since 1953, when the first survey was done, to 1993, the last year reported, some opinions readily recognized as characteristically Japanese held steady in their dominant status despite the many forces for change which might have been expected to erode their support. We cite here, to illustrate the pattern, four such persistent attitudes:[9]

1. Giving a job to the person who scored higher on a test rather than to a qualified relative who scored lower.[10]
2. Preferring a boss who would sometimes demand extra work despite rules to the contrary, but who looked after the employee personally in matters not connected with the work, over a boss who stuck to the rules and makes no unreasonable demands but never does things for you in matters not connected to the work.[11]
3. Preferring to work in a firm with a "family-like" atmosphere, even if it meant accepting lower wages.[12]
4. Preferring a picture of an attractive Japanese-style garden over an attractive English garden.[13]

Data to test for such persistence in other settings on the Pacific Rim is not readily available, because it is rare that studies are done over time using the same standard questions. However, when a traditional value readily identifiable as a characteristic element of Asian belief systems wins virtually unanimous support from a population as thoroughly modernized in its economic life, and as totally open to Western influence, as is the population of Hong Kong, it seems reasonable to interpret the result as evidence of the persistence of values. It is in this way we interpret the fact that in Hong Kong in 1987, some 91 percent of the people supported the principle that "officials should set a moral example."

CONTINUITY IN CHINESE THOUGHT PATTERNS

A rather different kind of evidence for the persistence of cultural patterns in the face of extensive economic, social and political change is offered by Thomas Metzger. His reading of a wide range of recent and contemporary philosophical, political, and sociological Chinese writing leads him to assert that there is a major Chinese cultural strand made up of a broad range of intellectual writing, whether the writer is Communist or

Kuomintang, left or right, conservator or modernizer. Across these otherwise important divisions, he argues, there is a shared style of intellectual discourse, which he characterizes as "an optimistic, transformative, Napoleonic belief that intellectuals can grasp the ultimate nature of reality and control history." Further elaborating on the common features of this type of discourse, which, he argues, can be traced far back in the history of Chinese thought, Metzger delineates four characteristic elements:

1. *Utopianism:* a way of defining the goal of human life.
2. *Epistemological optimism:* "holding that a total, objective, systematic understanding of human life can be obtained to guide action."
3. *History:* viewed as a *teleological process* moving inexorably toward the ultimate goals of humankind.
4. *Agency:* there is a socially visible group, usually seen as the intellectuals, who can grasp the right theoretical system *(t'i-hsi)* and use it to influence the course of development of China, and perhaps the whole world.[14]

THE ADAPTATION OF TRADITION

Some traditions truly persist. Others, however, may only seem to persist, maintaining their external form or their obedience to the religious or ritual calendar, but nevertheless in actual content are transformed into something quite different from their original nature. It is a moot point whether such phenomena should be counted as additional evidence of the persistence of tradition, or, on the contrary, should be weighed as evidence of how economic and social change engender change in a culture. We take no stand on the issue, but note that our survey of continuity and change in Asian values identified a number of instances of the seeming persistence of traditions which had been so profoundly adapted that in actuality they seemed quite different from the tradition they presumably continued. The phenomenon warrants further and fuller exploration, but we can only pause in our exposition for a single illustration.

Our example again involves the seemingly ubiquitous phenomenon of ancestor worship, with the evidence coming from the population of Shanghai. Forty-four percent of the people surveyed in 1990 evidently felt that it was a moral obligation to visit and sweep tombs. Given the long history of Communist opposition to this idea and its practice, it might certainly be argued that having so relatively high a proportion of Shanghai citizens still currently affirm the importance of tomb sweeping is evidence of the persistence of tradition. But Chu and Yu note the anomaly that this view is held in the face of the fact that in Shanghai today there a very few tombs one could possibly visit and sweep. Moreover, according to Chu and Yu, what people are talking about and doing has very little to do with ancestor worship in the sense in which it was practiced in earlier times. Rather, the practice has been transformed into a kind of social occasion and a way of expressing solidarity with living relatives. Instead of being true ancestor worship, the event has now become the occasion for a family gathering "usually meaning having a small family dinner with relatives on the birthday of a deceased parent."[15]

THE ABANDONMENT OF TRADITION

Although one can find some evidence of the strengthening, the persistence, and the adaptation of tradition, the frequency with which one can document such occurrences is very modest compared to the mountain of evidence that numerous Pacific Rim countries traditions are being massively abandoned in one realm of life after another. The Pacific Rim is being inundated by a flood of forces exposing it to industrialization, modernization, and globalization. Occupational systems are transformed, mass communication of all kinds washes over every shore and reaches every distant corner, transportation and associated human movement is extended, deepened, and greatly sped up, knowledge is redefined and revalued. In the process, many fundamental values are challenged and reformulated, basic human relationships are redefined and reordered, and numerous traditional ways of thinking and behaving are transformed.

To fully document this massive abandonment of tradition is beyond the scope of this chapter. However, a modest selection of the evidence across a series of realms may serve to suggest the depth, the scope, and force of the argument that would be felt by those confronting a more exhaustive mobilization of the evidence.

Family, Marriage, and Kinship

Few aspects of human relations can claim to be as fundamental as those often grouped under the rubric family, marriage, and kinship. Yet few realms exceed these in the degree of change in tradition which they manifest.

Continuing the lineage   Continuity of the family name in Japan has for centuries had the status of an almost sacred responsibility. When the head of a family produced no male heir, it was essential that an appropriate male be adopted to carry forward the family name. In the years immediately after World War II, despite the great upheaval Japan was experiencing, it was still the case that a striking 73 percent of a national sample affirmed the idea that it is necessary to adopt a child to continue the family line "even if there was no blood connection." However, in every subsequent five-year period fewer and fewer people supported this idea. After 20 years, in the 1973 survey, the proportion taking this position (36 percent) had been cut in half, and at the latest report, from the 1993 survey, it had further sunk to 22 percent, considerably less than one-third its original strength (Hayashi 1977: 44; Research Committee 1993: 56).[16]

Surveys taken on Taiwan indicate there too the population was responding in a manner similar to that of Japan. In this case we do not have numerous periodic reports, but do have information for two relatively widely separated points in time. In 1963, 70 percent of the Taiwanese considered it "very important" that one have a male heir "to transmit the lineage." By 1991 the percentage so rating the issue was down to only 32 percent (Marsh 1996: T6.5).

Choosing a marriage partner   Perhaps no decision in life is more important than that of choosing a marriage partner, and this is all the more so in societies in which divorce is infrequent and difficult to obtain. From Chengdu, on the mainland, comes evidence of a nearly total transformation over time in the practice of finding a mate.

Martin Whyte divided his sample from Chengdu according to the year individuals were actually married. For each event, he knew from his informants whether it had followed the tradition of arranged marriages or whether the matches has been made in some other way. The oldest cohort consisted of people who had married between 1933 and 1948. Thereafter they were grouped in five-year intervals, with the last cohort including all those whose marriage occurred between 1977 and 1987.

It is hard to imagine a more profound shift in fundamental human values and behavior than that reflected in the reports of the residents of Chengdu. In the cohorts married before the Communist victory, 68 percent reported that their marriage had been "arranged," but in the cohort married most recently the percent of arranged marriages had dwindled to a mere 2 percent! Almost equally dramatic was a shift in the proportion affirming the importance of being in love as a condition for marrying. In the oldest cohort love had been a factor in 17 percent of the cases, but by the 1977–87 cohort it was an important consideration in 67 percent of the marriages. Given both Chinese cultural mores and the puritanism of the Communist regime, it is particularly notable that having sex with one's proposed before the actual wedding rose from 4 percent in the marriages occurring in the earliest period to 18 percent of those entered into in the decade of the 1980s (Whyte 1995: T2).

It is very important to note that the striking pattern Whyte reported for Chengdu was evidently also manifested as well in Taiwan, although the data there covered a somewhat shorter span of time, the sample comprising six cohorts starting with those married in 1955 and ending with those married between 1980 and 1984. As on the mainland, in Taiwan marriages in which the parents decided on the marriage partner fell over time from 53 to 11 percent of the cases; marrying without dating fell from 51 percent to a mere 4 percent; and having sex before the actual marriage rose from 13 percent in the cohorts married early to 37 percent among those marrying after 1980. In short, the patterns of change in Taiwan were, broadly speaking, identical with those observe in Chengdu (Whyte 1995: T 3).

This evidence from Taiwan is particularly important because it makes it clear that the shift reported for Chengdu was not merely an artifact of Communist control of every aspect of life. Rather, we are led to conclude that broad forces of social change—occupational, educational, and spiritual—were at work in both places, and that they had the same effect despite the differences in the socioeconomic and political systems governing these two settings.

Basic Values and Life-Guiding Principles

In perhaps in no other realm is the evidence for a fundamental shift in values more extreme or more visible than in the basic values for living, in the goals and aspirations one holds out for oneself and one's children, and in the perception of the good and bad in human relations. In place of the dominance of the clan, the community, and the family, we find the individual and the self come increasingly to be the key points of reference for both the society and the person. In place of subordination of the self to common interests, and the enthronement of collective goals and collective good, we increasingly find a concern with self-fulfillment, with personal gratification, and with the assertion of individual rights.

The Shanghai story   We begin our exploration of the evidence with data from Shanghai. Unfortunately, measures over time are not available, and we must content ourselves with differences among age groups as a proxy. However, it will be apparent for a number of the topics covered that a true shift across the generations is a more likely explanation of the observed differences than would be one based on the presumed effects of aging alone.

Chu and Ju asked their Shanghai sample to make a series of choices about their basic hopes and aspirations and their fundamental goals in life. The proportion choosing the more modern idea of seeking "true love" as a goal in life rose from only 11 percent among those over 50 years of age to 49 percent among those under 29 years old. This difference might be interpreted as merely reflecting a characteristic of the aged, who may be assumed to feel that the search for true love as a meaningful goal is past for them. We see these statistics more as an expression of new values. To support our interpretation we note certain other results from the same survey which cannot so easily be explained by the mechanisms of aging, yet which also suggest the rising *general* importance of personal satisfaction—as against community harmony—as a central goal in life. For example, the proportion who chose "living happily" as the key to meaning in life rose from a mere 7 percent among those over 50 to 35 percent among those under the age of 29.[17]

Perhaps the most important evidence from Shanghai comes from a different phase of the study. In its interpretation we use as our standard the general acceptance which some value is presumed to have enjoyed earlier, and compare that with the level of support for that value expressed by a contemporary sample. The values tested by Chu and Ju were selected on expert advice as being those the Chinese people "cherished for thousands of years," and had been "nearly universally accepted in the past." A list of some 18 values considered at the heart and core of Chinese culture were presented to the sample in Shanghai, preceded by the question: "Of these elements of traditional Chinese culture . . . which ones do you feel proud of, which ones should be discarded, and which ones are you not sure of?"

Initially, for the total sample, the data were presented using a special scoring system, an index based on the percentage who were proud of a value minus the percentage who said it should be discarded. By this method "diligence and frugality" earned a top score of +86 percent. The lowest score was -64 percent, indicating the great majority voted to discard this principle of living while few voted to retain it. That dismal score was earned by the venerable value called "the three obediences and the four virtues."[18] Other outstandingly low scores, indicating a predominant opinion that the principle should be discarded, were earned by the value named "the way of the golden mean," at -60 percent on the index; "differentiation between men and women," at -60 percent; and "discretion for self-preservation," at -56 percent.[19] The authors found such a high level of rejection of these values, which for centuries had been the core of Chinese culture, to be "nothing short of phenomenal," and this outcome must have played a major role in their decision to give their book the title *The Great Wall in Ruins.*

There certainly is reason to attribute this rejection of key traditional values by the Shanghai population as reflecting conscious and intense efforts by the Communist regime to inculcate new values in the Chinese population. However, we feel it is significant that this study was based on the people of a city generally recognized as the most international and cosmopolitan, and as being the most subject to modernizing influences, in all of China. It is also important to note that studies of the younger generation, which had been much less exposed to concentrated Communist propaganda efforts directed against these values, also showed half to two-thirds rejecting them, albeit not quite so strongly as did the older generation.[20]

Life goals in Japan   By turning to Japan for further evidence regarding changes in life goals we escape the issue of systematic government pressure raised by the Shanghai data. But we find again the same pattern, namely that self-centered values come more and more to outweigh the commitment to group morality and public service.

In the Japanese national character survey respondents were given a list of six "attitudes towards life," and were asked to select one which "comes closest to your feeling." This design of the question of course meant that no value was likely to command a majority, because the total vote was divided across so many choices. Nonetheless, the pattern that emerged was fairly clear-cut, with the more self-centered, hedonistic values rising in strength, while the more moralistic and public-service goals lost support. Thus the attitude "Don't think about money or fame; just live a life that suits your own taste" more than doubled its support over the years, being endorsed by only 21 percent in 1953 but becoming the single most popular attitude by 1993, with 41 percent of the respondents casting their single vote for this way of life alone. By contrast, the value:

"Resist all evils in the world and live a pure and just life" steadily lost ground over the same period. It went from being the most selected attitude in 1953, at 29 percent, to being one of the least favored in 1993, chosen by a mere 6 percent. Taken together, the two community-service and public-morality items dominated the selection in 1953, jointly accounting for 39 percent of all the choices, but by 1993 they had progressively declined in popularity and accounted for only 10 percent of all first choices. By contrast, the two attitudes which suggested a more self-centered and hedonistic approach to life more than doubled their support over time. Together they accounted for 39 percent of all choices in 1953, but their popularity increased steadily, so that by 1993 they commanded an overpowering 67 percent of all first choices (Hayashi and Suzuki 1990: 101; Research Committee 1993: 39).[21]

Leisure Activities and Popular Tastes

We conclude our survey of the abandonment of tradition with some evidence concerning the use of leisure time and personal preferences for different kinds of popular entertainment. It is by now commonplace to note the worldwide diffusion of certain moving pictures and the music of certain bands and singers. Madonna, for example, is recognized worldwide and has an audience in virtually every country. But some countries, among which Communist China is perhaps most notable, sought for decades to do the equivalent of hermetically sealing off their populations from such influences considered not only foreign but also "polluting." It is, therefore, particularly revealing to discover how massive have been the shifts in popular taste across the generations in a provincial city such as Baoding on the Chinese mainland.

Martin Whyte asked his respondents to indicate their first and second choices in entertainment, providing them a list which included traditional opera and Hong Kong-Taiwan pop. As might be expected, in the older generation 68 percent gave their votes to Chinese opera, but their adult children made this choice in only 13 percent of the cases. By contrast, the older generation voted for pop music only 13 percent of the time, but their fully mature children gave 71 percent of their votes to this source of entertainment (Whyte 1996).

SOURCES OF INFLUENCE: CAUSE AND EFFECT

All of the countries are subject to a number of influences which have the potential for eroding tradition and fostering new attitudes, values, and behaviors. These streams of influence sometimes act independently, but usually they are combined in a great confluence, a sea of forces for change which washes over everyone and everything. Hong Kong perhaps exemplifies the most extreme case, where, according to Lau and Kuan "economic growth and the ensuing rise in the standard of living . . . in turn fuel the inexorable process of Westernization and modernization, the pervasive effects of which are evident in almost all spheres of life . . . discernible even among people in the lower strata, thus testifying to their penetrative potency." (Lau and Kuan 1988: 1)

It is, of course, a moot point whether the rise of industry and commerce should be considered "Westernization" in the same sense as certain films, music, and literature are more or less unambiguously identifiable as "Western." Much is to be gained if we are careful to *disaggregate* the different concrete forms of influence, and as well to study separately their *differential* impact on society, culture, and the individual. Moreover, we need to take into account the substantial cultural, economic and political variety of the nations and peoples in the Pacific Rim countries.

Educational Effects

The spread of modern education may well be the most pervasive and profound source of influence on many of the attitudes and behaviors we have assessed. As Lau and Kuan noted for Hong Kong: "The more educated had a more 'modernist' orientation toward society. . . . They had a stronger sense of personal efficacy, and believed much less in fatalism. They were more tolerant of social conflict, and more likely than the less educated to believe that conflict was a natural and integral part of social life. . . . They were less traditional in that they placed less emphasis on filial piety and kinship relations. They were more likely to give freedom of speech to others, less likely to ban newspapers that published false news, and less likely to prohibit meetings for an unorthodox cause. . . . The more educated believed in competition and individual effort, and they would oppose any organizational efforts to thwart the competitive process." (Lau and Kuan 1988: 161–162)

Among the examples of striking differences separating the more from the less educated in Hong Kong we note the response to the idea that the kind of government you have is immaterial, a view to which an overwhelming 81 percent of the least educated agreed, whereas this idea was affirmed by only 22 percent of the most educated (Lau and Kuan 1988: T 5.1). The effects of education were manifest not only under conditions of relative freedom, as in Hong Kong, but also under the more controlled conditions of life in Communist-dominated Shanghai. For example, the idea that one should plan to live with one's parents after marriage was favored by 57 percent of the less educated, but the proportion fell to about half, at 27 percent, among the more educated (Chu and Ju 1993: T. 9.3).

The Role of Changing Occupational Structures

The transformations of Pacific Rim societies in the recent past began, in most cases, not with political regime or social policy changes, but rather with economic development.[22] In particular they have experienced rapid industrialization, burgeoning trade and commerce, vast expansions of transportation networks, and great declines in the proportion of the national income accounted for by agriculture. Multitudes moved from the countryside and agricultural employment to take up city residence and nonagricultural work. These shifts in the composition of the labor force, and in the nature of the work performed, seem especially relevant to our concerns. First, the shift of the place and type of work from traditional agriculture to industrial labor has quite substantial effects in inducing more modern attitudes and values, including a greater sense of efficacy, a heightened openness to new experience, increased tolerance for departures from tradition, and greater appreciation and respect for the nature and rights of socially less powerful groups such as children and women. In my research on individual modernity I demonstrated these effects in six developing countries, two of which were in Asia, and there is every reason to believe that similar processes have been at work in the developing countries of the Pacific Rim.[23] These effects, furthermore, are not dependent on the fact that most industry is located in urban settings. The six-nation study of individual modernity and more recent work on factories in the countryside in Mainland China[24] demonstrate conclusively that industrial work in modern factories has a significant impact in fostering modern attitudes independent of the contribution of urban living.

Perhaps equally as important the general growth of industrial employment has been the massive movement of women out of the home and into the paid labor force. For example, in Taiwan, even after the first spurt of industrialization, only 16 percent of the respondents in the 1963 sample of men reported their wives to be in the paid labor force, the remainder working at home. But by 1991 the proportion having wives in paid employment had risen to 48 percent. Comparable and even more dramatic shifts in the extent of formal employment by women have been reported for other countries on the Pacific Rim. We believe the impact to have been profound, but our sources have paid less attention to the effects of female employment than they might have.[25]

Other Sources of Influence

Urban experience   As a key experience for those who do not find work in the urban setting, and as a supplement for those who do secure industrial employment, the urban setting as such seems to exert an influence on attitudes, values, and behaviors independent of the modernizing impact of employment itself. In the six-nation study of individual modernity we showed that in East Pakistan and India, as in the other nations studied, the longer men of rural origin lived and worked in urban areas the higher their scores rose on the attitudinal modernity (OM) scale. Moreover, this effect of urban living was clearly independent of the impact of factory experience in the Indian case, and was independent of mass-media exposure in both countries.[26] In his study of Taiwan, Robert Marsh also systematically took account of the extent of rural living and later urban contact his respondents had experienced. He found a number of attitudes and values to be reflected in the scores on his index of rural-urban exposure. For example, in response to the question whether physical punishment is necessary in raising children, the urban index showed a modest but consistent effect even with occupation held constant, those with more urban contact being less likely to believe in the necessity for physical punishment.[27]

Exposure to mass media and Western culture   In the six-nation study exposure to the mass media was generally second only to education as a force affecting men's attitudes and behavior. Even controlled for occupation and education, the Beta weight for mass-media exposure in a regression on the OM score stood at .20 in both India and East Pakistan (Inkeles and Smith 1974: T 19-2).

Much of what the mass media have been bringing to the populations of Asian-Pacific nations has been indigenous, but very large elements of the material they introduce is reasonably labeled "Western." It is of special interest that several of the relevant studies have sought to disentangle the effect of mass-media exposure in general from the specific influence of Western culture. In Shanghai, Chu and Ju found many instances in which the degree of contact with Western culture played a substantial role in shaping attitudes and behavior to a degree equal to, and sometimes greater than, the mere fact of exposure to the mass media.

For example, the view that divorce is something acceptable if the couple involved does not have children was affirmed by only 27 percent of those with low exposure to Western influence, whereas this more liberated view was manifested by 57 percent of those under high Western influence. Fifty-one percent of those with high exposure to the West said that if given the opportunity they would retire if they could live comfortably, whereas only 27 percent of those with little Western exposure said they would take that option, claiming that instead they would continue working (Chu and Ju 1993: T. 3.1 and T. 5.5).[28]

THE NEXT STEP

All the sources of influence we have examined are interrelated,[29] and often they produce their effects in a complex interaction. Regression analyses, which a number of the key investigators we cite have used extensively, can help considerably in identifying the general realms and the particular issues which are more or less sensitive to one or another source of influence. However, to understand in any depth the complex response of cultures, communities, and individuals to the sources of influence to which they are exposed, it would be highly desirable to undertake more fine-grained analyses with a battery of techniques to assess each of the important questions separately. Such analysis is the next step required to move us beyond the stage to which the documentation in this chapter has brought us. We have shown conclusively, we believe, that a number of the nations on the Pacific Rim have in the last decades of the twentieth century experienced great, often profound, shifts in values, attitudes, and behavior in various realms of life. But even in areas of greatest volatility, some attitudes change, and some values shift, but others do not. Attitudes may change, but behavior may not, and the reverse pattern is also observed. Moreover, many traditions persist unchanged, and some seem to enjoy a resurgence of commitment and support. A comprehensive, coherent, and convincing account of the complex and important process of social change currently being experienced by perhaps as much as a third of the human race awaits our efforts.

Ruth Hayhoe is at present Director of the Hong Kong Institute of Education. In 1996–1997 she was associate dean for Graduate Studies at the Ontario Institute for Studies in Education of the University of Toronto, where she has served as a professor for many years. Her most recent publications include *China's Universities 1895–1995: A Century of Cultural Conflict* (New York: Garland Publishing Inc., 1996) and *East-West Dialogue in Knowledge and Higher Education* (New York: M. E. Sharpe, 1996), co-edited with Julia Pan.

5. Education as Communication

Ruth Hayhoe

The role of modern education in both China and Japan has been an instrument for inculcating the state's values and visions. It has been a hotly contested struggle between those who advocated uncompromising modernity and the "Enlightenment" values of individualism and democracy (in the case of Japan) and Marxist ideals of a fully egalitarian society (in the case of China) and those who wished to preserve Confucian notions of hierarchy and order in an East Asian alternative version of modernity.

This chapter addresses the question of how values are communicated through education, both in Asia and in the context of relations between Asia and the West. The first section sketches out a civilizational perspective, considering education as communication within the conditions of civilizational transition that characterize our present age. Next, I present an approach to methodology in comparative education, proposing a systematic way of identifying and exploring core values in the Asian context, and reflecting on their relevance to the West. This methodology is illustrated by sketching out ideal types for Confucianism, Taoism, and Buddhism. The chapter concludes by considering the ways in which core values are communicated through education: legal frameworks and national educational structures, textbooks, and pedagogy. The illustrations drawn upon come mainly from China and Japan, the two Asian societies I know best, but the approach should be adaptable to other Asian societies.

CIVILIZATIONAL PERSPECTIVES

In the fascination with modernization and modernity in the sociological literature of the 1950s to the 1970s, including the work of Parsons, Inkeles, Rostow, and many others, these terms themselves had very positive connotations, and there was considerable consensus that modernization embodied a convergence of values and cultural patterns, reflecting the structures of industrialization that gave birth to modern values. Fukuyama's *End of History* (1992) expresses a widely held perception that the West had "arrived" and that other nations and regions simply had to follow in its steps. Historians, such as Carroll Quigley, however, saw the modernization of the West in terms of the rise and fall of civilizations. Quigley evaluated Western civilization in terms of six levels of culture and saw it as relatively advanced in the intellectual, military, and economic realms, in that order, while less advanced in the political and social dimensions of culture, and most backward in the area of religion. (Quigley 1961: 62).

In the 1980s and 1990s a rising chorus of critical voices has led to considerable soul-searching concerning some of the negative dimensions of the Western experience of modernization, such as environmental destruction, the fragmentation and loss of familial and social cohesion, and the erosion of mainstream religious practice as a common heritage of spirituality, the latter giving way to splintered and extremist forms of religious adherence. The emergence of postmodernism as a serious scholarly paradigm, or antiparadigmatic complex, has given academic sophistication to these voices. However, I see it as a somewhat defeatist acceptance of relativism, an unseemly eagerness to relinquish the rich heritage of scientific thought from the Enlightenment which underlay Western modernity, and relegate it to the status of one among many metaphors. Juergen Habermas's approach is a more constructive one, affirming the positive contribution of European modernization while identifying certain distortions which led to its "jagged profile." (Habermas 1984, 1987)

Habermas addresses the problem of a one-sided development of scientific-technical forms of rationality, and the concomitant underdevelopment of moral-practical and practical-aesthetic forms of rationality. In his "Theory of Communicative Action" he proposes a revitalization of cultural life that would nurture these areas to make possible a broader and more all-embracing rationality. He also identifies moments in individuals' religious development that illustrate the choices that were made and demonstrate the noninevitability of any one pattern of modernization.

A fascinating example is the victory of Calvinism, with its extreme individualism, over the communitarianism of the Anabaptists (Habermas 1987: 2, 232).

Habermas provides a profound critical analysis of the Western modernization experience that carries with it a prescription for positive change—in the areas of knowledge, a realignment of moral, aesthetic, and scientific-technical fields, and in the area of social organization, a revitalization of the life-world in relation to the system. But what resources are we to draw upon in this process? If we consider Asian core values from the perspective of the Western need for a rethinking of modern values, this will bring a certain degree of engagement to our scrutiny. The dimension of education and cross-cultural communication is added to our efforts to understand the communication of core values through Asian patterns of education.

Samuel Huntington's recent examination, *The Clash of Civilizations*, set a framework for thinking about the Western understanding of Asian values. Huntington challenges the West to come to terms with the fact that civilizational differences much more profound than the ideological differences of the Cold War are likely to be the main source of conflict in the future. From this he derives the need for the West to develop a much deeper understanding of other civilizations, most particularly Confucian civilization in East Asia and Islamic civilization in the Middle East, which he sees as exercising the greatest potential economic and geopolitical threat to the West's security and well-being (Huntington 1993, 1996).

Huntington's realist perspective is somewhat harsh, and to make a point he tends to exaggerate the importance of culture, yet his main message is an interesting and new one for the West. It signals a kind of reversal of our traditional relationship to East Asia. In the late nineteenth and early twentieth centuries the West was the provider of knowledge that made possible the modernization of countries such as Japan and China. Now people of the West face a situation where their ability to understand and learn from East Asian culture and civilization may be as essential to future economic well-being as was the scientific knowledge of the Enlightenment to Japan and China a hundred years ago. This puts the study of core Asian values in a somewhat different light. It also brings us to the question of how this kind of understanding can be gained.

For a long time, Chinese and Japanese universities were bent upon absorbing the best from the West, and traditional texts and values were seen at best as a heritage to be critically examined, ordered, and preserved, and at worst as a set of beliefs that should be thoroughly repudiated to make way for science and democracy. China's May 4th Movement set a tone of radicalism and rejection of Confucian values for China that has persisted up to the present time (Schwarcz 1986), while Japan has taken a more moderate course, but, giving little overt attention to traditional values as a living source of inspiration.

There have, however, been some voices that have maintained a sympathetic interest in the study of Confucianism in East Asia over a long period, including a group around Theodore de Bary at Columbia University, and a second group at the Chinese University of Hong Kong. Furthermore, the work of Tu Wei-ming over the last two decades in developing what he calls the Confucian project represents a fascinating effort to present Confucianism as a world religion or moral/ethical system that has a message not only for East Asia but also for the West. Tu's work elaborates Confucianism both in its traditional historical, philosophical setting, with his early focus on the work of the radical philosopher Wang Yangming, (Tu 1974) and in the way it has underlain the modern development of China and Japan (Tu 1996). He further sets the Confucian project against the "Habermas project," emphasizing its attention to spirituality and ability to promote social harmony and cohesion, as elements of ethical rationality that may be valuable for the West (Tu 1993). There is thus a contemporary literature that is available to us for the study of core Asian values.

THE COMPARATIVE METHOD AND THE STUDY OF VALUES

For nearly a century, scholars of comparative education have struggled with the question of how to take into account the context of educational systems. On one side were positivists, gathering statistics and developing data bases that would juxtapose patterns of education across different societies and make possible a formulation of general laws or principles of education and societal development; on the other were historians and philosophers interested in the "living spirit" that informed education systems, the religious values that shaped them differently in different contexts (Hans 1967), and the ways in which they were an expression of "national character" (Mallinson 1975). For the one group, comparative education made possible a science of education with pretensions to universality, while for the other profound cultural differences dictated an approach that depended more on disciplines such as history, philosophy, and anthropology than economics or positivistic sociology.

One of the leading figures in the 1960s and 1970s, Brian Holmes, pioneered a "problem approach" to comparative education that adapted Karl Popper's critical dualism and hypothetico-deductive approach to scientific method for comparative studies in education. He made use of Dewey's five stages of problem analysis for educational research. An educational problem was identified, and cross-national or cross-cultural cases were drawn upon in proposing hypothetical solutions to it. Through a process of deduction, one or several potential solutions were tested in the specific conditions of a particular context.

The aspect of the context which needed the closest scrutiny, from Holmes's perspective, was that of values and beliefs. He proposed the use of Weberian ideal types for analyzing patterns of value and making possible fairly accurate predictions about the effectiveness of particular policy solutions in a defined context. He suggested three or four levels that might be identified and clarified through the construction of ideal types in a society or region. The ideas of classical philosophers such as Plato or Aristotle could be used to formulate broad normative ideal types for Europe, and these could be modified and made more specific to a particular country, region, or time period by reference to later philosophers: for example, Locke or Hume for Britain, Descartes or Condorcet for France, Dewey for the United States. These would be the first two layers of normative patterning. Constitutions or other national legislation were seen as the source of actual ideal types, a kind of third layer, setting out the practical ideals of a given nation, and often informed explicitly and/or differentially by the ideas of classical or national philosophers. Considerable attention was also given to a fourth layer, what he defined as the realm of "mental states." These are persistent values that motivate behavior yet may be in clear opposition to the proclaimed normative values of a particular society: they may draw upon value patterns of an earlier period. Myrdal's "lower valuations" in *An American Dilemma* were examples Holmes often used, showing how the ideals of the American constitution were undermined in actual behavior by persisting deeply held notions of class and racial difference that go back as far as Plato (Holmes 1981).

If we apply this approach to East Asia, there is no doubt that Confucianism has provided an enduring set of values for the high culture of the whole East Asian region, including Japan, China, Korea, and Vietnam (Rozman 1991). While the literature about Confucianism is immense, it lends itself to the identification of core values that could provide a kind of overarching ideal, typical normative model. Modifying this model for different regions and periods would be Taoism in China, Shintoism in Japan, various schools of Buddhism in all four East Asian societies, and possibly Christianity and Islam in selected regions. These middle-range value systems have borne an interesting relationship to Confucianism over time, in some cases providing a set of countervalues—anarchism as against a clear familial hierarchy in terms of Taoism and Confucianism, for example—and in other cases melding with and reinforcing aspects of Confucian values. The ultimate effect of the tensions and interactions among these persisting value systems has been a process in which Confucianism has been challenged, penetrated, and transformed, but has managed to survive to the present (Ding and Liu 1996: 11).

In the modern period, Confucianism has largely gone underground, with the adoption of value complexes from the West as the framework for modern development—parliamentary democracy along with constitutional monarchy in Japan, Marxism-Leninism in China. Actual ideal types can be constructed for these two countries on the basis of modern constitutions—Japan's postwar constitution and education law (Beauchamp and Vardaman 1994), as well as China's Common Program adopted in 1949, its first constitution of 1952, and subsequent constitutions (Hu and Seifman 1976). These documents might be seen as the program of the state for constructing a modern society, or as the product of struggle among political factions, representing traditionalists at one pole and those who wished to oppose tradition with modern values of individualism and equality at the other.

The role of modern education in both China and Japan has been as an instrument for inculcating the state's values and vision. It has been a hotly contested struggle between those who advocated uncompromising modernity and the "Enlightenment" values of individualism and democracy (in the case of Japan), and Marxist ideals of a fully egalitarian society (in the case of China) and those who wished to preserve Confucian notions of hierarchy and order in an East Asian alternative version of modernity. In between these two opposing poles lie values and ideas from Taoism, Shintoism, and Buddhism which over a long period had succeeded in undermining and softening Confucianism while facilitating its survival. More recently introduced religions such as Christianity and Islam may also have played a role.

In the modern schooling systems of East Asia, most of which were established in the late nineteenth century or early in the twentieth, we can see these conflicts working themselves out, with the behavior of different groups informed by particular value complexes. The creation and use of ideal types for each of these configurations may help us in understanding both successful change and successful resistance to change. On the top level are the policymakers or legislators, who formulate and adopt particular approaches to education and enshrine them in national laws or administrative regulations and often also control the development and approval of textbooks. On the next level are the managerial groups who implement policy at their particular region or level and may either carry out or frustrate the purposes of the policymakers. At the grass roots are teachers themselves, who are the direct communicators of the values the state wishes to inculcate, or contrarily, of deeply held values of their own which may have successfully resisted state efforts to bring them in line (Holmes 1981: chapter 5).

Clearly developed ideal types, containing a synthesis of core ideas based on the main value complexes which continue to have an influence in East Asia, could be extremely useful in identifying conflict; making comparisons among groups, societies, and time periods; understanding how values are communicated; and discovering which ones are communicated through the school system. The ideal types could be constructed from the wealth of existing literature. They should aim at simplicity and logical coherence, so they can be used in a heuristic way, as precision instruments that help us to identify and interpret observed value patterns in educational and broader societal settings. They would be useful for analyzing laws, policy documents, and textbooks, on the one hand, and also for constructing appropriate questionnaire or interview instruments for the empirical study of values.

CORE VALUES OF CONFUCIANISM, TAOISM, AND BUDDHISM

In *The World of Thought In Ancient China,* Benjamin Schwartz provides us with a masterly overview of traditional Chinese values and beliefs, setting them out in contrast to core ideas of Western classical civilization. For Confucius, the good society was one in which *li* ceremonies hold together an entire normative order derived from the relations of the ideal family. Through *li,* each member of society learns to contribute to the overall harmony of the sociopolitical order in ways appropriate to their role, status, rank, or position, within an explicit and many-layered hierarchy. While Plato saw the family as private and particularistic, a threat to the overall order of the republic, for Confucius "it is precisely in the family that humans learn those virtues which redeem the society, or the family is precisely the domain within which authority comes to be accepted and exercised not through reliance on physical coercion but through the binding power of religious, moral sentiments based on kinship ties" (Schwartz 1985: 70).

For Confucius, knowledge begins "with the empirical cumulative knowledge of masses of particulars and then includes the ability to link these particulars first to one's own experience and ultimately with the underlying 'unity' that binds this thought together." The past achievements of sage kings and noble men provide the pattern to be studied for reforming the present. In Plato's view, knowledge is achieved through mathematical reasoning and the perception of eternal abstract forms, and is accessible only to philosopher-kings. For Confucius, learning takes place mainly through the mastery of texts and their application to contemporary problems of society, while for Plato abstract reasoning and the use of the dialectic are at the heart of knowledge acquisition.

In terms of the human person, Confucius called for a lifelong pursuit of *ren* (humanheartedness), a personal cultivation that involves achieving inner equanimity and outer integrity and responsibility to society. It was different for men and women, and for the four classes (scholar, farmer, craftsman, merchant), with only male scholars having access to the kinds of learning that could make leadership possible. Confucius was perhaps closest to Plato in his conception of the human person, as Plato also emphasized fundamental differences of class, and focused on the education of philosopher-kings, with a greater emphasis on abstract reasoning, and a transcendental vision of deity. Confucianism has often been depicted as more a moral philosophy than a religion, but Schwartz notes that Confucanism includes a strong belief in heaven and a sense of personal relation to heaven, though no theology.

In Taoism, the good society is one that orders itself in a spontaneous unintentional way, in harmony with the dynamics of the natural world, with inaction or *wuwei* as the leading principle, and fluidity or horizontal relationships contrasting to the hierarchy and structured order of the Confucian polity. Knowledge is gained through observation of the natural world, leading to protoscientific tendencies, in Needham's view; much less confidence is placed in words and the study of texts than is the case with Confucianism. The most radical Taoist thinker, Zhuang Zi, was a master in seeing the relativity of all things. "If we know that heaven and earth are grains and the tip of a hair is a range of mountains, then we have perceived the law of difference." (Zhuang Zi in Schwartz 1985: 219) The concise, penetrating stories found in his work open up profound flashes of insight into the natural order and human behavior. As for the human person, within Taoism, the mysterious female, with her passivity, stillness, and waterlike or valleylike role, is perceived as far more effective than the dominant, purposive male.

In these two ideal types—the Confucian and the Taoist—we can see a remarkable set of opposites which have given tremendous vitality and flexibility to Chinese society. The tension between these two extremes was never resolved in a Western-style synthesis, based on linear logical development, but rather remained as a creative balancing force, with Taoism both challenging and revitalizing Confucianism over time.

The only other belief system which had a profound and long-lasting importance in Chinese education and society was that of Buddhism, which also linked China in significant ways with Japan, Korea, and the countries of Southeast Asia. In *East Asian Civilizations: A Dialogue in Five Stages,* de Bary devotes one chapter to the Buddhist Age and sketches out the introduction of Mahayana Buddhism to China and Japan at a time of political and military disarray in the fifth–sixth centuries C.E., showing how a Buddhist conception of democratic equality made itself felt in a new emphasis on public discussion and the people's cooperation in consensus building (de Bary 1988: 33). A contemporary Buddhist scholar describes good society: "The Buddhist tradition of education, right from its inception, has concentrated all its energies to found a society where there are neither cultural nor social identities among its members. Men and women, irrespective of their stations of life, when bound together by unity and concord give rise to a homogeneous society." (Weerasinghe 1992: 49–50) It is a society formed by both religious and lay persons, who come to understand that castes and classes, and every other type of identity, are man-made and who practice the democracy of interdependence and mutual respect.

The Buddha's teaching, *Dharma,* is seen as the most important source of knowledge, and followers are expected to listen, reflect, and meditate on that teaching. There is thus an inwardness, sometimes described as *mindfulness,* that involves both precise inner awareness and external observation skills. Inner peace, through meditation, is seen as the basis for both spiritual and material progress.

The human person, in Buddhist thinking, does not have an unchanging soul with a persistent identity. Rather, personality implies "a bundle of mere physical and psychical elements conditioned into a certain conventional shape . . . an ever expanding, ever changing and ever renewing phenomenon . . ." (Weerasinghe: 30). Men and women are treated equally, and Buddhism was even more important than Taoism in offering opportunities for women's education and scholarship in the Chinese context (Tsai 1981).

These three brief sketches of Confucian, Taoist, and Buddhist views of society, knowledge, and the human person should be useful in helping us to identify core values that have persisted in modern education in East Asia. These values might be seen as constituting an important and often neglected resource in the modernization process, a resource that is shaping a quite distinctive modernization trajectory that may have useful lessons for the West. The degree to which this resource is available to the West, as we rethink some of the values of Western modernity, is an interesting question. One clear place we can see it is in the increasing number of Asian immigrants in Western populations, and the various channels whereby they are introducing their values to North American society. A second intriguing possibility is in the links between Asian philosophies and both feminist and First Nations' ways of thinking. Third, we might look to Asian Christianity, as an expression of the influence of Asian values on some of the core values of our culture.

EDUCATION AND THE COMMUNICATION OF VALUES

In this section I suggest four areas where the communication of values takes place in education: national structures as set in place by constitutions and legislation, textbooks, pedagogy, and the mass media. For the first two I will take examples from China and Japan, to illustrate how the ideal type may help in understanding core values.

Constitutions, legislation, and policy documentation tell us a great deal about the intentions of the state and how they have changed in the five decades of postwar development. An extensive literature exists, particularly for the modern educational development of East Asian societies. To illustrate how an ideal type can help us in identifying core values and how they are communicated, there is the case of China in the 1950s. In developing this case, I am inspired by a point which underlies much of Alex Inkeles' work, that it is the structures of the modern factory that communicate and shape modern values, far more than any conscious effort to inculcate these values through formal or informal education.

In 1949, China adopted the "Common Program" as a sort of draft constitution, until a new constitution was formulated and adopted in 1954. Little attention was given to education specifically in these two documents, but there was a commitment to the development of the natural sciences, in the service of industrial, agricultural, and national defense construction in Article 43 of the Common Program, and a commitment to applying a "scientific-historical viewpoint to the study and interpretation of history, economics, politics, culture, and international affairs" in Article 44 (Fraser 1965: 83–84). The overall context was one of establishing a new socialist state, a people's republic committed to social equality, working-class rule, and economic construction under Soviet tutelage. The proclaimed normative patterns were those of Marxism-Leninism, with the addition of Mao Zedong thought as the expression of a Chinese version of socialist thought. These proclaimed normative patterns should have led to the creation of institutions that promoted equity of access, the integration of theory and practice in the curriculum, and a fairly horizontal set of structures. What emerged from the restructuring of higher education in the early 1950s, however, was an extremely hierarchical set of structures, headed by a small number of elite institutions in major cities, with theoretical, applied, and professional fields isolated from one another. Academically rigorous entrance requirements were established, and cadre appointments were guaranteed to all graduates, in a descending order that reflected the level and quality of the institution from the center down to the locality.

I have discussed elsewhere how faithfully these patterns reflected Confucian values: higher education was fully integrated into the bureaucracy; a hierarchy similar to that of the traditional civil service examination system distributed leadership positions; and the patterns of knowledge reflected the age-old separation of mental and manual labor in Confucianism (Hayhoe 1989: 12–14, 32–34). Exacerbating some of the negative dimensions of these Confucian patterns were traditional European patterns which, ironically, had retained much greater strength within the Soviet system than in European capitalist societies. Thus the actual structures of the new socialist higher education system proclaimed very different values from those enunciated in the Common Program and constitution.

A closer look at selected features of the system will bear this out. Moral-political education was a core concern, and President Liu Shaoqi's text "How to Be a Good Communist" had strong Confucian overtones. People's University, founded in 1950 on the basis of some of the former higher institutions from the border regions and modelled after the Moscow Planning Institute, had an exclusive focus on such social science areas as planning, finance, economics, political science, and law, all within a Soviet paradigm. At its founding Liu justified this focus by explicit reference to Confucius and the fact that no one had had the right to compete with him for students (Liu 1969: 238). In other words the approach to social sciences, a new version of the Confucian concept of "mental labor" developed at People's, was the one orthodox approach, to be adopted throughout the whole national system. This was made possible by the establishment of regional institutes of political science, law, economics, and finance, whose faculty members were all trained at People's University, and by the way in which People's undertook the task of preparing political education textbooks and training teachers in this area for higher education throughout the country.

The Hanlin Academy had been the arbiter of classical knowledge under the imperial system, linking the emperor with the class of scholar-officials who managed the bureaucracy, and People's University took on a parallel function in the new People's Republic. The high degree of centralization and central ideological control through classical knowledge which had characterized the imperial system was now buttressed by a scientific legitimacy drawn from Marxism and Soviet academic patterns.

It is my view that most attempts to understand the educational radicalism of the Great Leap Forward and the Cultural Revolution underestimate the degree to which they were a reaction to the hierarchy and centralization of the new Confucian-Soviet orthodoxy which had taken shape. It was a reaction that can best be understood by reference to Taoist thought and the ways in which Taoism had consistently undermined and questioned Confucianism in a kind of polar dialectic that held the two in balanced opposition. Through his deep understanding of the Chinese psyche, Mao was able to mobilize young people to attack these patterns of elitism, privilege, and oppression through the enshrinement of Marxist dogma in these two movements. Patriarchal familialism, the separation of mental and manual labor, the predilection for hierarchy, were all attacked, with some justification, and new spaces were opened up for women and other underrepresented groups during the Great Leap Forward of 1957 and the Cultural Revolution of 1966–68. Tragically, both movements failed to provide a democratic alternative and opened the way for even more blatant abuses of power.

This consideration of the tensions of the 1950s and 1960s in Chinese higher education illustrates the way in which ideal types of core value complexes can help us to understand policy conflicts. We can probe beneath the political factionalism that shaped conflicting policies and uncover some of the deep-rooted cultural patterns which underlay these conflicts. By examining them, we may be helped in anticipating and avoiding future conflicts.

Much of my work over the past decade in studying Chinese higher education has been predicated on the need to gain an understanding of the cultural context of this process. China's experience with the Soviet Union in the 1950s has an important lesson for the West. Technically and economically it could be defined as a highly successful project of educational borrowing, which led to rapid economic growth and the successful building of a planned socialist economy. Culturally and in terms of deep-rooted values, however, it was a disaster, erupting in conflict more destructive than China had known for decades.

The lesson for all who are participating in the present phase of technology transfer to China, through massive World Bank projects and a wide range of bilateral activities, is the necessity to understand the cultural context on a deeper level, analyze the ways in which specific interventions are being integrated within that context, and anticipate potential areas of conflict before they erupt. We need to understand the tension and balance that exists between Confucian patterns of order, hierarchy, and authority on the one hand and Taoist patterns of radical anarchism on the other. Both are important facets of the Chinese cultural heritage, which underlie the normative statements of policy shaping the higher education system and international interactions.

From this consideration of core values as expressed in systemic features of education, I turn to the question of textbooks as a medium for the communication of values. In both China and Japan, textbooks have tended to be standardized across the country, with strong central control over their content, and intense contestation at times of radical change. Textbooks were a major flashpoint of controversy in China's Cultural Revolution decade, and postwar Japanese educational history has also been marked by intense debates over the content and control of textbooks (Horio 1989: 171–199).

A comparative study of the content of textbooks could be extremely helpful for the identification of core values and the elucidation of cultural differences between Asian and Western societies. The ongoing struggle for economic supremacy between Japan and the United States has led to a wealth of literature on management styles, scientific research resources, educational practices, and so forth. Yet how do we reach beneath the differences evident on all these levels to identify core value differences?

A recent article by Elaine Gerbert analyzing Japan's Kokugo readers, the language texts used for children in their first three years of school, illustrates how the comparative study of textbooks can contribute to this kind of deep-level understanding. Gerbert's article demonstrates how different is the world which Japanese children learn to observe and name in their early years from that of American children. Japanese children are introduced to a world of nature, plants, and animals, depicted in a harmonious way. They are taught to develop habits of introspection, and to reflect on their own feelings and those of others.

> Human actions are not analysed and critiqued from a perspective of right and wrong, just and unjust. Children are taught instead to observe closely, to be sensitive to the nuances of the feelings of others, to imagine and to empathize with those feelings and to be understanding and cooperative. . . . The kokugo textbooks teach children to attune their sensitivities not only to the feelings of other people but also to nature (Gerbert 1993: 162).

> The specific consciousness of the individual self, so central and consistently present from beginning to end in American stories, becomes a neutral, general consciousness that presides over but does not intrude into the world of the kokugo story (Gerbert 1993: 163).

By contrast, American children are taught through primary-school textbooks an active rather than a contemplative approach to nature, and a strong sense of the self and individual volition. They are introduced to a society marked by diversity and social conflict and encouraged to respect difference and intervene on behalf of the disadvantaged. They are educated to be problem solvers and activists. Little guidance is given for introspection, the exploration and nurture of the feelings, or the ability to observe with care and precision.

Gerbert's article is richly illustrated with examples from Japanese language readers that give profound insights into the development of character in the early years of Japanese childhood. Buddhist beliefs clearly lie at the heart of the understanding of self and society that is encouraged in these textbooks. The ideal type of Buddhism sketched out earlier brings into focus a set of core values in Japanese society that stand in direct contrast to the values of individualism, activism, and social equity that characterize American education and can best be understood by reference to John Dewey's educational theories.

Textbooks are also of great importance for understanding dynamics of political interaction within East Asia, with one persistent issue being the teaching of history, and how Japan's role in World War II is depicted in Japanese texts. Here a great deal of work has been done by Japanese educators, who have worked with the Foreign Ministry to translate texts from other Asian societies depicting the war and struggled with the Ministry of Education Science and Culture for a more detailed and accurate depiction of Japan's historic aggression. This one issue is a kind of flashpoint of political controversy.

Of even greater interest is the project of writing a textbook of East Asian history that could be used in schools throughout the region. Obviously, serious work on such a project will become possible only when the Korean and Chinese representatives feel the issue of Japanese texts has been resolved, but issues around the selection of materials, and the interpretative content of such a series of texts, relate closely to the character of core Asian values. It is likely that Confucianism, Taoism, and Buddhism will all influence the process of selection. Clearly developed ideal types would be helpful in identifying core values, and the degree to which they find support in one or several of these belief systems, as well as in religions such as Shintoism, Christianity, and Islam, whose influence has been limited to more specific regions and time periods.

If textbooks are a major channel of communication in education, styles of pedagogy are also important and probably less open to manipulation by the state. Within Confucianism there is a long tradition of the teacher as personal mentor, fostering the moral formation of students and setting an example of how to be a gentleman and fulfill one's social and familial obligations (de Bary 1996). Recent literature has shown how women in Confucian societies fulfilled similar roles in a separate set of social institutions, cloistered within family and clan yet finding clear institutional expression in study groups, poetry clubs, and even publishing networks (Ko 1994). Buddhism and Taoism may give less emphasis to elements of moral formation and more to spiritual and affective aspects of the master-disciple relationship, but these too are important for under-standing the dynamics of Asian pedagogy.

In terms of the communication of values in education, clearly the teacher's style of pedagogy and the kinds of relationships teachers develop with their students are very important variables. Some literature exists on teaching styles and teachers' roles in modern China and Japan; generally the expectation that teachers will exert moral influence through affective connection with their pupils, in addition to their cognitive responsibility, remains in force. In their daily work, teachers face the difficult task of bridging the values extolled in textbooks in areas such as political educa-tion in China, as well as those values which are rewarded in a society increasingly permeated by a market philosophy. In Japan the Buddhist philosophy of peace and adaptation to nature, expressed in the language texts, is far from consonant with the values of the consumer society.

What bears study is the perceptions of teachers about their responsi-bilities towards students in the arena of fostering values, the pedagogies and relationships they develop in order to carry out their task, and the difficulties they face as they build bridges between the relatively safe and sheltered world of the classroom and that of the wider society, both national and international.

A final area that calls for attention is the mass media—television, radio, the press—and, increasingly, the integrated access to all of these through the Internet and various new technologies. What kinds of values do these media present to young people and how far do these values accord or clash with those inculcated by teachers and through the texts they study in school? One would expect the answer to be very different in the context of a socialist as against a capitalist society, yet the parallels among Singapore, Taiwan up to the end of martial law, and China indicate that regimes that control the press fairly tightly use it for communicating state-approved values. The degree of interconnection between education, and the media, and the ways in which the media are used in education, would certainly be a topic worthy of study and would yield insights into core values in Asia and their transmission through education.

CONCLUSION

A convincing study of core Asian values must be set in the context of a vast literature, both a philosophical literature about Asian religions and belief systems, and a historical literature on Asian modernization. In this chap-ter, I have tried to illustrate how ideal types that draw upon this literature may help social scientists to apply its insights to such studies and to perceive core values in their original setting. These ideal types may also be useful for comparison with core values as identified in the international literature. They may be used to explore the degree to which UN statements on human rights find resonance in Asian thought and the nuances they take on in the Asian context.

I have made the point that the study of core Asian values should be seen as having substantive interest and importance for the West, as Westerners look to a common global future. In this conclusion, I would like to point to some of the core values that have been discussed, and that are notably absent in the dominant approach to education in North America. I would also like to discuss how one might approach the task of fostering these values.

North American education teaches children and young people to develop a strong sense of individualism, to be efficacious in problem solving and social action, and to have fairly highly developed cognitive skills in the areas of abstract reasoning and logic. What is done far less effectively, in my view, is teaching young people how to create space within themselves for introspection and meditation, and how to make this the basis for developing profound and penetrating powers of observation and analysis, both of the natural and of the social world. Facility in this Asian-style "active passivity" could make our often impatient and volitional activism far more effective. We also tend to neglect other aspects of education. We teach young people to take community responsibility on the basis of the ethics of equity and participation, yet we fail to nurture the kinds of affective connection and understanding of the other that are described so compellingly by Gerbert.

We should try to foster these values into North American education, not merely in response to Huntington's realist concerns about economic and geopolitical survival in a future dominated by Asia, but for the more intrinsic concerns expressed by Habermas in his project of "redeeming modernity." Tu Wei-ming's Confucian project offers one approach, and I believe the work done by Asian scholars in North American universities, as they elucidate core dimensions of Asian thought, is critical to us. As such work finds its way into the common curriculum at secondary and tertiary levels, it will provide a context in the classroom where young people of Asian descent are given the opportunity of communicating some of the values that have often lain hidden in the past.

It is increasingly important for us to understand core aspects of Confucianism, Taoism, and Buddhism in North America, but mass conversions to these belief systems are unlikely; nor would they be particulary desirable. Rather, we may pursue the kind of understanding that helps us in recovering lost or neglected dimensions of our own cultural heritage—Jewish, Sufi, and Christian mysticism may have points in common with that of Asia, and Christian communalism has a long history. A study of Asian Christianity might be extremely helpful in seeing the points of intersection between Asian core values and those of our own spiritual traditions.

REFERENCES

Beauchamp, Edward and James Vardaman. 1994. *Japanese Education since 1945: A Documentary Survey.* New York: M. E. Sharpe.

Chen, Jingpan. 1990. *Confucius as a Teacher—Philosophy of Confucius with Special Reference to its Educational Implications.* Beijing; Foreign Language Press.

de Bary, W. Theodore. 1988. *East Asian Civilizations: A Dialogue in Five Stages.* Cambridge, MA: Harvard University Press.

———. 1996. "Confucian Education in Premodern East Asia." In *Confucian Traditions in East Asian Modernity.* ed. Tu Wei-ming. Cambridge, MA: Harvard University Press.

Fraser, Stewart. 1965. *Chinese Communist Education: Records of the First Decade.* Nashville: Vanderbilt University Press.

Fukuyama, Francis. 1992. *The End of History and the Last Man.* New York: Free Press.

Gerbert, Elaine. 1993. "Lessons from the Kokugo (National Language) Readers." *Comparative Education Review* 37, (2).

Habermas, Juergen. 1984. *The Theory of Communicative Action.* Vol. 1. Boston: Beacon Press.

———. 1987. *The Theory of Communicative Action.* Vol. 2. Boston: Beacon Press.

Hans, Nicholas. 1967. *Comparative Education.* London: Routledge and Kegan Paul.

Hayhoe, Ruth. 1986. "Penetration or Mutuality? China's Educational Relations with Europe, Japan and North America." *Comparative Education Review* 30:2.

Holmes, Brian. 1981. *Comparative Education: Some Considerations of Method.* London: George Allen and Unwin.

Horio, Teruhisa. 1988. *Educational Thought and Ideology in Modern Japan: State Authority and Intellectual Freedom.* Edited and translated by Steven Platzer. Tokyo: University of Tokyo Press.

Hu, Shiming and Eli Seifman. 1976. *Towards a New World Outlook: A Documentary History of Education in the P.R.C. 1949–1976.* New York: AMS Press.

Huntington, Samuel. 1993. "The Clash of Civilizations?" *Foreign Affairs* 72: 3.

———. 1996. *The Clash of Civilizations and the Remaking of World Order.* New York: Simon and Schuster.

Ko, Dorothy. 1994. *Teachers of the Inner Chambers.* Berkeley: University of California Press.

Liu Shaoqi. 1969. *Collected Works of Liu Shao-ch'i.* Vol. 2, 1945–57. Hong Kong: Union Research Institute.

Mallinson, Vernon. 1975. *An Introduction to the Study of Comparative Education.* London: Heinemann.

Needham, Joseph. 1978. *A Shorter Science and Civilization in China.* Edited by Colin Ronan. Cambridge, MA: Cambridge University Press.

Quigley, Carroll. 1961. *The Evolution of Civilizations: An Introduction to Historical Analysis.* New York: Macmillan.

Rozman, Gilbert. 1991. *The East Asia Region: Confucian Heritage and Its Modern Adaptation.* Princeton, NJ: Princeton University Press.

Schwarcz, Vera. 1986. *The Chinese Enlightenment: Intellectuals and the Legacy of the May 4th Movement.* Berkeley: University of California Press.

Schwartz, Benjamin. 1985. *The World of Thought in Ancient China.* Cambridge, MA: Harvard University Press.

Tsai, Kathryn. 1981. "The Chinese Buddhist Monastic Order for Women: The First Two Centuries." In *Women in China: Current Directions in Historical Scholarship.*, ed. R. Guisso and S. Johannesen. Lewiston, NY: Edwin Mellen Press.

Tu Wei-ming. 1976. *Neo-Confucian Thought in Action: Wang Yangming's Youth (1474–1509).* Berkeley, CA: University of California Press.

———. 1993. *The Way, Learning and Politics.* Albany, NY: State University of New York Press.

———, ed. 1994. *China in Transformation.* Cambridge, MA: Harvard University Press.

———. 1996. *Confucian Traditions and East Asian Modernity: Moral Education and Economic Culture in Japan and the Four Mini-Dragons.* Cambridge, MA: Harvard University Press.

Tu Wei-ming, Milan Hejtmanek and Alan Wachman, eds. 1992. *The Confucian World Observed: A Contemporary Discussion of Confucian Humanism in East Asia.* Honolulu, HI: Institute of Culture and Communication, The East-West Centre.

Weerasinghe, Henry. 1992. *Education for Peace: The Buddha's Way.* Ratmalana, Sri Lanka: Sarvodaya Book Publishing Services.

Wing-On Lee is Associate Professor, Department of Education, University of Hong Kong, and is currently chairman of the department's Hong Kong Centre for IEA Studies and Associate Dean of Faculty of Education. He is also president of the Comparative Education Society of Hong Kong. He has published widely in the areas of comparative education, values education, and civic education. He is at present national coordinator for an IEA Civic Education Study in Hong Kong and is a member of the project's International Steering Committee. He played a key role in drafting the *Hong Kong Guidelines on Civic Education in Schools* (1996), and is the editor of *Moral Education Policy: Developments since 1978* (a special issue of *Chinese Education and Society,* Jul/Aug 1996) and a co-editor, with Mark Bray, of *Education and Socio-political Transitions in Asia* (a special issue of the *Asia Pacific Journal of Education,* 1996) and *Education and Political Transition: Implications of Hong Kong's Change of Sovereignty* (a special issue of *Comparative Education,* 1997).

6. MEASURING IMPACT OF SOCIAL VALUE AND CHANGE[1]

Wing-On Lee

> *. . . [I]mpacts on value cannot be seen only from a top-down perspective even in such an ideologically centralized country as China. Economic liberalization, as well as certain decentralization policies in administration, has actually opened up a possibility for values to be influenced from a bottom-up direction.*

Values and value transmission are important subjects for investigation in a variety of fields: philosophy, anthropology, sociology, and psychology have all touched on the subjects. They have also been investigated from a variety of perspectives. From a sociocultural perspective, value is regarded as a key element in the socialization process, and is the subject of cultural, religious, political, educational, and occupational research. From an individual perspective, value is regarded as a key element in belief systems and attitude formation, and even as a determinant of behavior and a key component of studies dealing with attitudes, personality, and self-esteem. Researchers in these areas usually begin with a remark of the broad nature of the study. An example is Schwartz's article "Studying Human Values":

> Previous theoretical and empirical programs of research on values have agreed in defining values as broad, transsituational goals,

113

varying in importance, that serve as guiding principles in life (e.g., wisdom, health, freedom, security, obedience). Some programs have focused on the values of individuals, others on values of cultures. All view values as playing a central role in the social sciences as key antecedents, consequences, and correlates of human action and experience . . ."(1994: 239).

This chapter will begin with a review of the various ways values are measured. Then it looks at social impacts, which can be measured in terms of the relationships of social change to value, of value to social change, and also in terms of the impact of education as a means of value transmission. The chapter will conclude with a discussion of directions in the measuring of values and the limitations and directions of measuring impact.

MEASURING VALUES: A LITERATURE REVIEW

There have been an impressive number of instruments developed to measure values in the last four decades. These instruments represent diverse perspectives and orientations. Braithwaite and Scott (1991: 666) list 15 multi-item scales that are representative of a variety of perspectives and orientations, namely:

1. The Study of Values, by G. W. Allport, P. E. Vernon, and G. Lindzey (1960)
2. The Value Survey, by Milton Rokeach (1967)
3. The Goal and Mode Values Inventories, by V. A. Braithwaite and H. G. Law (1985)
4. The Paths of Life Survey, by C. W. Morris (1956)
5. The Revised Paths of Life Survey, by P. Dempsey and W. Dukes (1966)
6. Value Profile, by R. Bales and A. Couch (1969)
7. Life Role Inventory Value Scales, by G. Fitzsimmons, D. Macnab, and C. Casserly (1985)
8. Conceptions of the Desirable, by M. Lorr, A. Suziedelis, and X. Tonesk (1973)
9. Empirically Derived Value Constructions, by L. Gorlow and G. A. Noll (1967)
10. The East-West Questionnaire, by A. R. Gilgen and J. H. Cho (1979)
11. Value Orientations, by F. R. Kluckhohn and F. L. Strodtbeck (1961)
12. Personal Value Scales, by W. A. Scott (1965)
13. Survey of Interpersonal Values, by L. Gordon (1960)

14. The Moral Behavior Scale, by S. Rettig and B. Pasamanick (1959)
15. The Morally Debatable Behaviors Scales, by Harding and Phillips (1986).

The instruments vary in the way value is defined—in terms of preference (1, 4), agreement (6, 10), importance (7, 13), goodness (14), justifiability (15), guiding principles (2, 3), or consistent admiration (12). The instruments vary in scope: instruments 1–11 represent a broad conceptualization of the value domain, 12 and 13 are restricted in scope to interpersonal values, and 14 and 15 more narrowly to moral values. They also represent a variety of interests and foci, as the value emphases that can be drawn from the 15 instruments cover the following aspects:

1. Concern for the welfare of others: benevolence (13), kindness (12), social orientation (1, 7), egalitarian orientation (6), humanistic orientation (8), positive orientation to others (3), and receptivity and concern (4).
2. Status desired or respected: recognition and leadership (13), status (12), personal achievement and development (7), acceptance of authority (6), status-security values (9), an authoritarian orientation (8), and social standing (3).
3. Self-control: self-control (12) and social restraint (12).
4. Unrestrained pleasure: self-indulgence (4), need-determined expression vs. value-determined restraint (6), and a hedonistic orientation (8).
5. Individualism: independence (13, 12, 7), withdrawal and self-sufficiency (4), individualism (6, 9), and work ethic (8).
6. Social adeptness: social skills (12) and conformity (13).
7. Religiosity: religious orientation (1), traditional religiosity (3), and religiousness (12) (Braithwaite and Scott 1991: 666–667).

The instruments cited above represent earlier efforts at the measurement of values among scholars and researchers, mostly biased toward Western values. However, some of them are still very influential, not only in the Western world but also in the East. For example, the scales developed by Rokeach and Morris are still being replicated in many of the value surveys conducted today in different parts of China, including Hong Kong. But new instruments continue to be developed, some looking at different sets of value, others looking at cross-cultural value items. These new instruments will be introduced later in this chapter.

MEASURING IMPACTS

There are two major approaches to evaluating impacts: one investigates the impact of the sociocultural context on values, the other, its converse, looks at the impact of values on the sociocultural context. Their interrelationship is illustrated by Figure 6-1.

Figure 6-1. The Relationship between the Value System and the Ideological System

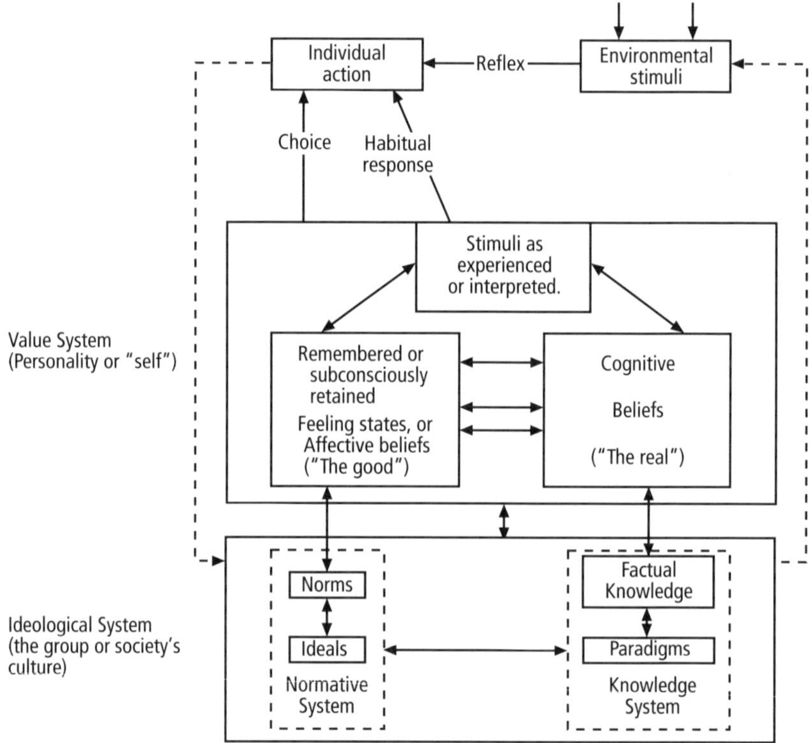

Source: Hutcheon (1972)

The value system and the ideological or cultural system are interdependent on each other. Chief among the environmental stimuli initiating the individual's acts are responses to factors that are partly based on his value system and partly on the larger ideological and cultural system. These factors include the cognitive, affective, belief, normative, ideal, and knowledge systems. Each individual social act, in turn, affects the culture of which it forms a part. Beliefs about the "real" and "good" are twin aspects of the personality, or value system, while the knowledge and normative systems interact at the cultural or ideological level. The knowledge and normative systems of the group and the cognitive and affective systems of the individual continually shape one another in their parallel evolution (Hutcheon 1972: 182–183).

While Hutcheon's model provides a conceptual framework for understanding bidirectional impacts of value and personality at societal and individual levels, Walsh and Charalambides's (1992) study examines the impacts of values from the perspective of self-consciousness. Their study of American undergraduates suggests that repeated exposure to different belief structures will influence individual belief structure. Such exposure will change not only the "mask" of the person, but even the "face" behind the mask.

MEASURING THE IMPACT OF SOCIAL CHANGE ON VALUES

The impact of social change on values is an important concern among sociologists (such as Talcott Parsons), social psychologists (such as Alex Inkeles), anthropologists (such as Robert Bellah), and futurologists (such as Alvin Toffler). The tone of discussion was set largely by Parsons' distinction of modernity vs. tradition and Inkeles' notion of modern man, a tone that persists today, despite increased attention paid to postmodernity in the 1980s and 1990s. An instance of such influence can be seen in the European Value Systems Study Group (EVSSG) surveys conducted in 1981 and 1990. The first study covered 26 European countries and the second covered almost all countries of Europe and the Canada and the United States. This research was based on the hypothesis that modernization has created significant impacts on value change. The four fundamental hypotheses are:

1. As countries advance economically, the values of their populations increasingly shift in the direction of individualization.
2. In the long run, modern societies will converge in the direction of individualized value systems in religion, morality, politics, primary relations, and work.
3. The value systems of individuals in modern societies tend to be fragmented.
4. In the long run, modern societies will show a coherent pattern of individualized value systems in all domains of behavior (Ester, Halman, and de Moor 1994).

The report on the EVSSG, entitled "The Individualizing Society: Value Change in Europe and North America," clearly associates individualization with modernization; the authors argue that modernization and individualization are basic features of advanced society and that both lead to reduction in traditional religiosity, de-ideologization of politics, aspiration for work satisfaction, and noncommitment in primary relationships (such as marriage and family).

The issue of individualization is also a central issue for many other studies on value changes and modernization. For example, Singh (1981), looking at the intrapsychic predictors of modernization among Indian farmers, emphasizes individual-level variables rather than village-level characteristics in explaining peasant modernization in India. He reports high correlation between achievement motivation and self-awareness, and agricultural productivity.

Hofstede's (1984: 168–171) study of cultural consequences also chooses individualism/collectivism as one of the four major variables for analysis. His findings suggest that individualism correlates positively with wealth and social mobility and middle-class values, and is very much a universal norm. Moreover, the thesis of cultural consequences is that we can find the origin of the norm of individualism in the capitalist market economy and the nuclear family structure. While Hofstede looks at how individualism is related to a specific cultural phenomenon, such as the market economy, Triandis, McCusker, and Hui's (1990) study of individualism looks at how the development of specific individualistic/collectivist orientations can be a result of cultural factors. They argue that individualistic/collectivist orientations are affected by external factors, such as exposure to the mass media, affluence of the society, social mobility, and geographical mobility. Their focus of study is quite different from Hofstede's, but both regard individualism as one of the major elements of the modern society.

MEASURING CULTURAL VARIATIONS IN SOCIAL CHANGE

While most studies focus on the impact of social change on values, others have investigated how different cultures behave in the social change or modernization process. When looking at the impact of social change on values, Triandis et al. (1990: 1018) define delicate distinctions of various levels of individualism that are associated with different cultures. For example, their distinction between self-reliance and individualism argues that self-reliance can serve either the group (by the individual not being a burden on the group) or the individual (freedom to do one's own thing), whereas the benefits of individualism tend to be restricted to the individual. In this context, they then argue that "self-reliance is not a good indicator of the construct of individualism . . . ." They examine how the impact of social change on value allows for the understanding of cultural variations in social change and modernization.

The most widely quoted study on the influences of Chinese values on social change is the Chinese Value Survey (CVS), conducted by Michael Bond. The study was administered to 100 students in a variety of disciplines in 22 countries selected from all the five continents. Three of the CVS dimensions are actually very similar to Hofstede's dimensions of Power, Distance, Individualism/Collectivism, and Masculinity/Feminity. The distinctiveness of the study lies in the introduction of a dimension called "Confucian Dynamism" (covering such value indicators as persistence, ordering relationships by status, thrift, and sense of shame), a measure in which the Four Little Dragons, (Hong Kong, Taiwan, Japan, and South Korea) ranked at the top. Results of this study have added considerable credence to the post-Confucian thesis and have helped explain how Confucian values can be predictive of economic growth (Hofstede and Bond 1988: 16–17; Chinese Culture Connection 1987: 158–159). The post-Confucian thesis argues that the prevalence of "vulgar-Confucian" values in today's Eastern societies is significant to the development of East Asian societies. These values include pragmatism, familial orientation, group orientation, and hard work. While most Western explanations of achievements refer to individual orientation, the post-Confucian thesis argues that dedication to the collective (family, group, company) is an important motivational factor for collective prosperity. These post-Confucian values, sometimes termed "Confucian ethics," often are compared to Weber's Protestant ethics.

As mentioned at the beginning of the chapter, many of the earlier developed value measurement instruments are still being used in Eastern societies today. Among these instruments, Rokeach's Value Survey is the most widely employed scale, and, to a lesser extent, Morris's Paths of Life scale has also attracted some attention. In Hong Kong, Lau (1985) polled 1,463 university students in both the University of Hong Kong and the Chinese University of Hong Kong, applying the Rokeach Value Survey instrument. They found that the students at both universities tended to place greater emphasis on personal and competency-oriented values. The four most important terminal values were "true friendship," "wisdom," "self-respect," and "happiness," whereas the four least important were "pleasure," "salvation," "a comfortable life," and "social recognition." Regarding instrumental values, the four most important qualities were "responsible," "courageous," "intellectual," and "capable," and the four least important were "clean," "obedient," "imaginative," and "polite." Lau and Wong (1992) later applied Rokeach's scale to secondary students. They found that Hong Kong adolescents have value emphases very similar to those of their older peers, that is, placing greater emphasis on personal and competency-oriented values. Of the terminal values, "freedom," "true friendship," "happiness," and "a comfortable life" were ranked highly. Of the instrumental values, "capable," "cheerful," "broad-minded," and "intellectual" were ranked most important; the terminal values "mature love," "national security," "an exciting life," and "salvation" and the instrumental values "logical," "imaginative," "clean," and "obedient" were ranked least important. These findings seem to suggest that Hong Kong youngsters favor a joyous, comfortable, free, and enjoyable lifestyle, a picture in line with the features of modernization and individualization.

Studies conducted by other researchers have led to very different observations. Wong and Cheng (1992) conducted a survey on "Value System of Youth," administered to 535 students, 11 to 17 years old, from four secondary schools. The test-makers developed their instrument by combining the scales of Rokeach, Allport et al., Shorr, and Bales and Couch. Their findings showed "family relationship," "freedom," "family members," "friends," "filial piety," and "knowledge" at the top among the 46 items. Although freedom is rated as extremely important, results of this study showed that the youngsters still upheld very traditional Chinese or Confucian values. Similarly, Kwan and Tse (1991) surveyed Hong Kong youth aged 11 to 22. They found that "contribution to society" and "having a happy family" were regarded by the respondents as two important criteria of judging a person's success. Moreover, a large majority of the respondents regarded "to build up one's career" and "to repay your parents' love" as the most important objectives of life, whereas "freedom" and "family relationship" were considered the most important tasks in life. These studies suggest that Hong Kong youngsters are on the one hand achievement-oriented and fond of freedom, but on the other hand uphold significant traditional Chinese or Confucian values, such as filial piety (to both family and society) and familialism.

In Taiwan, Yang (1989) applied a revised Paths of Life Questionnaire to students in Taiwan. The students expressed a strong preference to "preserve the best that man has achieved" and "show sympathetic concern for others," with moderate preference to "enjoy group and social participation." Li and Yang (1989) revised the "Study of Value Instrument" of Singh, Huang and Thompson, using it to measure Taiwanese university students' preference for six types of values. The findings were that the "theoretical" values (e.g., rational and empirical) were most preferred, and the "religious" values (e.g., unity and wholeness) were least preferred. The findings fit extremely well to the modernity framework, which is associated with such attributes as rationality and secularization.

In the People's Republic, Morris (1956) applied the Paths to Life Questionnaire to examine university students' ranking of 13 life goals. According to the study, the life goals most preferred by male students were to "obey the cosmic purposes," "constantly master changing conditions," and "act and enjoy life through group participation." The female students preferred "obey the cosmic purposes," "show sympathetic concern for others," and "preserve the best that man has attained." The life goals least preferred were the same for both male and female students, namely, "cultivate independence of persons and things," "wait in quiet receptivity," and "meditate on the inner life." Using the individualistic/collectivist framework, the P.R.C. students in the 1950s clearly expressed a strong collectivist orientation. Feather (1972) applied the Rokeach scale to 68 university students in Mainland China, and found that the most important terminal values expressed were "true friendship," "wisdom," "freedom," and "mature love," whereas the least important were "family security," "a comfortable life," "an exciting life," and "salvation." Among the instrumental values, the most important were "ambitious," "broadminded," "intellectual," and "courageous," while the least important were "forgiving," "helpful," "clean," and "obedient." The two studies cited above took place more than two decades ago and were conducted by Westerners, but corroborative studies by Chinese scholars include the surveys conducted by Wang (1987), Kou (1989), and Zhao, Chen, and Liu (1993). For illustration purposes, only the study of Zhao et al. is elaborated here.

Zhao et al. administered the Rokeach scale to 483 secondary students from three ethnic groups—Han, Hui, and Zhang. Looking at the four most important terminal values, the study found that "a sense of accomplishment" and "national security" were commonly considered the most important terminal values by all the three ethnic groups; "self-respect" was ranked high by the Hans and the Huis, "a world at peace" was ranked high by the Huis, and the Zangs, "true friendship" was ranked high among the Hans, and "equality" was ranked high only among the Zangs. There is a clear commonality in the rating of instrumental values among the three ethnic groups, as "ambitious," "broad-minded," and "honest" were all regarded as the most important. "Capable" was ranked high only among the Hans, "courageous" only among the Huis and "helpful" only among the Zangs. In respect to the least important terminal values, only "an exciting life" and "salvation" were shared among the three ethnic groups; "a comfortable life" and "salvation" were regarded as the least important among the Hans and the Huis, "mature love" among the Huis and the Zangs, "inner harmony" only among the Hans, and "freedom" only among the Hans of the instrumental values, "logical" and "obedient" were ranked low by all the three ethnic groups, and "independent" and "loving" were ranked low by the Huis and Zangs. Only the Hans ranked "clean" and "self-controlled" at the lowest level.

The study of Zhao et al. has significant implications, as the test was meant for cross-cultural comparisons, and the differences in value emphases reflect social and cultural background. For example, the Zangs are fond of "equality," but this is not a matter of concern among the Huis and the Hans, which may reflect the Tibetan situation. "Capable" is ranked high among the Hans, but not by the Huis and the Zangs, which may reflect the relative availability for professional achievements. Comparing the findings from the mainland and Hong Kong is most instructive. While Hong Kong students rate "freedom" and "happiness" and "a comfortable life" as the most important values, "freedom" is one of the least important values to the mainland Hans, as is "a comfortable life" to all the three ethnic groups in the P.R.C. Moreover, "imaginative" is an important instrumental value among the Hong Kong students, but not at all to the mainland students. This may reflect different value emphases in different social and cultural circumstances.

The above studies, which measure value orientations or preference of students in Hong Kong, Taiwan, and the People's Republic, were not designed specifically for measuring impacts of social change on values, or values on social change. However, they are helpful for interpreting values of youth in the "modern" society, and give an insight into the impacts of modernization. Moreover, the variations in value preference across cultures can be helpful for understanding the impacts of culture on the modernization process.

MEASURING IMPACTS OF EDUCATION

Works measuring the impact of education on values can easily be found in the literature of sociology of education. Many of these studies discuss how students are influenced by the education system at large (Paulo Freire and Pierre Bourdieu); the hidden curriculum (Michael Apple and Jean Anyon); and the teaching/learning process, the classroom language used, and the curriculum textbooks adopted (Basil Bernstein). In pre-turnover Hong Kong, the major focus of sociological studies has been equality of opportunity in education rather than the impact of values on education. Some conclusions, however, can be drawn from content analysis of curricula or textbooks in the People's Republic, Taiwan, and Hong Kong. Although this is not specifically a measurement of how values are transmitted and the impact of values, a conclusion can be made regarding what values are expected to be transmitted in the intended curriculum and therefore what the expected impact of values will be. A number of studies focus on the values conveyed in children's books. For example, Blumenthal's (1976) "Models in Chinese Moral Education: Perspective from Children's Books" showed that the content of moral education in China placed emphasis on Communist morality and devotion to the revolution as well as to the new society. Chang's "Children's Literature and Political Socialization" (1979) showed that children's picture storybooks were used after 1949 as a tool to transmit officially approved messages to readers. In Taiwan, studies of textbooks include R. Martin's (1975) "The Socialization of Children in China and in Taiwan: An Analysis of Elementary School Textbooks" and L. C. Li's (1989) "An Analysis of the Political Socialization Content in the Chinese Textbooks of the Junior High School, Taiwan." Martin's work suggested that the Taiwan government promoted a revitalization of the traditional Confucian value system, whereas the mainland government advocated a new socialist system and separation from the Confucian traditions. Li's work found obvious political orientations in the Taiwan curriculum.

While these studies have dealt with political socialization in China and Taiwan, content analyses of curricula in Hong Kong are mainly focused on value orientations. These include works by Y. M. Wen (1987),

K. C. Au (1991), Y. Y. Au (1994), and S. K. Leung (1996). The concern for identifying modern values and traditional values in the textbooks in Taiwan and Hong Kong further demonstrates the dominance of the theme of social change and modernization in value study. According to K. C. Au's study, textbooks in Taiwan and Hong Kong both emphasize three modern values, namely, concern for public affairs and current events within and outside the country, confidence in science and technology, and receptivity to change and creativity. On the other hand, they also teach three traditional values, namely family and nostalgic homesickness, obedience/respect for authority, and gender bias.

Using a different framework, Y. Y. Au (1994) and Leung (1996) conduct content analyses of Hong Kong Chinese language textbooks according to four sets of values, namely, self-oriented values, group-oriented values, society-oriented values, and nation-oriented values; Leung's study also includes nature-oriented values. It is interesting to note that self-oriented values are distinctive in the Chinese language curriculum, as they represent the highest percentage of themes across the five categories of value orientations (see Table 6-1). Self-oriented values are even more important at the junior secondary level, as this category of values represents 60.4 percent of all themes in the junior secondary curriculum and 38.4 percent in the senior secondary curriculum. It is also interesting to note that the percentages of themes decline accordingly from group-oriented values to society-oriented values and nation-oriented values.

Table 6-1. Themes in the Chinese Language Curriculum (%)

	Junior Secondary	Senior Secondary
Self-oriented values	60.37	38.41
Group-oriented values	24.60	26.09
Society-oriented values	11.03	17.67
Nation-oriented values	4.00	16.05
Nature-oriented values	—	1.78

Source: Leung (1996, p. 118)

It would be tempting to identify a clear illustration of individualization process in the Hong Kong curriculum. However, both Au and Leung contend that this instead shows a significant emphasis of Confucian values on self-cultivation. For example, Leung (1996: 119) argues that the cultivation of self is actually the foundation of all virtues. As mentioned earlier, the "self" is the source and the focus of motivation. Human relationships are extended from the self. Au (1995: 194) also argues:

> self-cultivation" is the foundation of being a human, and the fundamental requirement of attaining order and harmony of human relationships. "Self-cultivation" stimulates "self-reflection," "self-critique," "seeking one's own self" and "seeking one's truthfulness" from "self-awareness" to "self-love" and "self-control." All this should go further to attain self-determination, [a higher degree of] cultivating oneself, self-enrichment, and to attain the four virtues of "benevolence, righteousness, rite, and intelligence.

On the other hand, it is obvious that nation-oriented values are rather weak in the Chinese language curriculum, but the significance of this category rises conspicuously at the senior secondary level. Comparing the old curriculum that Wen examined and the new one that Leung analyzed, there are some obvious differences in value orientations between the two. Table 6-2 shows a clear change in the value emphases, if not value orientations. There is an obvious change in the presentation of father image, an awareness of the issue of gender equality, an addition of international perspective in addressing the issue of national pride, and also a more direct discussion of the government behavior which is a prerequisite for participatory citizenship. The moral virtues remain important, although there is a shift in the way that these virtues are presented. The comparison of the old and the new curricula has added a longitudinal perspective to the measuring of social change and value change in time. Once again, the issue of value change in modernization and cultural variations stands out as a significant theme in the measuring of impact of education on values.

LIMITATIONS AND POSSIBLE DIRECTIONS OF MEASURING IMPACTS

The study of the impact of values can be addressed by looking at three issues: the values of the originators of value preferences, such as students, teachers, and political leaders; the impact of these educational experiences as manifested by changes in belief structures among those affected; and the ultimate effect of value changes.

Table 6-2. Value Orientations in the Old and New Chinese Language Curriculum

	Old Curriculum	New Curriculum
Father Image	• stern • affection not expressed	• not stern or strict • affection expressed
Women's status	• low status • associated with inferior jobs • incidents of discrimination	• women with strong and firm character • associated with optimistic and positive attitudes • incidents of discrimination cannot be indentified
Aspirations and meaning of life	• greatest motivation of study: becoming a government official and upward social mobility • emphasizing the political significance of education: for the country's glory	 • the international dimension glorifying the country added, e.g., comparing the Three Gorges of Yangtze River project with that of the Tennessee Valley.
Sociopolitical values	• presenting a gloomy picture from corrupt policy	• obvious passages of exposing the wrongdoing of the government and the disastrous effect of wars
Nostalgia, homesickness	• focusing on the motherland cuisine, and scenery	• extending the focus to the Chinese culture and nation
Moral virtues	• theoretical mention of such virtues as filial piety, a sense of shame, willingness to correct mistakes, self-confidence, and perseverance	• presenting these virtues through historical stories

Source: Leung (1996, 121–129)

The values of those originating value preferences   Most of the existing studies use students as subjects or respondents. As such, these studies represent measurement of the values or value changes among students, especially students at the tertiary level of studies. These studies have already considered the impact of education in one way or another; however, they can only test the result of change, rather than identify causal relationships. Moreover, the process is still more or less unknown.

Despite the involvement of students at large, few studies use teachers as subjects, and there is obviously a dearth of study on the values of political leaders. Future projects on the impact of values should include teachers, political or social leaders, and school administrators as the targets of studies. In this context, there should be delphi studies on the value preferences of the political and social leaders in order to give a clearer direction for the shaping of values in the society.

Impacts of changes in belief structure   This can be assessed partly by content analyses of textbooks and curricula, looking at the shift of value emphases, belief systems, or ideological changes presented in the texts. The author's study of "changing ideopolitical emphases in moral education in China" attempted to track the sociopolitical climate of a country and relate it to ideopolitical shifts in education (Lee 1996). The study was done at the level of documentary analysis; however, we still lack empirical studies of the relationships between educational experiences and belief structures in the wider society, with both quantitative and qualitative methods of inquiry, touching upon the areas of social psychology and social anthropology.

Ultimate effect of value changes   We need to explore both impacts from the top and impacts from the bottom, studying how government policies can create impacts on value changes at the societal level, as well as examining impacts of movements taking place at the grass-roots level. For example, in the area of moral education in China, the government has been exerting its influences in the direction of development of moral education. However, impacts on value cannot be seen only from a top-down perspective even in such a ideologically centralized country as China. Economic liberalization, as well as certain decentralization policies in administration, has actually opened up a possibility for values to be influenced from a bottom-up direction. Recent local and provincial initiatives in southern China developing a series of rhymed moral education texts, namely, *The Three Character Classics, The Four Character Song of Social Ethics,* and *The Five Character Rhyme of Family Ethics,* have spread influences to the northern part of China.

Research methods   Most of the researches cited above used the questionnaire survey technique, with a few of them supplemented by interviews and content analyses of interviews and textbooks. The study of impact requires an extension of research methods, borrowing from other fields including anthropology and psychology. A direction that Boruch proposes is the adoption of randomized field experiments to test the effects of a particular program, policy, or service at both the individual and institutional levels. This will involve random allocation of individuals, neighborhoods, clinics, sectors, or other entities among alternative regimens, each group receiving a different regimen or a different level of treatment (Dennis and Boruch 1989: 293–294). Boruch proposes that this method can be applied to measuring educational effects, such as programs for drug education, delinquents, and at-risk students (Boruch 1997). Boruch's methodology and other observational techniques in social psychology are important in assessing not only the outcome but also the process of impacts.

Another direction of future research is the adoption of qualitative methods in social anthropology, with a particular focus on understanding the cultural perspectives of value changes. This will become a significant complement and qualification of the general picture derived from quantitative findings, especially in understanding the cultural context for value changes and the subtle residuum of tradition in an obvious change of value. For example, in Hong Kong, the limitation of accommodation in cities has composed a clear threat to the Chinese tradition of extended family. However, do people in Hong Kong simply give up the customs of extended family and welcome those of the nuclear family? A closer look shows that small families still live close to each other for mutual support, and many old people are still being taken care of by the younger generation at home. Qualitative study can help provide an in-depth look at the characteristics of such other values as individualism and achievement orientation that are assumed to develop in the course of modernization. Moreover, as mentioned, the need for a focus on studying not only students but also the views of social or political leaders has opened up a need for investigating the major value preferences among leaders of the various sectors in the society.

Another consideration is the time factor. As effects usually cannot be seen within a short span of time, longitudinal studies are necessary for measuring impacts. During this symposium, Inkeles has cited some of his longitudinal studies on value changes in various countries, applying the same instrument to people in an interval of five or ten years. This is an important strategy for assessing change according to a standard framework of measurement. Leung's (1996) effort to compare curricula is another way to look at value change across time (see Table 6-2). There is certainly a need for more serious content analyses on textbooks of the same subject across time to see how value emphases have changed.

This chapter has cited numerous existing works on impacts of values on social change and the impacts of social change on values; however, these studies have been mainly confined to studies at a macroscopic level, with mainly quantitative approaches. Further consideration of the three questions posed here suggests that there is a need for changing the scope of research: from a macroscopic level to a microscopic level, from looking at impacts from the top to looking at them from the bottom, from a time-static focus to a progressive focus. Research methods can also be extended to consider the application of other social sciences research methods, such as the random experiments and qualitative approaches of social anthropology. All this means that despite the existence of a large body of literature on impact, there are many dimensions of research yet to be addressed, and research approaches yet to be attempted for further understanding the impacts of value changes.

REFERENCES

Allport, G. W., P. E. Vernon, and G. Lindzey, 1960. *Study of Values: Manual and Test Booklet.* Boston: Houghton Mifflin.

Au, K.C. 1991. "The Relationship between Primary School Curricular Content and Individual Modernity." *CUHK Education Journal* 19 (1):9–40 (in Chinese).

Au, Y. Y. 1994. "Value Orientations in Junior Secondary (S1-S3) Chinese Language Curriculum of Hong Kong." M.Ed. dissertation, Faculty of Education, University of Hong Kong,

———. 1995. "Value Orientations in Hong Kong Junior Secondary Chinese Language Curriculum [Xianggang Zhongguo Yuwen Chuzhong Kecheng de Jiaozhi Quxiang]." In *Essays on Chinese Education* [*Zhongwen Jiaoyu Lunwenji*], ed. S. K. Tse, Y. C. Lee, and A. L. S. Fung, 187–200. Hong Kong: Department of Curriculum Studies, University of Hong Kong.

Bales, R. and A. Couch. 1969. "The Value Profile: A Factor Analytic Study of Value Statements." *Sociological Analysis* 39:3–17.

Blumenthal, E. P. 1976. "Models in Chinese Moral Education: Perspectives from Children's Books." Ph.D. dissertation, University of Michigan.

Boruch, Robert. 1997. "Randomized Controlled Experiments for Evaluation and Planning." In *Handbook on Evaluation,* ed. L. Bickman and D. Rog. Newbury Park, CA: Sage.

Braithwaite, V. A., and H. G. Law. 1985. "Structure of Human Values: Testing the Adequacy of the Rokeach Value Survey." *Journal of Personality and Social Psychology* 49:250–263.

Braithwaite, V. A., and W. A. Scott. 1991. "Values." In *Measures of Personality and Social Psychological Attitudes,* ed. J. P. Robinson, P. R. Shaver, and L. S. Wrightsman, 661–745. San Diego: Academic Press.

Chang, P. H. "Children's Literature and Political Socialization" In *Moving a Mountain,* ed. G. C. Chiu and F. L. K. Hsu, 238–256. Honolulu: The University of Hawaii Press.

Chinese Culture Connection, The. 1987. "Chinese Values and the Search for Culture-free Dimensions of Culture." *Journal of Cross-Cultural Psychology, 1987,* 18 (2):143–164.

Dempsey, P., and W. Dukes. 1966. "Judging Complex Value Stimuli: An Examination and Revision of Morris's 'Paths of Life.'" *Educational and Psychological Measurement* 26:871–882.

Dennis, Michael L., and Robert F. Boruch. 1989. "Randomized Experiments for Planning and Testing Projects in Developing Countries." *Evaluation Review* 13, (3):292–309.

Ester, P., L. Halman, and R. de Moor. 1994. "Value Shift in Western Societies." In *The Individualizing Society: Value Change in Europe and North America, 2nd ed.*, ed. P. Ester, L. Halman, and R. de Moor, 1–20. Tilburg, The Netherlands: Tilburg University Press.

Fitzsimmons, G., D. MacNab, and C. Casserly. 1985. *Technical Manual for the Life Roles Inventory Values Scale and the Salience Inventory.* Edmonton, Alberta: PsiCan Consulting Limited.

Gordon, L. V. *Survey of Interpersonal Values.* Chicago: Science Research Associates, 1960.

Gorlow, L. and G. A. Noll. 1967. "A Study of Empirically Derived Values." *Journal of Social Psychology* 73:261–269.

Harding, S. and D. Phillips. 1986. *Contrasting Values in Western Europe: Unity, Diversity and Change.* London: Macmillan.

Hofstede, G. 1984. *Culture's Consequence: International Differences in Work-related Values.* Newbury Park: SAGE Publications.

Hofstede, G. and M. H. Bond. 1988. "The Confucius Connection: From Cultural Roots to Economic Growth." *Organizational Dynamics*, 16, 4–21.

Hutcheon, P. D. 1972. "Value Theory: Towards Conceptual Clarification." *British Journal of Sociology* 23 (2):172–187.

Kluckholm, F. R., and F. L. Strodtbeck. 1961. *Variations in Value Orientations.* Evanston, IL: Row, Peterson.

Kou Yu. 1989. "A Survey Study of the Vocational Values and the Value Systems of Secondary Students [Guanyu Zhongxuesheng de Zhiye Jiazhiguan ji qi Jiazhi Xitong de Diaocha Yanjiu]." *Periodical of Beijing Normal University* [*Beijing Shifan Daxue Xuebao*], Additional Issue.

Kwan, Y. H. and W. L. Tse. 1991. *A Study of the Attitudes of Secondary Students on Values in Life in Hong Kong.* Hong Kong: YWCA.

Lau, S. 1985. "A Value Profile of Chinese University Students in Hong Kong." In *Selected Papers on Youth Studies in Hong Kong 1984–87*, ed. A. M. C. Ng and F. M. Cheung. Hong Kong: Centre for Hong Kong Studies, Chinese University of Hong Kong.

Lau, S. and A. K. Wong. 1992. "Value and Sex-role Orientation of Chinese Adolescents." *International Journal of Psychology* 27:3–17.

Lee, W. O. 1996. "Changing Ideopolitical Emphases in Moral Education in China: An Analysis of the CCP Central Committee Documents." *Asia Pacific Journal of Education* 16 (1):106–121.

Leung, S. K. 1996. "Value Orientations in Senior Secondary (S4-S5). Chinese Language Curriculum of Hong Kong and Perceptions of Teachers on Values Education." M.Ed. dissertation, Faculty of Education, University of Hong Kong.

Li, L. C. 1989. "An Analysis of the Political Socialization Content in the Chinese Textbooks of the Junior High School." *Bulletin of Graduate Institute of Education* (Taiwan Normal University) 32:449–466.

Li, M. C. and K. S. Yang. 1989. "A Study of Values among Chinese College Students [Zhongguo Daxuesheng de Jiazhiquan]." In *The Character of the Chinese* [Zhongguoren de Xingge], 2nd ed., ed. Y. Y. Li and K. S. Yang, 324–345. Taipei: Institute of Ethnology.

Lorr, M. A. Suziedelis, and X. Tonesk. 1973. "The Structure of Values: Conceptions of the Desirable." *Journal of Research in Personality* 7:137–147.

Martins, R. 1975. "The Socialization of Children in China and in Taiwan: Analysis of Elementary School Textbooks." *The China Quarterly* 62:242–262.

Morris, C. W. 1956. *Varieties of Human Values.* Chicago: University of Chicago Press.

Rettig, S. and B. Pasamanick. 1959. "Changes in Moral Values among College Students: A Factorial Study." *American Sociological Review,* 24:856–863.

Scott, W. A. 1965. *Values and Organizations: A Study of Fraternities and Sororities.* Chicago: Rand McNally.

Schwartz, Shalom H. 1994. "Studying Human Values." In *Journeys into Cross-cultural Psychology,* ed. Anne-Marie Bouvy et al., 239–253. Lisse: Swets & Zeitlinger.

Singh, S. 1981. "Intra-psychic Predictors of Modernization among Indian Farmers." In *Perspectives in Asian Cross-Cultural Psychology,* ed. J. L. M. Binnie-Dawson, G. H. Blowers, and R. Hoosain, 183–192. Lisse: Swets and Zeitlinger B.V.

Triandis, H. C., C. McCusker, and C. H. Hui. 1990. "Multimethod Probes of Individualism and Collectivism." *Journal of Personality and Psychology* 59 (5):1006–1020.

Walsh, J. P., and L. C. Charalambides. 1992. "Individual and Social Origins of Belief Structure Change." *Journal of Social Psychology* 130 (4): 517–532.

Wang Xinling. 1987. "A Report on Survey of the Value System and Moral Judgement of Students in a Secondary School in Beijing [Guanyu Beijing Yisuo Zhongxue Xuesheng de Jiazhi Baogao yu Daode Panduan de Diaocha Baogao]." *Journal of Psychology* [*Xinli Xuebao*], 4.

Wen, Y. M. 1987. "A Study from the Comparative Education Perspective of the Development of Secondary Level Chinese Language Teaching Materials from the Late Ching Dynasty to the Present Day." M.Ed. dissertation, Faculty of Education, Chinese University of Hong Kong.

Wong, S. W. and H. K. Cheng. 1992. *Value System of Youth: An Exploratory Study of Configuration and Structure.* Hong Kong: City Polytechnic of Hong Kong.

Yang, K. S. 1989. "Expressed Values of Chinese College Students [Zhongguo Daxuesheng de Renshengguan]." In *The Character of the Chinese* [Zhongguoren de Xingge], 2nd ed., ed. Y. Y. Li and K. S. Yang, 269–323. Taipei: Institute of Ethnology.

Zhao Zhiyi, Chen Sheqing and Liu Hongyun. 1993. "A Report on the Survey of the Value Orientations of the Adolescent Students of Three Ethnic Groups in China [Woguo Sange Minzu Qingshaonian Xuesheng Jiazhiquxiang de Diaocha Baogao]." *Studies in Ethnic Education* [*Minzu Jiaoyu Yanjiu*], 1:34–44.

William K. Cummings, Director and Professor, Center for Comparative and Global Studies in Education of SUNY-Buffalo, will be president of the Comparative and International Education Society in 1998. He has worked for development organizations or universities in Asia for over ten years, and in the United States has served on the faculties of Harvard, the University of Hawaii, and the University of Chicago as well as at the National Science Foundation. He is the author of *Education and Equality in Japan* (Princeton, 1980), co-editor of *The Challenge of Eastern Asian Education* (SUNY Press, 1996), and coordinator of the recent policy study, Towards Transnational Competence (IIE, 1997).

7. Promoting Human Rights in East Asian Values: Basic Education's Role[1]

William K. Cummings

Our Imperial Ancestors have founded Our Empire on a basis broad
and everlasting, and have deeply and firmly implanted virtue;
Our Subjects ever united in loyalty and filial piety have from
generation to generation illustrated the beauty thereof. This is
the glory of the fundamental character of Our Empire,
and herein also lies the source of Our education.
—The Imperial Rescript on Education, 1890

Today's world leaders recognize that basic education can promote positive human values, but in the early modern era, opinion among the Western powers was mixed. It is useful to examine the case of Japan, which in 1872, against the counsel of certain foreign advisors, vigorously launched a program of basic education. Japan was among the first nations to declare a policy of universal primary education (Weiner 1992). It was also among the most efficient in implementing such a policy, achieving virtually full enrollment of eligible youth within 40 years, or about the time the United Kingdom first announced a national policy of compulsory education. Over subsequent decades Japan introduced various changes in its compulsory education requirements, extending it to six (1907) and later nine years (1946) to keep up with changing times.[2]

Japan's flexible development and support of basic education contributed in many direct and indirect ways to the development of the Japanese people as well as to the nation's progress. But the record is not perfect; one particular blemish was the role basic education played in motivating young people to commit themselves uncritically to the war effort from the mid-1930s to 1940s. Japan's basic education was significantly reformed after World War II to emphasize developing a rich personality that respects peace and democracy. Young people have benefited from this new emphasis, whether one makes comparison to prewar Japan or to young people in Western societies. Other nations in East Asia have imitated the Japanese example and are achieving similar benefits (World Bank 1993).

THE ARGUMENT

Human endeavor is guided by the pursuit of values, and the Lasswellian list of eight core values is a useful summary. It is suggested, particularly in recent Western discourse, that individuals have the right to realize these various values; actions that add to the realization of values can be considered to promote human rights (Montgomery 1995).

Governments, through the policies they develop and implement, play a pivotal role in the realization of human values. Lasswell's schema (Lasswell 1976) goes into considerable detail in relating government policies to the core values. The international human rights community pays particular attention to the actions of governments in the areas of political and civil rights, which is only a subset of the full range of rights. Given that government policies may promote some rights at the expense of others, it is inappropriate to judge a government for the effects of its policies in only one area.

Most governments' policies can be evaluated in terms of the values they influence. Educational policy, the focus of this chapter, can have a direct influence on the Lasswellian values of Skill, Enlightenment, Rectitude, Respect, Well-Being, and Affection (Carnoy 1993), and may have an indirect effect on other values including Wealth (Jencks 1972) and Power (McGinn 1996). The policy vehicles available to educators include school provision, curricular content, teacher training and instructional supervision, and pupil selection and promotion. Through these policies, educators can have a profound impact on social capital.

In the nineteenth century, governments differed in their orientation to basic education. In Reformation Germany, education was favored as a means of nurturing piety, while in revolutionary France, it was seen as a form of power for the common person (Glenn 1988). In the United States, Thomas Jefferson argued that public education was a crucial underpinning of democratic government, but others worried that it would corrupt the natural spirit. The aristocratic leaders of the United Kingdom, having witnessed the revolutions in France and the United States, opposed public education out of a fear that it would give the commoner dangerous ideas; the Tsar feared educating the Russian peasant for similar reasons.

Japan, starting with the Meiji restoration (1868), provides a distinct contrast to these Western examples. Japan's leaders displayed extraordinary faith in basic education as well as flexibility in periodically modifying its structure and content. It is generally recognized that the outputs from these policies, successive generations of literate, disciplined, and eager young people, provided the backbone for Japan's amazing accomplishments (and failures) in industry, war, and peace. Among the many distinctive features of Japanese basic education is its egalitarian structure, especially notably after the post–World War II reforms. This egalitarian structure has fostered a relatively equal distribution of several of the values identified by Lasswell, most notably Skill, Enlightenment, Respect, and Well-Being. It may also be that the exceptionally equal distribution of Wealth in Japan when compared with distribution in other advanced capitalist societies may be related to the unique nature of Japan's basic education (Cummings 1980).

We will begin with the Japanese case, then review Japan's influence on the basic education of neighboring countries, noting how these countries came to share some of Japan's characteristics. We conclude by considering some of the civilizational implications of Japan/East Asia's great policy of basic education.

MEIJI JAPAN'S APPROACH IN BASIC EDUCATION

The Meiji or "Old System" of Education

The Japanese story begins with the extraordinary aristocratic revolution of 1868, and its battle cry, "Restore the Emperor and Expel the Barbarians," that cast aside the feudal Tokugawa regime. The young warriors who took control of Japan were deeply conscious of the prime importance of mass education and advanced knowledge to achieving modernization. In the Charter Oath, issued soon after their accession to central power, they announced the need to "seek knowledge widely throughout the world" (Tsuneichi 1958: 643). Upon consolidating the traditional governmental units, they began in 1872 to construct a modern educational system that would promote Skill and Enlightenment. The Fundamental Code of Education issued that year declared: "There shall, in the future, be no community with an illiterate family, nor a family with an illiterate person. Every guardian, acting in accordance with this, shall bring up his children with tender care, never failing to have them attend school" (Passin 1965: 209–211).

At this formative stage, the government looked to education as a means for forging a closer integration of the diverse feudal loyalties and for training a technical elite. Factions in the government disagreed only on the basic tenet of shaping the educational philosophy. After a decade of unrewarding experimentation with Western liberal ideas, from the early 1880s, the government shifted toward a more traditional elitist and pragmatic conception. Mori Arinori (Hall 1973), who from 1885 to 1889 served as Minister of Education, played a key role in articulating the new policy that was to remain as the framework for Japanese education through World War II. The main characteristics of Mori's educational system included:

Spiritual training   All youth throughout the nation were required to spend a minimum of four years in primary schools to learn basic cognitive skills and the principles of the national morality. Mori repeatedly emphasized the necessity of spiritual education, for fostering Rectitude and Respect. An opening paper presented for the consideration of the cabinet put forth the following rationale:

> Civilization is gradually spreading as can be seen by the progressive changes in the objects we use for our daily activities. Is the spirit of our people sufficiently hardened and trained that they may withstand adversity, bear up and endure under pain, and shoulder the heavy burdens of the long road ahead? This must be doubted. Since the Middle Ages, in our country only the warriors have performed civil and military duties. Now, as a result, only one portion of the

people adequately understands and supports the modernization of the state. In contrast, the great majority are confused and may lack those qualities of strong character essential for guaranteeing the independence of the state.

We have identified those general moral principles which we hope the educational system will instill in the people, but what is the detailed educational program that will realize these principles? Consider for a moment. Our country has never been subject to indignity from a foreign nation thanks to the authority of the Imperial Throne which has been occupied by an unbroken line of Emperors from ancient times. The people's traditional spirit of defending the fatherland and of total loyalty to the emperor still remains firm. This is the essential foundation for national wealth and strength. If this is made the goal of education and the character of the people is advanced according to this spirit, there will be no need for fear. The people will feel a strong sense of loyalty to the throne and love for their country; they will have strong character, and be pure in thought. We must establish through education the principle of abhorring those who are insulting and evil. If we are successful, there is no doubt that the people will be able to endure much difficulty and will be prepared to strive together to carry out their tasks. . . . This vitality if channeled into productive labor will develop the national wealth. There is not one element in advancing the fate of the state and casting away all danger which does not come from this vital spirit. The elderly pass this vital spirit to the young. Fathers and ancestors pass this vital spirit to posterity. From person to person and household to household, all are made the same according to this vital spirit. The vital spirit of our nation becomes fixed, and the nation naturally becomes something of great strength (Mombusho 1972: 270–276).

In 1891, after extensive discussion within the government, the main themes to be stressed in the school's program of spiritual training were summarized from the Imperial Rescript on Education:

Know Ye, Our Subjects:

Our Imperial Ancestors have founded Our Empire on a basis broad and everlasting, and have deeply and firmly implanted virtue; Our Subjects ever united in loyalty and filial piety have from generation to generation illustrated the beauty thereof. This is the glory of the fundamental character of Our Empire, and herein also lies the source of Our education. Ye, Our subjects, be filial to your parents, affectionate to your brothers and sisters; as husbands and wives be harmonious, as friends true; bear yourselves in modesty and moderation; extend your benevolence to all; pursue learning and cultivate arts, and thereby develop intellectual faculties and perfect moral powers; furthermore advance public good and promote common interests; always respect the Constitution and observe the laws; should emergency arise, offer yourselves courageously to the State; and thus guard and maintain the prosperity of Our Imperial Throne coeval with heaven and earth. So shall ye not only be Our good and faithful subjects, but render illustrious the best traditions of your forefathers.

The Way here set forth is indeed the teaching bequeathed by Our Imperial Ancestors, to be observed alike by Their Descendants and the subjects, infallible for all ages and true in all places. It is Our wish to lay it to heart in all reverence, in common with you. Our subjects, that we may all thus attain to the same virtue.

Source: (Hall 1949: 27–28).

Every school child was required to memorize and recite these short paragraphs, and they provided the foundation for the moral education curriculum. Among the themes emphasized in the morals curriculum were the respective ways in which men and women could contribute to the national purpose. While men were urged to assume their place in the world of work, women were directed to the home. After completion of the second grade, the sexes were placed in different classrooms. From that point on, the curriculum for young girls emphasized domestic arts such as cooking, sewing, and flower arranging. Girls were discouraged from attending school beyond the compulsory level, and the educational opportunities that were available to them were not equal to those for men. One official report stated: "Our female high education may be said to have the object of forming character in women and of imparting knowledge well-calculated to make good wives and wise mothers, able to contribute to the peace and happiness of the family into which they marry" (Fujita 1938: 121). Until after World War II, a Japanese woman could not seek a degree at most of the indigenous universities. The majority who studied beyond the compulsory level ended up as temporary teachers in primary schools.

National integration   Until the Meiji Restoration, political power in Japan had been fragmented into nearly three hundred distinct units. The loyalties of warriors and common people had been to their local lords rather than to the national government. One of the greatest challenges faced by the young Meiji government was to alter this pattern of local allegiances and shift the focus of Affection upwards to fixate on the Imperial State. The new curriculum of spiritual training, richly infused with themes of loyalty to the emperor and allegiance to the national purpose, was a principal means towards this goal of national integration. To ensure that local areas received the message, the young government quickly moved to a system whereby the central government exercised extensive control over local schools—texts were authorized by the central government, school principals were appointed by government, expenses in the compulsory schools were supported by central government subsidies, and central government inspectors made annual visits to each local school. In these ways the government encourage local schools to adhere to national policy.

Prior to the formation of this policy of state dominance, however, many private groups established modern schools, including several reputable institutions supported by foreign Christian missions. To avoid antagonizing the Western nations, the Meiji government allowed these mission schools to carry on, but after the turn of the century the government took steps to reduce the attractiveness of private schools (Burnstein 1967). Among these actions were provisions making it difficult for private school graduates to sit for the exams at higher-level government schools and universities. Because graduation from a government school or university was a requisite for many civil service jobs, these actions restricted the career prospects of private school students. As with the public schools, the government sent inspectors to private schools. Some private schools were forced to dismiss personnel who were considered objectionable by the government. In these ways, the government sought to realize a uniform educational program that would foster national integration.

Meritocratic selection of an elite   At the top of the old system was the Imperial University (after 1897, Tokyo Imperial University), the function of which was to select the national elite and provide them with the broad education appropriate to elite roles. In contrast with the compulsory primary school, virtually no restrictions were placed on the manner in which the members of the Imperial University conducted their educational or research activities. The assumption was that those who gained admittance to this institution would already have developed such a strong commitment to national goals that further indoctrination would be unnecessary. Admission to this elite institution was to be based solely on a competitive entrance examination that anyone with the appropriate level of educational achievement could take. Through the nineteenth century, the Imperial University accepted fewer than one person out of every thousand in a given age-group who attended primary school. Even as late as the 1930s, when several additional Imperial Universities were established, the ratio of primary school entrants to places at the Imperial Universities for new students remained over a hundred to one; the government restricted the scale of the most prestigious higher educational institutions so that their degrees would confer honor and advantageous career prospects.

Technically competent labor force   Between the primary schools and the Imperial Universities, Mori Arinori had established a framework for the development of a diverse multitrack post-compulsory educational system wherein Skills and Enlightenment were to be fostered. The most prestigious track led through a middle school and higher school into an Imperial University. Other tracks pointed the way to various vocational schools, normal schools, and technical and semiprofessional schools. Once an individual began on one track, he could not normally transfer onto a different track; for example, an individual who started in a secondary vocational school could not upon completion of its program compete for admission to a college, but would first have to go back to complete the middle school course.

Mori and others of the Meiji government highly valued the potential contribution of the various schools comprising this intermediate sector. They appreciated the need that Japan would have for competent, trained specialists and skilled workers if the nation intended to succeed in its industrialization effort. At the same time, Mori was concerned that the students who attended the postcompulsory schools should continue to receive spiritual education. During his tenure as Minister of Education, he devoted particular attention to the curriculum of the normal schools where primary school teachers were trained. Special morals texts were designed for these schools, as was a Spartan schedule that included early morning calisthenics conducted by military officers. Mori believed their exemplary presence would help in cultivating the loyal and disciplined character appropriate for teachers. Insofar as the state maintained a monopoly of the teacher training schools, these provisions were certain to reinforce the official policy of providing systematic spiritual training to primary school students. Similar provisions for spiritual training were built into the curricula of the other intermediate schools.

Strains in the Old System

The educational policies promoting national integration, spiritual training, development of a core of competent technicians, and the meritocratic selection of a national elite were established by the central government to serve the interests of the state and those social groups closest to the state. These policies were designed to bend the people into conformity with the program established at the center. As Mori Armari often asserted, "Education is not for the sake of the student but for the sake of the state." The central elites believed that the ordinary Japanese subject was backward and needed to be guided into the modern world.

The central government retained its commitment to these basic policies through World War II. Yet vast internal social changes in this period modified policy specifics. For example, with industrialization, the demand for technically trained manpower increased. Events following World War I encouraged a more militaristic national tone, and this led to an intensification of spiritual training. Most historical accounts imply that the policies designed by the government to cope with these social changes were successful. This was not always the case.

Primary school enrollments   While the central government declared as early as 1872 that it intended to achieve universal attendance in primary schools, this goal was not realized until about 1910, nearly forty years later (Mombusho 1972: 192 ff.). The government initially required attendance and compelled parents to underwrite the educational costs. Upon realizing that these policies actually caused a decline in enrollment, the government ordered local governments to collect revenues to support compulsory education; and at the same time, it allowed those localities facing fiscal problems to forgo an educational program. Only as the central government began, from the late 1880s, to subsidize compulsory education was there significant progress toward the realization of universal enrollment. The growing popular recognition that education offered career alternatives also contributed to the increase in attendance.

Spiritual training   Although the central government was concerned from the beginning with introducing moral education into the curriculum, it took time to develop acceptable texts. The views of diverse traditions, including religious groups and the Meiji oligarchs, clashed substantially, leading, to long and divisive debate. It was not until 1891, with the proclamation of the Imperial Rescript, that some agreement was achieved. The early curriculum essentially emphasized the values of a nineteenth-century liberal society committed to national development and the preservation of family values. Over time, as the compilers of the texts became increasingly zealous in their identification with the national purpose, increasingly biased and nationalistic themes were introduced. A favorite example of this trend concerns the treatment of Socrates. In the earlier morals texts, Socrates was merely described as a wise man in ancient Greece who lived an ascetic life of the mind. However, by the 1930s, Socrates became a Greek soldier who "went to war three times to fight bravely for his country" (Hall 1949: 105).

Despite these intensified efforts to use education in channeling the moral inclinations of the populace, many young people failed to conform with the official morality. Especially from 1917 to the mid-1930s, there were frequent student protests, labor revolts, and other expressions of ideological deviance. The central government responded in a manner that would shock contemporary defenders of civil rights; teachers at all levels in the education system were relieved of their positions, and many intellectuals were imprisoned and subjected to brainwashing treatments. Christian schools were forbidden to teach doctrines that the state considered incompatible with its official ideology, and some Christians were persecuted. Communists, in particular, were subjected to intense harassment. It was only as Japan moved into full-scale war against the Allied Powers that the incidence of deviance and rebellion subsided.

The Impact of Old-System Values Education

The primary stress of early Meiji education was on Skill and Enlightenment to enable the new nation to build a dynamic modern economy. But the first decade of the new education brought concern about the moral fiber and loyalty of the common people, so from the early 1880s a new emphasis was placed on values education, with a special stress on Rectitude and Respect. Following World War I and the growing popular interest in Marxist concepts of class struggle, national leaders increased the emphasis on loyalty to the state (Lasswell's Affection value). Unfortunately, in Japan patriotism became superpatriotism and Japan became embroiled in a great and ultimately unwinnable war. The next section reviews Japan's efforts to define and realize a new set of values.

VALUES EDUCATION IN POSTWAR JAPAN

Background for the Occupation Reforms

Japanese society made impressive strides toward realizing the goals designated by the Meiji rebels. By the mid-1930s, national institutions were effectively unified under a strong central regime. The economy was diversified, the military was strong, and the people were loyal. Basic education had supported each of these developments. If Japan had achieved its aims in World War II, the central government might have retained the old system in essentially unaltered form.

By September of 1945, however, Japan had no choice but to declare unconditional surrender. In anticipation of Japan's fall, on July 26, 1945, the Allied Powers issued the Potsdam Declaration, which declared their intent to remove "all obstacles to the survival and strengthening of democratic tendencies among the Japanese people. Freedom of speech, religion, and of thought, as well as respect for the fundamental rights shall be established" (Anderson 1975: 61).

Although Japan had surrendered to the Allied forces as a whole, the actual task of implementing the spirit of the Potsdam Declaration was assumed by a U.S. Occupation government headed by Gen. Douglas MacArthur. The Occupation was instructed to work through the existing

Japanese government and emperor but not to support them. In the early months, the Occupation issued several directives to the Japanese government that were intended to remove all militaristic and ultranationalistic influences. Courses in moral education, geography, and Japanese history that were considered supportive of the wartime ideology were temporarily suspended. A purge of educational officials and teachers who had played key roles in promoting the wartime ideology was begun. Over 120,000 teachers, or a quarter of those in the profession, were either purged or removed themselves to avoid the purge. Similar steps were taken to remove officials and responsible individuals in all sectors of life from business to the arts. The removal of these nationalistic elements from former positions of prominence and the appointment of "liberals" in their stead considerably facilitated the Occupation's reform program.

One of the first goals of the Occupation was to establish the foundation for a more democratic mode of government. A special committee of the Diet was charged with the task of drafting a new constitution, and when it faltered, the Occupation submitted its own proposal. Ultimately, a version identical in most respects to that proposed by the Occupation was ratified in November of 1946 by the Diet. The preamble clearly reflects its American authorship:

> We, the Japanese people, acting through our duly elected representatives in the National Diet, determined that we shall secure for ourselves and our posterity the fruits of peaceful cooperation with all nations and the blessings of liberty throughout this land, and resolved that never again shall we be visited with the horrors of war through the action of government, do proclaim that sovereign power resides with the people and do firmly establish this Constitution. Government is a sacred trust of the people, the authority for which is derived from the people, the powers of which are exercised by the representatives of the people, and the benefits of which are enjoyed by the people. This is a universal principal of mankind upon which this Constitution is founded (Beckmann 1962: 673).

In contrast with the Meiji constitution, several articles of the new "Peace Constitution" dealt with educational matters. Article 20 declared, "The State and its organs shall refrain from religious education." Article 23 stated, "Academic freedom is guaranteed." And Article 26 stated, "All people shall have the right to receive an equal education correspondent to their ability."

Whereas the old system had been created through a series of imperial decrees and administrative orders, the new educational system was based in the constitution and in laws that had been debated and legislated by the national Diet. The change to a legislative basis in combination with the emergence of progressive political parties that developed an interest in educational policy resulted in a lively postwar educational dialogue.

A New Educational Philosophy

To aid in the development of proposals for educational reforms, the Occupation invited 27 distinguished U.S. educators to Japan in March 1947. This team, known as the U.S. Education Mission to Japan, produced a report that provides the clearest statement of the philosophy underlying the subsequent reform. The opening statement echoed the Occupation's goal of helping Japan to develop a new education appropriate to a liberal democratic society. It urged the development of an educational philosophy that recognized "the worth and dignity of the individual" and that would "prepare the individual to become a responsible and cooperating member of society." Evident in these statements is a determination to shift popular Affection away from the imperial state and towards each citizen and his/her community. The mission enumerated several weaknesses of the old system.

The Japanese system of education in its organization and curricular provisions would have been due for reform in accordance with modern theories of education even if there had not been injected into it ultra-nationalism and militarism. The system was based on a nineteenth-century pattern which was highly centralized, providing one type of education for the masses and another for the privileged few. It held that at each level of instruction there is a fixed quantum of knowledge to be absorbed, and tended to disregard differences in the ability and interests of pupils. Through prescription, textbooks, examinations and inspection, the system lessened the opportunities of teachers to exercise professional freedom. The measure of efficiency was the degree to which standardization and uniformity were secured (U.S. Education Mission to Japan 1946: 4).

To translate the mission's recommendation into concrete reform proposals, an Educational Reform Council was established with official status equivalent to the Ministry of Education. As its first task, the council considered the development of a statement of the philosophy of the new system that might replace the old system's Imperial Rescript. The council ultimately decided that the specifics of the new education should be worked out by the local communities, school boards, and schools, so as to reflect more closely the desires of the people, and that it would be inappropriate to draft such statements from above. Nevertheless, in the Fundamental Law of Education, one of the first laws drafted by the council, the new aim of education is stated:

> Education shall aim at the full development of personality, striving for the rearing of the people, sound in mind and body, who shall love truth and justice, esteem individual value, respect labour, and have a deep sense of responsibility, and be imbued with an independent spirit, as builders of a peaceful state and society (Anderson 1975: 349).

Post-Occupation Changes in Japanese Education

Over the postwar period, Japanese education has undergone dramatic expansion in response to the rapid growth of the economy and private demand. After the U.S. Occupation, the national government began to introduce reforms designed both to increase administrative efficiency and strengthen central control. Among the most important were a substantial reduction of the role of local governments and school boards (1956), a strengthening of the Ministry of Education in curriculum development and textbook review (1957), and the formal revival of moral education in the curriculum (1958). Each of these reforms was firmly opposed by the leftist political parties, and the most controversial aspects were somewhat neutralized.

The curriculum has been revised on three occasions. The most recent changes followed upon a major review of Japanese education requested in 1984 by Prime Minister Nakasone. This review was authorized in view of pressing changes including the maturation of society, the rapid progress of science and technology, and new developments in communications and transport (Chiba 1991). It confirmed the principles of the Fundamental Law of Education of 1947, and elaborated three elements of a vision for the twenty-first century: to form a broad mind, healthy body, and rich creativity; to foster a spirit of freedom, self-discipline, and public welfare; and to realize Japanese as members of the World Community. These principles have given rise to "internationalization" as the principal new dimension of moral education in Japan. In other areas of the curriculum, there has been an effort to reduce academic pressure while encouraging greater diversity and creativity.

Impact of the Japanese Program

Japan's leaders invested in basic education because they believed it provided the foundation for a harmonious and productive society. More recently, they also have come to value basic education's potential for nurturing "rich personalities" that are individualistic and creative. The pattern of evidence reviewed below suggests the wisdom of Japanese pedagogy. Of course, it may be that some of the outcomes noted here are in part due to other influences.

Respect   Possibly the most outstanding aspect of Japanese moral education is the emphasis it places on respect for others. Young people are encouraged to listen to the opinions of others and to avoid interrupting others when they speak. Young children are also taught to respect the dignity of labor, whether manual or mental, and whether by young people or old. These lessons seem to have some impact; for example, in a comparative study of occupational prestige, Japanese samples are likely to make weaker discriminations between high- and low-prestige occupations (Ishida 1992). Concerning intergenerational respect, public opinion polls show that there are wide intergenerational gaps in Japan; nevertheless, younger Japanese still show respect for their elders. And younger Japanese are much more willing to include older Japanese in their households than are the younger generations of Western societies. While Japan must rank rather high in instilling respect for others, a recent worrisome trend is the increasing incidence of bullying among young people.

Enlightenment and skills   In recent years, Japanese education has received high marks for its success in teaching the cognitive curriculum. In comparative tests, Japanese young people score at or near the top. For example, in the second international math test Japanese seventh graders were first among 19 nations and twelfth graders were second (IEA 1988). Japanese young people were equally distinguished in the second international science test (IEA 1992).

The great majority of Japanese young people attend the general course of secondary schools and nearly half go on for tertiary education. Thus only a minority of Japanese young people receive a formal school education that concentrates on specialized skills. Whether or not Japanese young people receive skill-training while in school, they inevitably encounter such training in the workplace. Comparative studies suggest that Japanese young people are quick to master these skills, because at school they have been trained in how to learn. Their academic experience provides them both with a solid foundation of basic education and a determination to do their best when confronted with a challenge. Various observers, impressed with the learning of the Japanese worker, have stated that Japan has the best rank-and-file labor force in the world (Dore and Sako 1989).

Well-being   One of the keys to well-being is sound knowledge of the conditions that foster good physical and mental health. The Japanese curriculum includes systematic instruction on physical health from the early grades as well as periodic school-based examination of eyesight, dental hygiene, and other conditions. The curriculum stresses such habits as tooth-brushing, boiling water, and frequent exercise. These habits are supported by the extensive availability of neighborhood clinics and an excellent system of national health insurance. By most indicators, Japanese enjoy good health. For example, since the mid-1970s the Japanese population has led the world in average life expectancy for both men and women (World Bank 1995).

The rapid pace of change in Japan and the highly demanding work ethic generate a high level of stress. Mental well-being is fostered in Japan by an emphasis on harmony in group relations and an encouragement of contemplation and self-reflection. While Japan is reputed to have a high suicide rate, in fact the rate is no higher than the world average.

Affection   Affection implies commitment to others, whether at the family, local, or national level. A major thrust of Meiji education was to instill the ethic of loyalty to the emperor and his servant, the national state. Sharp criticism of this emphasis following World War II, led to a new stress on the importance of the individual, friends, and family. As one indication of the change, a recent cross-national study of the attitudes of youth show that only 40 percent of Japanese young people report feeling a strong sense of emotion to their national flag, compared with over 90 percent of Koreans. On the other hand, Japanese young people report a high level of commitment to their friends, to the point of placing even greater weight on the views of friends than of teachers or parents (Prime Minister's Office, 1992).

Rectitude   Japan's legal system follows on the French model in terms of many of the major legal codes as well as in the system of training and appointing judges and certifying lawyers. The Japanese people are even more law-abiding than their French counterparts. Comparative studies of incidents such as rape, homicide, burglary, and mugging generally point to a low incidence of deviance in Japan.

THE "DIFFUSION" OF THE JAPANESE MODEL

In parallel with Japan's early modern efforts, Korean, Chinese, and Thai political leaders initiated more or less independent efforts of educational modernization. The imperialistic policies of Japan and various Western nations terminated most of these autonomous efforts, however, leaving Japan and Thailand as the only independent Asian innovators.

Whereas Thailand did not pursue a policy of regional influence, Japan aggressively occupied various Asian nations and through its colonial policies stamped the imprint of its human resource model (Tsurumi 1977; Hong 1992). Japan's influence was strongest in the Korean and Taiwanese systems, but it also affected other nations through the visitations of students (as in the case of China) and through more limited periods of occupation (as in the case of Indonesia, Vietnam, the Philippines, and China). In this section, we review the diffusion of the Japanese model, first through colonial policy and in more recent years through diplomacy and technical cooperation.

Japanese Colonialism

Japan's first colony was Taiwan, acquired as part of the settlement of Japan's successful war with China of 1894–95. Tsurumi, who has carried out the most comprehensive study of this experience, indicates that Japan went about establishing an educational system in Taiwan along essentially the same lines as the system it had already established in Japan over 25 years. Education was a servant of the state. Its largest task, that of universal elementary schooling, was twofold. It was to unite the entire population psychologically and instill loyalty to the state in each of its members, and at the same time to provide them with the discipline, skills, and attitudes Japan's version of modernization required of its people (Tsurumi 1977: 212).[3]

What the Japanese colonialists did not reckon with was the difficulty of inducing the Taiwanese people to undergo education in an alien language. After some thought about relying on the local language for education, such a step was soon abandoned. Thus progress in Taiwan was slow and far more costly than the Japanese had anticipated. As Japanese policy proceeded and success in education proved to lead to better employment, pressure began to mount for expanded opportunities at the secondary and tertiary level. For example, Japan decided to establish institutions for the training teachers, agricultural scientists, and doctors. Tsurumi stresses the human cost to the Taiwanese people of undergoing education in a foreign language that featured a foreign culture. But she also notes some positive benefits, such as the equal inclusion of women in basic education, compared with their exclusion in nearby China. By virtue of Japan's involvement, Taiwan was relatively well educated by the end of the Japanese occupation. The human resources developed during the occupation have served Taiwan well in its drive for industrialization and economic development over the past four decades.

Korea was Japan's second major colony. The Japanese colonial authorities encountered much stiffer resistance to their rule there and thus had to commit a much more substantial military presence. Hong (1992) reports on the protests of the Korean people and the often harsh reactions of the Japanese colonial authorities; but he agrees with Tsurumi that Japanese educational policy in Korea was essentially a mirror of its own educational policy at home. He notes how the colonial authorities extended elementary education to six years in Korea, following the precedent of Japan and that reforms in Korea of moral and education and of tertiary education (both in 1922) followed soon after similar reforms in Japan.

The Korean public was and continues to be resentful of the Japanese occupation and of the Japanese restructuring of various Korean institutions, including education. Even five decades after Japan's departure, the imprint is unmistakable. The Korean educational structure with a six-year primary school, a three-year middle school, and a three-year high school resembles the Japanese model. So do the courses taught in these schools as well as many of the daily rituals.

Japanese colonialism left a profound imprint on the educational systems of Taiwan and Korea. Japan occupied other Asian nations for a briefer period, and in most instances took preliminary steps to implement the same colonial policies as it had carried out in Taiwan and Korea, though Japan lacked the staff to go very far in advancing them. The memories do linger in the older generations, in places as far-flung as Burma and Indonesia.

Diplomacy and Aid

Following World War II, Japan had to relinquish its colonies. Moreover, the Japanese economy and its impact on Asia were diminished. But from the mid-1950s the Japanese economy began to gain strength through a new strategy of rapid growth fueled by the export of high-quality industrial goods to the West and Asia. As its economy progressed, Japan came to involve nearby Asian economies in this strategy, targeting them for exports as well as selectively sharing technology. Taiwan and Korea were early partners in the Japanese recovery. Gradually, Japan expanded its economic ties to other Asian nations—Thailand was an early favorite, with Singapore, Hong Kong, Malaysia, Indonesia, and the Philippines also receiving much attention.

With some of these countries, Japan also established ties of Overseas Development Assistance (ODA) to carry out its obligation to provide reparations for the damages inflicted in World War II. As its economy progressed, Japan began to expand its ODA activities in line with the expectations for countries attaining the status of advanced industrialism. ODA was channeled through bilateral programs and through the Asian Development Bank, over which Japan exerted considerable influence. Japan also began to influence other multilateral agencies such as the World Bank and those of the United Nations.

While it would be a gross overstatement to argue that the major objective of these postwar transactions was to diffuse a Japanese approach to development, it nevertheless can be argued that a by-product of many of these transactions has been to increase the influence of Japanese ideas of development and the role of education (Yamashita 1991; Stewart and Nihei 1992). Taiwan and Korea continue to operate educational systems similar to those established in the colonial period. Other Asian nations have been sufficiently impressed with the Japanese model to establish policies of "Learning from Japan" (Singapore) and of "Looking East" (Malaysia).

In sum, Japanese relations with Asia have had two distinctive patterns, one based on colonial ties and a second based on postwar economic ties. Figure 7-1 (page 154) characterizes the two groups of Eastern Asian nations as two wings of an Eastern Asian development flock led by Japan (Hong Kong, often considered an Asian Tiger, is not included in this grouping, as at the policy level the leadership has expressed little interest in the Japanese model. China also is not included as it, until recently, has relied on a controlled economy; further China has consciously restrained the development of human resources).[4] In the analysis that follows, several indicators will be cited to illustrate how the nations in the Japanese flock differ in important respects from other Asian nations (e.g., the Socialist and Communist republics of East and and Southeast Asia as well as the South Asian nations, all of which have relatively weak ties to Japan) as well as other developing countries and the major industrial nations of the West. The relevant data are included in the Appendix to this chapter. Grouping Asian nations in this way is not intended to suggest any formal agreement; rather the grouping is analytical, based on differences in levels of mutual trade, investment, and political affinity.

Figure 7-1. The Eastern Asian Development Flock

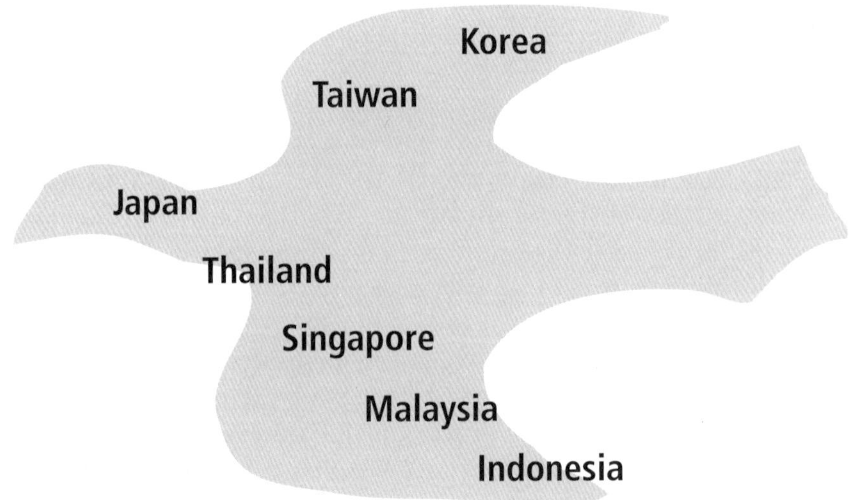

Just as Japan has consciously or unconsciously exported its educational ideals to other parts of Asia, it too has also been the recipient of various Asian cultural exports. Perhaps of greatest consequence has been the Asian demand that Japanese textbooks be amended to show greater and more accurate recognition of Japan's ongoing relationship with Asian countries (current hot issues include Japanese wartime atrocities and the forced recruitment of "comfort women"). Asian student flows to Japan accompanied by demands that Japanese universities and communities internationalize their services are another channel for Asian influence on Japan (Hook and Weiner 1992).

The expanding postwar interactions among the various Asian nations, with Japan as a key player, have resulted in a growing Asian consensus on the efficacy of many of the features of the development model pioneered by Japan, including those elements intended for developing human resources and values.

This is not to deny the persistence of major intraregional variations in the practice of human resource development. China's socialist approach (Carnoy and Samoff 1990) and Malaysia's multiracial approach (Mukherjee 1988) are two distinctive deviants from the main pattern. Also, there are important points of variation closer to the Asian mainstream; for example, Korea and Taiwan place greater stress on the public sector than does Japan, and the Korean state places more emphasis on national unity than do most of the other Eastern Asian countries. These differences form the basis for important human resource competition within the region.

Core Features of the Eastern Asian Approach

The first outlines of the Eastern Asian approach emerged in the late nineteenth century as Japan and other Eastern Asian nations responded to the Western challenge. But only Japan and Thailand were able to escape the shackles of Western imperialism and develop distinctive approaches (Altbach and Selvaratnam 1989). Since Japan has enjoyed greater developmental success over time, the Japanese approach has been the most influential. Thus it helps to focus first on Japan when seeking to identify the core features of the Eastern Asian prototype; but, as will be indicated below, other East Asian nations have developed important variations on the Japanese model that deserve note. The core features of the Japanese/ East Asian approach insofar as they relate to educational policy are as follows:

The state is strong but lean. In view of potential external threats, East Asian states have usually mobilized substantial resources for national defense, somewhat above the average level of other nations. For example, Taiwan and Korea devote about 10 percent of GDP for defense. But in most other areas, the government's expenses are modest compared both to Western industrial societies and the average for developing societies; for example, Asian expenditures in the field of welfare are negligible, and in public health the expenditures are comparatively low. Indeed, East Asian leaders are often explicit in their disdain for the Western welfare state, arguing that the safety net is too generous and discourages hard work. While expenditures in these areas are low, the state nevertheless takes a directive role through its mobilization of community organizations and its emphasis on family and community responsibility. Apart from defense, the two policy areas where the East Asian state allocates relatively large sums are industrial policy and human resources. The limited commitments of the East Asian state result in government budgets that absorb smaller proportions of GNP than are typical of Western industrial societies or of many developing societies (Tan and Mingat 1992). As noted in Appendix Table A, government expenses absorb 10 percent of Japan's GDP, an average of 20 percent of Taiwan and Korea's, and 22 percent of the other Asian NICs, compared to an average of 44 percent for the countries of Western Europe and 30 percent for other developing countries.

Human resources are critical for national development.   Key leaders in Japan, and later those in other Asian nations who perceived the need to respond to the Western challenge, concluded that a major cultural and human transformation would be necessary (Smith 1955; Hall 1973). Surveying the factors behind Western political and economic pre-eminence, Asian leaders recognized the scarcity of their resources. Whereas the leading Western nations were blessed with generous natural resources, East Asian leaders concluded that people were their major resource. Thus, as indicated in Appendix Table A, Japan and the countries closest to it spend relatively large proportions of the lean national budget on education, and this leads to relatively high enrollment rates in primary and secondary education.

In East Asia, stress has been placed not only on the development of human resources but also on their utilization; the Asian states have placed educational and cultural policy at the center of plans for national development. In the public sector, educational streams were tightly linked to projected manpower requirements. Governments assumed a coordinating role in the transition from education to work, and in several instances routinely carried out annual surveys to evaluate the success of schools in placing their graduates in workplaces. This legacy of planned utilization of scarce human resources endures.

The state is responsible for the educational framework.   Given the concern for maximizing the impact of scarce human resources, the state assumed a central role in their development (Black et al. 1975). Central authorities sought to lay out educational goals and a curriculum as well as to provide textbooks and staff (Ministry of Education 1980). With these contributions, the Asian state was satisfied it could shape the educational process: given a slim budget, the state minimized its involvement in the everyday management of schools. Principals and staff were trusted to do their jobs; hence, within the centrally prescribed framework, there remained much school-level autonomy in implementation.

Seeking knowledge throughout the world   Entering late and reluctantly into the modern era, Asia recognized a need to catch up to the leading Western nations (Levy 1972). Seeking knowledge particularly from the West became a core element in the Asian catch-up strategy (Braisted 1976; Teng and Fairbank 1954). Western knowledge, particularly in the areas of science, medicine, and technology was seen as the essential means for developing national strength and competitiveness. The schools were expected to provide a solid foundation in these areas by featuring mathematics and science as required subjects from the first grades of the primary school. Colleges and universities were also expected to stress these fields. The earliest human resource institutions were established to import and transmit scientific and technical knowledge rather than to create it (Bartholomew 1989); applied faculties such as agriculture, engineering, and medicine were far more prominent than faculties in the basic sciences. This legacy endures.

Western science/Eastern values   While Western knowledge was considered valuable, Asian leaders had reservations about the broader societal framework of the West. They believed that Asia's familistic and political values provided a better foundation for the good society (Hall 1973). Thus, they sought through schooling and other means to foster continuity in the values realm. Schools included moral education as a core component of their curriculum, and educators were expected to set proper examples to lead young people to respect Asia's enduring traditions.

In contrast with the off-and-on Western interest in multicultural-ism, Asian states identified a common core of values which they sought to convey in the national language to all young people; bilingualism was typically eschewed. The common normative core mainly focused on behavior stressing honesty, hard work, respect for parents and authority, and cleanliness (Befu 1993; NIER 1981). Religious commitments were left up to the individual, so long as they did not conflict with state priorities:

thus the Japanese state made no distinction between Christians and Confucianists and the Indonesian Pansacila emphasized respect for God, without placing priority on any particular religion.

Educational leaders in Asia have frequently convened conferences to review their programs in values education, and there has been a tendency toward a convergence in the values curriculum of the different nations. For example, whereas moral education was not stressed in Singapore 15 years ago, it now is featured at both the primary and secondary level. In both Indonesia and Malaysia, which have large Islamic populations, there has been a tendency to infuse a common morals curriculum into the distinctive programs of religious education for the various ethnic religious groups.

While a process of convergence can be observed, the challenges confronting each Asian nations differs. The two Koreas are locked in a military stalemate and there is considerable tension between China and Taiwan; several of the nations of Southeast Asia have only recently achieved internal peace after years of secessionist rebellion. To the extent a nation is threatened, whether by internal or external forces, it is likely to place a higher priority on values of loyalty and political and social conformity. Japan is perhaps the most relaxed Asian nation in this regard, while the two Koreas and China are perhaps the most cautious. Appendix Table B attempts to summarize the stress in the moral curricula of several Eastern Asian nations as of the early 1990s.

Public primary schooling provides the foundation.   Reflecting the Asian conviction that excellence derives from a command of basics, Asian educators placed special emphasis on the development of effective primary schools (Passin 1965). Much care was devoted to the curriculum and teaching methods at this level, and adequate funding was provided to insure a solid basic education for all. Asian nations have tended to realize universal enrollment faster than nations in most other parts of the world (Williamson 1993: 149). As indicated in Appendix Table A, the average gross enrollment ratio of 1970 for those nations associated with Japan was close to 100 percent, well ahead of the average for South Asia (54 percent) or for other developing nations. The stress on primary education meant that advanced educational levels were sometimes given lower priority, at least in the public sector (James and Benjamin 1988). But through a combination of public and private effort, Asian enrollment ratios at the secondary level were comparatively high as early as 1970.

The public school teaches; the pupil has to learn.   Always conscious of scarce resources, Asian educators placed limits on the school's responsibilities. The school's job was to present the curriculum in as effective a manner as possible for the average pupil (Cummings 1980). It was up to the pupil and the parents to take advantage of the school's presentation. The school was not required to make special efforts to accommodate slow students or to stimulate the gifted. The responsibility for learning rested on the pupil. To insure this common understanding, the school worked closely with local leaders and parents so as to gain their cooperation. Thus, considerable pressure was exerted on young people to exert their best efforts for learning. When young people encountered difficulties, parents sought through extra tutoring to help them master the required material (Stevenson and Stigler 1992).

Public secondary and tertiary education focus on national priorities. The Asian state's concern was to catch up and then move ahead. Public resources were allocated in accordance with that objective. Thus in education beyond the foundation level, the public sector had the limited objective of developing critical manpower and training elites (Cummings 1980; Fong 1982). The public sector set up a limited number of educational opportunities in critical areas and heavily subsidized them to keep tuition low and attract good students; in some fields such as engineering, the state actually funded a surplus of opportunities in anticipation of future expansion in the related labor markets. Despite an overall policy of restraint, public institutions oversupplied in certain specialties.

"Society" is welcome to fill the gaps.   The Asian state sought to limit its provision in schooling (and other social services), but it recognized that the public might demand more. Rather than contain this popular demand, the state assumed a permissive policy, only intervening when the private response began to conflict with public objectives. Thus a vigorous private sector often emerged to complement the public sector (Geiger 1987).

One area of private response was at the preschool level. Also, because of the limited public provision of public-sector opportunities relative to the number of qualified students, entrepreneurs established competing private secondary and tertiary institutions. In several Asian societies (Japan, Taiwan, Korea, Indonesia, the Philippines) the private sector provides over 75 percent of all places at the tertiary level. Private schools emerged to accommodate the excess demand, which was sometimes very sizable (James and Benjamin 1988).

A distinctive East Asian creation is the private *juku* or supplementary courses to help pupils keep up with the curriculum provided in basic education (Kitamura 1986; Russell 1997). These schools, which first flourished in Japan, are now prevalent in most East Asian societies. Private schools also have emerged to help young people prepare for post-compulsory level entrance exams.

Yet another area of private initiative was in the utilization of human resources for research and development. While the public sector trained human resources to a high level and supported research in certain critical areas such as health and munitions, it left commercially relevant research and development to the private sector. As the Asian corporate sector expanded, it became increasingly involved in the self-sponsorship of major research efforts. Thus, in contrast with Western nations where national R&D budgets tend to be heavily subsidized by the state, in Asia typically three-quarters or more of all R&D activities are supported by the private sector. (Johnson 1993; Ushiogi 1993).

Education and research should be coordinated.   While the public sector limited its provision, it retained comprehensive responsibility. Thus private schools were required to observe public regulations. And periodically public officials intervened in the private sector to curb excesses, such as unreasonable prices or poor quality. A particular challenge for the public sector was the education provided by nonschool media such as journals, the cinema, and lately the TV industry. In these areas as well, the state was likely to intervene so as to achieve overall consistency in the educational experience.

Similarly, while state funding of research and development was comparatively modest, the state made important contributions to the coordination of research. Most notable was state sponsorship of overseas research trips and of national facilities for the import and translation of foreign research journals. In more recent years, the Asian state has come to play a more prominent role in targeting technologies for development by the private sector (Vogel 1991).

SOME IMPLICATIONS OF THE EAST ASIAN APPROACH

The East Asian approach provides sharp contrasts with the approaches to education that have evolved in leading Western industrial nations (Cummings 1992). For example, the East Asian educational ideal places greater stress on cooperation and cohesion relative to the Western stress on individualism. East Asian pedagogy assumes that the key to learning is individual effort rather than inherent genetic endowment or talent. And East Asian systems place more emphasis on insuring that every child receives a standard education than on enabling each child to obtain an education suited to his or her needs; similarly, teachers are expected to teach the common curriculum rather than to introduce innovations that express their unique strengths. East Asian educational systems tend to place their greatest stress on basic education, rather than on elite public schools or great universities, though in the schools that provide basic education, some educational conditions, such as the numbers of students in a classroom, do not conform with the standards characteristic of Western systems.

In these various ways, the East Asian approach constitutes an alternative to Western approaches, and a denial of the proposition that education around the world is becoming more homogeneous. The distinctiveness of the East Asian approach has provoked a variety of assessments. Many are critical, focusing on lack of quality and on "human costs." In contrast are assessments that take the East Asian approach on its own terms, evaluate its effectiveness in promoting cultural and political autonomy in the face of the Western challenge, and consider its comparative success in promoting national development. Since the East Asian approach has proved to have impressive development effects, this line of assessment inevitably leads to a consideration of their global implications.

Social Stability

A major concern of the East Asian approach is to instill accepted social values. Whereas Western educators lean towards a cognitive reasoning approach to values education (Kohlberg 1981), Asian educators favor a directive approach involving explicit teaching and consistent reinforcement (Cummings et al. 1988). The school is viewed as the primary vehicle for conveying the values curriculum, and it is partly for this reason that the school calendar is long and the atmosphere is constrained. But "constrained" is not the same as joyless or inhuman. Observation studies indicate that Asian children enjoy their schooling (Tobin 1989), and comparative statistics suggest that their school days are at least as humane as those experienced by children in other industrial societies. East Asian schools have low absenteeism; high completion rates (see Appendix Table A); abundant evidence of healthy youth; a comparatively low incidence of neurosis-suicide, as well as a low incidence of other forms of deviance (drugs, delinquency, juvenile pregnancy). The social savings from these healthy and stable child and adolescent years are substantial (UNICEF 1992; UNESCO 1992).

The Human Resource Edge

A second set of implications is what might be called the Eastern Asian Human Resource Edge. A relatively uncontroversial theme is that these educational systems are slanted towards the provision of math and science education and that they produce relatively large numbers of upper secondary and university graduates in technical and scientific fields. For example, Japan, with only half the population, trains as many engineers as the U.S. (Johnson 1993; U.S. Department of Education 1987). Despite the comparatively large number of Asian students specializing in these fields, nearly all obtain employment on graduation. Many of the best end up as researchers in Asia's corporate laboratories and universities. Some of the less qualified of these graduates take up positions in the lower levels of the modern manufacturing sector. But what about the rest? All find employment, but many are by standard human resource measurements "underemployed"; that is, they work in positions that do not require their professional skills such as in sales jobs or as stockbrokers and analysts (Kodama and Chiaki 1991; Muta 1990). But perhaps the underemployed provide unique perspectives to their coworkers that enhance the productivity of these nontechnological units (Cole 1989; Lynn et al. 1993).

Not an insignificant number of East Asia's underemployed graduates decide to leave the Asian labor market and seek opportunities in Western labor markets, especially the United States. Indeed one of the least heralded outcomes of Asian education's excess production is the extraordinary extent to which it has supplied scientific and technical workers to Western corporations and universities (Cummings 1984, 1985; Lee 1993).

While East Asia supplies both indigenous and overseas markets with large numbers of scientific and technical workers, it is sometimes asserted that these workers are not particularly gifted, that they are unable to make creative contributions (Miyanaga 1991). But the evidence supporting these assertions comes from earlier years when Asian researchers and laboratories were underfunded. That constraint is rapidly disappearing, and it remains to be seen how impressive will be the productivity of the Asian researcher under more favorable conditions. Recent indications (based on numbers of scientific articles, patent submissions, high-tech product sales) are that East Asian scientists may be highly competitive (Bloom 1990; Science and Technology Agency 1991). Their hard-work ethic combined with their openness to cooperate in joint projects may even give them an edge in some creative endeavors.

The Pacific Rim Connection

A third set of implications might be labeled as the Pacific Rim Connection. Over the past three decades, Asian human resources have become extensively developed and diffused throughout the Pacific Rim.

One facet of the rapid expansion of East Asian human resources has been a fostering of a new level of competitiveness as Asian corporations seek to outdo each other in the international marketplace. This competitiveness, often fueled by feelings of chauvinism, as between Korean and Japanese construction firms competing for the same contract, pushes Asian human resources to ever higher levels of productivity.

But an equally interesting and virtually unexplored theme is the extent of cooperation that emerges among Asian scientists, particularly when they are located in foreign settings. For example, a recent study documents that many Asian-born scientists working in American research universities retain relatively fluid scientific ties with colleagues in their countries of origin (Choi 1993). This cooperation across national boundaries may provide an important impetus to the quality of Asian scientific and technical work.

Another feature of the Asian connection is the rapidly expanding level of communication between scholars and scientists within the Eastern Asian region, particularly stimulated by Japan's new commitment to overseas development assistance. Over the past five years, Japan has trebled its intake of students from other Asian countries. Even more impressive has been the fivefold increase in the number of Asian scholars spending short study visits in Japan (Science and Technology Agency 1991).

There still remains the question of the East Asian limit, particularly in the area of research. Will there be an East Asian research edge? Can the East Asian approach move beyond knowledge-seeking to indigenous knowledge creation (Cummings 1994)? This may be a false question—for if Asian corporations can buy the other brains and labs of overseas competitors, why do they have to do the work on their own? Thus an extension of the Pacific Rim Connection analysis would be to look into Asian (and non-Asian) strategies for securing control of offshore knowledge/

value production. In the new era of weaker states, the nationality of knowledge workers has reduced meaning—but there still is interest in who benefits.

Human Rights

From the perspective of this study, the most critical example of a difference in the Asian and Western perspectives is with respect to human rights (Awanohara 1993). The East Asian approach places considerable emphasis on the family group and the community, often urging the individual to subordinate personal interests so as to advance the welfare of these broader collectivities. Even more, the individual identifies his/her well-being with that of the broader collective. The welfare of the broader group, it is proposed, results in a better situation for each of the members. Harmony and the consensual negotiation of differences are emphasized as means to reconcile individual and social rights. As suggested earlier, the East Asian record in terms of such human values as Skills, Enlightenment, Well-Being, and Respect is quite impressive. Several of the East Asian nations are also outstanding in terms of the distribution of Wealth.

In contrast to the East Asian approach, in recent years Western ideologues have urged East Asian states to make greater efforts to conform to universal (or are they Western?) concepts of human rights. The Western critics insist that East Asian nations should foster greater personal freedom and institute more representative forms of democratic government. In Lasswellian terms, perhaps the most critical issue is the distribution of Power. Western criticism of repressive governmental actions such as those in East Timor and at Tiananmen Square has been rebutted by East Asian leaders, who argue that their approach places its first priority on social welfare or development, and only as these conditions are realized does it become meaningful to encourage democracy and Western concepts of human rights. Sometimes the Asian leaders go so far as to point out how much more stable and crime-free their societies are compared with those of the Western nations that place such high priority on human rights. It may be that these differences in the notion of what constitutes a "good" society will lead to sharp conflicts between the East Asian and Western approaches to human rights over the next decades (*Japan Echo* 1993).

REFERENCES

Altbach, Philip, and Viswanathan Selvaratnam. 1989. *From Dependence to Autonomy: The Development of Asian Universities.* Dodrecht: Kluwer Academic Publishers.

Anderson, Ronald S. 1975. *Education in Japan: A Century of Modern Development.* Washington: U.S. Government Printing Office.

Awanohara, Susumu, et al. 1993. "Human Rights: Vienna Showdown," *Far Eastern Economic Review.* June 17:16ff.

Bartholomew, James. 1989. *The Formation of Science in Japan.* New Haven: Yale University Press.

Beckman, George M. 1962. *The Modernization of China and Japan.* New York: Harper and Row.

Befu, Harumi. 1993. *Cultural Nationalism in East Asia.* London: Curzon Press.

Black, Cyril E., et al. 1975. *The Modernization of Japan and Russia.* New York: Free Press.

Bloom, Justin. 1990. *Japan as a Scientific and Technological Superpower.* Washington: U.S. Department of Commerce.

Braisted, William R., trans. 1976. *Meiroku Zasshi: Journal of the Japanese Enlightenment.* Cambridge, MA: Harvard University Press.

Burnstein, Ira J. 1967. *The American Movement to Develop Protestant Colleges for Men in Japan, 1868–1912.* Comparative Education Dissertation Series, No. 11. University of Michigan.

Carnoy, Martin, and Joel Samoff. 1990. *Education and Social Transition in the Third World.* Princeton: Princeton University Press.

Carnoy, Martin. 1992. *The Case for Investing in Basic Education.* New York: UNICEF.

Chiba, Akihori. 1994. "Trends of Thought in Japan's Values Education: Japan's Perspective." In Ministry of Education Malaysia, *Values Education in ASEAN.* Kuala Lumpur: Ministry of Education Malaysia, 123–130.

Choi, Hyaeweol. 1993. "Asian Scholars in the United States: Roles, Careers and Contributions to the International Knowledge System." Ph.D. dissertation. Buffalo: Graduate School of Education, University at Buffalo.

Cole, Robert. 1989. *Strategies for Learning.* Berkeley: University of California Press.

Cummings, William K. 1980. *Education and Equality in Japan.* Princeton, N.J.: Princeton University Press.

———. 1984. "Going Overseas for Higher Education: The Asian Experience." *Comparative Education Review,* May 28:241–257.

———. 1992. "Examining the Educational Production Function: U.K. U.S. and Japanese Models." In *International Perspectives in Educational Productivity,* ed. Herbert Walberg and David W. Chapman, 4–21. Greenwich, CT: JAI Press.

Cummings, William K. (with Wing-Cheung So). 1985. "The Preference of Asian Overseas Students for the United States: An Examination of the Context." *Higher Education* 14:403–423

Cummings, William K. et al., eds. 1988. *The Revival of Values Education in East and West*. London: Pergamon.

———. 1994. "From Knowledge Seeking to Knowledge Creation: The Japanese University's Challenge," *Higher Education*.

Dore, Ronald and Mari Sako. 1989. *How the Japanese Learn to Work*. London: Routledge.

Eng Fong, Pang. 1982. *Education, Manpower and Development in Singapore*. Singapore: Singapore University Press.

Fujita,Taki. 1938. "The Higher Education of Women in Japan," in *Education in Japan,* papers presented at the World Federation of Educational Associations Seventh Biennial Conference, Tokyo, 1937. Tokyo: Tokyo Printing Co.

Geiger, Roger L. 1987. *Private Sectors in Higher Education*. Ann Arbor: University of Michigan Press.

Glenn Jr, Charles L. 1988. *The Myth of the Common School*. Amherst, MA: University of Massachusetts Press.

Hall, Ivan Parker. 1973. *Mori Arinori*. Cambridge, MA: Harvard University Press.

Hall, Robert K. 1949. *Shushin: The Ethics of a Defeated Nation*. New York: Teachers College Bureau of Publications,

Hong, Moon-Jong. 1992. "Japanese Colonial Education Policy in Korea." Ed.D. dissertation. Harvard University.

Hook, Glenn D., and Michael A. Weiner. 1992. *The Internationalization of Japan*. London: Routledge.

Horio, Teruhisa. 1988. *Educational Thought and Ideology in Modern Japan*. Steven Platzer, tran. Tokyo: University of Tokyo Press.

International Association for the Evaluation of Educational Achievement (IEA). 1988. *Science Achievement in Seventeen Countries: A Preliminary Report*. Oxford: Pergamon Press.

——— 1992. *Science Achievement in 17 Countries*. Oxford: Pergamon Press.

Ishida, Hiroshi. 1993. *Social Mobility in Contemporary Japan*. Stanford: Stanford University Press.

Iwasa, Nobumichi, and Keiji Suwanai. 1995. "Report of Results of Questionnaire in Moral Education in Each Country," mimeo.

James, Estelle, and Gail Benjamin. 1988. *Public Policy and Private Education in Japan*. New York: St. Martin's Press.

Japan Echo. 1993. *The Human Rights Debate*. Special Issue. September.

Jencks, Christopher. 1972. *Inequality*. New York: Basic Books.

Johnson, Jean M. 1993. *Human Resources for Science and Technology: The Asian Region*. Washington, DC: National Science Foundation.

Kitamura, Kazuyuki. 1986. "Japan's Informal Education System." In *Educational Policies in Crisis*. ed. William K. Cummings et al. New York: Praeger.

Kodama, Fumio, and Chiaki Nishigata. 1991. "Structural Changes in the Japanese Supply/Employment System of Engineers: Are We Losing or Gaining?" In *The Changing University,* ed. D.S. Zinberg. Amsterdam: Kluwer Publishers.

Kohlberg, Lawrence. 1981. *The Meaning and Measurement of Moral Development.* Worcester, MA: Clark University Press.

Lasswell, Harold D. 1976. "The Continuing Revision of Conceptual and Operational Maps." In *Values and Development: Appraising Asian Experience,* Harold Lasswell, Daniel Lerner, and John D. Montgomery. 261–283. Cambridge, MA: MIT Press.

Lee, Myoung-Jin. 1993. "Asian-Born Scientists and Engineers: Their Immigration Flow and Labor Market Adjustment." *Korea Journal of Population and Development.* July 22.

Lee, W. O. 1991. *Social Change and Educational Problems in Japan, Singapore and Hong Kong.* New York: St. Martin's Press.

Levy, Jr., Marion J. 1972. *Modernization: Latecomers and Survivors.* New York: Basic Books.

Lynn, Leonard H., Henry R. Piehler, and Mark Kieler. 1993. "Engineering Careers, Job Rotation, and Gatekeepers in Japan and the United States." *Journal of Engineering and Technology Management* 10:53–72

McGinn, Noel. 1996. "Education, Democratization, and Globalization: A Challenge for Comparative Education." *Comparative Education Review* 40(4):341–357.

Ministry of Education, Science and Culture. 1972. *Japan's Modern Educational System. Tokyo, 1980.* Translated from Mombusho. *Gakusei Hyakunenshi.* One Hundred Year History of Japanese Education, 2 Vols. Tokyo: Teikoku Chiho Gyosei Gakkai.

Miyanaga, Kuniko. 1991. *The Creative Edge: Emerging Individualism in Japan.* New Brunswick, NJ: Transaction Publishers.

Montgomery, John. 1995. "Human Values as Human Rights," mimeo.

Montgomery, John, and Dennis A. Rondinelli, eds. 1995. *Great Policies: Strategic Innovations in Asia and the Pacific Basin.* Westport, CT: Praeger, 1995.

Mukherjee, Hena. 1988. "Moral Education in a Developing Society: The Malaysian Case." In *The Revival of Values Education in Asia and the West,* William K. Cummings et al. New York: Pergamon Press.

Muta, Hiromitsu, ed. 1990. *Educated Unemployment in Asia. Tokyo: Asian Productivity Organization.*

National Institute for Educational Research. 1981. *Moral Education in Asia.* Research Bulletin No. 20. Tokyo.

———. 1990. *A New Decade of Moral Education.* Tokyo: NIER.

———. 1991. *Education for Humanistic, Ethical/Moral and Cultural Values: Final Report of a Regional Meeting.* Tokyo: NIER.

Passin, Herbert. 1965. *Society and Education in Japan.* New York: Teachers College.

Prime Minister's Office. 1992. *Nihon no Seinen* (Fourth Survey). Tokyo: Okurasho Insatsukyoku.

Science and Technology Agency, Japan. 1991. *White Paper on Science and Technology 1991: Globalization of Scientific and Technological Activities and Issues Japan is Encountering.* Tokyo.

Smith, Thomas C. 1955. *Political Change and Industrial Development in Japan: Government Enterprise, 1868–1880.* Stanford: Stanford University Press.

Stevenson, Harold W., and James W. Stigle. 1992. *The Learning Gap.* New York: Summit Books.

Stewart, Charles T., and Yasumitsu Nihei. 1992. *Technology Transfer and Human Factors.* Lexington, MA: D.C. Heath and Co.

Tan, Jee-Peng, and Alain Mingat. 1992. *Education in Asia—A Comparative Study of Cost and Financing.* Washington, DC: The World Bank.

Teng, SSu-yu, and John K. Fairbank. 1954. *China's Response to the West.* Cambridge, MA: Harvard University Press.

Tobin, Joseph. 1989. *Preschool in Three Cultures: Japan, China and the United States.* New Haven: Yale University Press.

Tsuneichi, Warren, et al. 1958. *Sources of Japanese Tradition.* New York: Columbia University Press.

Tsurumi, Patricia E. 1977. *Japanese Colonial Education in Taiwan, 1895–1945.* Cambridge, MA: Harvard University Press.

UNESCO. 1992. *World Education Report 1991.* Paris: UNESCO.

UNICEF. 1992. *The State of the World's Children.* New York: Oxford University Press.

U.S. Dept. of Education. 1987. *Japanese Education Today.* Washington, DC: U.S. Government Printing Office.

U.S. Education Mission to Japan. 1946. *Report.* Mimeo. Tokyo, March 30.

Ushiogi, Morikazu. 1993. "Graduate Education and Research Organization in Japan." In *The Research Foundations of Graduate Education,* ed. Burton R. Clark. Berkeley: University of California Press.

Weiner, Myron. 1991. *The Child and the State in India.* Princeton: Princeton University Press.

Williamson, Jeffrey G. 1993. "Human Capital Deepening, Inequality, and Demographic Events along the Pacific Rim." In *Human Resources in Development Along the Pacific Rim,* Naohiro Ogawa et al., 129–158. Oxford: Oxford University Press.

World Bank. 1993. *The East Asian Miracle: Economic Growth and Public Policy.* New York: Oxford University Press.

———. 1995. *World Development Report.* New York: Oxford University Press.

Yamashita, Shoichi. 1991. *Transfer of Japanese Technology and Management to the ASEAN Countries.* Tokyo: University of Tokyo Press.

APPENDIX

Table A. Comparison of Japan and Japan-related Asian Nations with Other Asian Nations, Europe, and the Developing World circa 1988 (unless otherwise indicated)

Indicator	Japan	Taiwan Korea	Other NICs	Other Asian	South Asia	West Europe	Developing Nation
Lean Government:							
Govt. Expense as % GNP	10	20	22	11	19	44	30
Ed. as % Govt.	34	19	25	17	9	10	13
Science							
Science/Eng. Students as % in Higher Education	22	37	23	29	24	29	29
Human Resources							
Primary GRE '70	99	107	89	86	54	103	76
Secondary GRE '70	86	48	28	28	20	70	27
Tertiary GRE '90	31	13	7	8	3	21	9
Society Fills Gap							
Private % 2nd	13	33	0	54	49	23	25
Private % H.Ed.	80	75	26	22	35	25	15
Efficiency							
2nd Student/Teacher	19	30	20	17	22	14	22
% Finish 4th Grade	100	96	82	83	58	95	83
% Primary Repeat	0	0	6	6	10	4	14

Source: Primary source is UNESCO (1992). Additional indicators are from World Bank and SPIE data bank at the University at Buffalo.

Table B. The Emphasis in the Values Education Curriculum of Selected Asian Nations

Country	Themes	Values Stressed
Japan-1	Per/Social Ed. Civic Ed. Character Ed.	Respect for human dignity, characteristic culture, democratic society and state, contributing to a peaceful international society.
Taiwan-1	Per/Social Ed. Character Ed. Civic Ed. Political Ed.	Benevolence, justice, courtesy, sincerity, thrift and diligence, respect elders, obey the law, patriotism.
Korea-1	Character Ed. Civic Ed. Per/Social Ed. Political Ed.	Honesty, diligence, filial piety, patriotism.
China-2	Political Ed. Character Ed. Per/Social Ed	Think of others collectively, revere the people and the nation, respect others and yourself.
Thailand-3	Character Ed Per/Social Ed. Religious Ed. Political Ed.	Self-reliance, diligence and responsibility, frugality and endurance, self-discipline and awareness of rules, practice religious ethics, patriotism.
Singapore-3	Character Ed. Per/Social Ed. Political Ed.	Habit formation and development of character, sense of belonging to the community and respect for cultural heritage (including Asian values), love of country and spirit of nation building.
Malaysia-3	Character Ed. Per/Social Ed. Religious Ed.	Cleanliness of body and mind, sympathy and tolerance, moderation, diligence, gratitude, justice, honesty, respect, love, public spiritness and community relations, freedom, modesty, bravery, rationality, self-reliance, cooperation.

Indonesia-2	Religious Ed.	Belief in God, civilized human being, good
	Character Ed.	Indonesian personality, disciplined, hard-
	Per/Social Ed.	working, tough, responsible, self-confident,
	Political Ed.	intelligent, skillful, healthy, patriotic,
		empathetic, self-reliant, innovative.
Philippines-3	Per/Social Ed.	Health, truth, love, social responsibility,
	Political Ed.	economic efficiency, nationalism and
	Character Ed.	patriotism, global solidarity.

Sources: 1 is Iwasa and Suwanai (1995) ; 2 is NIER (1991); 3 is NIER (1990).

Note: The value education themes presented here are in rank order of priority from a list including character, civic, religious, political/ideological, personal/ social, and other (e.g., peace, social studies).

Kai-ming Cheng, Chair Professor of Education and Pro-Vice-Chancellor, University of Hong Kong, and recently Visiting Professor of Education at the Harvard Graduate School of Education, Honorary Fellow of the University of London Institute of Education, and Fellow of the Commonwealth Council for Educational Administration. His most recent publication, *Quality of Basic Education in China: Case Study of the Province of Zhejiang,* was published by the International Institute for Educational Planning.

8. Engineering Values: Education Policies and Values Transmission

Kai-ming Cheng

One explanation for the late acknowledgement of the cultural role of education is that educators usually teach in only one culture and hence are often less sensitive to others—as the saying goes, "It is the fish who is the last to discover water." . . . Value-related assumptions are mostly taken for granted. But if education is the realm that best preserves cultural values, then current systems are worthy of serious study and evaluation.

Character education was one of the ten major educational items that President Clinton included in his 1997 State of the Union address to the United States Congress. He emphasized the need to teach citizenship skills and to promote order and discipline, support communities that introduce school uniforms, impose curfews, enforce truancy laws, remove disruptive students from the classroom, and have zero tolerance for guns and drugs.

It is unusual for a political leader in the West to include "character education" as a policy goal, although the teaching of values is commonplace in East Asian cultures. The inclusion of character education raises important questions: Can character be taught? What is the role of the state in character education? What kind of character should it aim for? What are the relations between value and education? Are values transmitted through education? If so, can they be transmitted through policies in education?

This chapter will discuss the role of values in education. It argues that the essential issue is the relative position of the individual in a community; that education plays a key role in transmitting cultural values; that values are an essential part of the culture and are often *presumed* rather than *engineered;* that values are transmitted by education implicitly rather than explicitly and that the role of government policy in transmitting values is ambivalent.

VALUES AND CULTURE

Values and culture are closely related. Social scientists analyze elements of culture such as artifacts, rituals and ceremonies, heroes, behavioral norms, shared values, and basic assumptions (Schein 1992: 3–27; Hofstede 1991: 3–19), at different levels of abstraction; however, deeper-rooted cultural elements are less visible and less often probed. Robert LeVine writes:

> The more general ideas—basic assumptions—are less accessible to verbal formulation because the social consensus in a community protects them from challenge. (1984: 76)

In this sense, the invisible but fundamental dimensions of culture start with values.

Although individual value systems differ within any one culture, the community shares some norms that distinguish one culture from another (Hofstede 1980: chapter 1). While this proposition may invite some statistical or conceptual debates, there are basic facts that are generally observed: where there is only one system in a culture, the operating systems (social, health, welfare, or education) tend to reflect the value choices it favors.

Most investigations of values in society look at culture, concentrating on the values shared among members of the society. Although the study of culture is nothing new in various disciplines of the humanities and social sciences, relating culture to education, especially to the formal education system, is relatively recent, and still rare, a rather strange situation given that education is a fundamental human activity and by nature clearly related to culture.

One explanation for the late acknowledgement of the cultural role of education is that educators usually teach in only one culture and hence are often less sensitive to others—as the saying goes, "it is the fish who is the last to discover water." Most educators work in an environment unpolluted by alternative cultural values. Value-related assumptions are mostly taken for granted. But if education is to be the realm that best preserves cultural values, then current systems are worthy of serious study and evaluation. Anthropologists have long regarded child-rearing as a key to understanding native cultures and as an essential stage of a person's education; it is in this context that the literature about education and values appears most significant.

VALUES AND SOCIALIZATION

The relation between education and values is frequently touched on in discussions about socialization. Socialization represents the process in which cultural values are transmitted from one generation to another. LeVine (1982: 61–68) has discerned three alternative perceptions of socialization—as *enculturation,* as *acquisition of impulse control,* and as *role training.* Enculturation is an anthropological concept representing a culture-deterministic approach. "It is seen as an automatic process of absorption in which the child as *tabula rasa* acquires culture simply by exposure to it" (ibid.). A young person acquires the cultural values of a society because he or she is in that society and has no experience of alternative value systems. Here, education is conceived in the broadest sense: everything in the society plays an educational role. The formal education system is but part of the culture, and values in the education system are inevitably determined by the culture.

The notion of acquisition of impulse control represents a psychological approach. It conceives of humans "as born with drives that are potentially disruptive to social life," and it sees "the problem of socialization in terms of taming disruptive impulses and channeling them into socially useful forms" (ibid.). Here, the issue of values is taken for granted; there is a tacit assumption of constant value norms according to which humans have to be controlled. Education is then seen as an instrument for harnessing human drives, and as a consequence it becomes to some extent a method of behavioral modification. Under these assumptions, education *preserves* rather than *changes* social values.

The conception of socialization as role training is sociological and political. It interprets socialization "as a process conceived as designed to achieve the conformity of, individuals to social norms and rules" (ibid.). As a contrast to the Freudian formulation, role theory emphasizes positive prescriptions. There is also the tacit framework that personality and social structure are two separate systems, and socialization is a promoter of conformity by integrating the two systems. In this view, education again is seen to abide by existing cultural norms in the society.

LeVine's categories are by no means exhaustive, but still allow us to examine the notion of social capital in the context of socialization. If values are seen as a matter of social capital, then we are concerned about how "good" or "useful" values are preserved, transmitted, or created, and how "bad" and "evil" values can be harnessed, reduced, or eliminated. In this context, the focus is on education as a system. If we regard values as a matter of social capital, then our concern should be whether or not values can be created and accumulated as capital should be, and what role education plays in such a process. All these converge to suggest the title of this chapter: Can values be engineered?

VALUES AND INDIVIDUALS

There can be no easy definition for value, but it is safe to say that values involve priorities, choices, and decisions about dilemmas. Value issues frequently encountered include equity vs. efficiency, aspiration vs. economic needs, individual vs. community needs, majority benefits vs. minority needs, and so on. Central to all these issues is the dichotomy between individual goals and goals of a larger collective—the family, firms or institutions, neighborhood, city, nation, or even the entire world.

Writers often run the risk of oversimplification and debate value issues along the continuum between individualism and collectivism (Kim 1994; Triandis 1989). On the one hand, extreme individualism makes individual needs central to all social considerations: a nation's worth or success, for example, is based on its satisfaction of the needs of each individual citizen. On the other hand, extreme collectivism requires individual needs to be subordinate to or identical with collective needs.

This issue is as the center of discussion in most of the comparisons between the East Asian culture and the mainstream Western culture. Fei Hsiao-tung, a leading sociologist in China, discerned in the 1940s a defining difference between Chinese and Western societies, the former being a configuration of hierarchy, and the latter a configuration of association. For example, a person born into a Chinese society is born into a predetermined social hierarchy. The person is to live within this hierarchy and to live up to its expectations. By contrast, in Western society each person is first and foremost an individual; his future relations with other members of the society are contingent upon practical needs whereby people associate with one another.

It is perhaps appropriate at this juncture to look at cases in specific cultures. Numerous writers share the perception that in East Asian societies, individuals are expected to conform to societal norms that pay very little respect to individual characteristics, whereas in the West, the respect for individual needs prevails over and indeed underpins societal norms. F. L. K. Hsu even concludes that the concepts of self and personality, as understood in Western psychology, are foreign to Chinese thinking. Hsu argues that "the concept of personality is an expression of the western ideal of individualism." (Hsu 1985: 24)

In this context, education plays a key role as the major means of socialization. I have shown elsewhere that education reflects such a cultural difference, comparing education in the East Asian culture and that in the mainstream Western culture (Cheng 1990; 1994b; 1997a). In China and other East Asian societies, the education system is so structured that different individuals are supposed to follow more or less the same curriculum, compete in the same examination, and be assessed and rewarded according to the same set of criteria. In other words, students are educated under uniform expectations and they are expected to develop themselves along a uniform track reflecting a collective desire. The civil examination in the imperial court, which had a history of about one thousand years, was typical of such a system; writers tend to view contemporary education systems in East Asia as just a variation of the ancient system (e.g., Solomon 1971: chapters 2 and 3; Cleverly 1991: chapter 2).

In mainstream Western societies, the education systems are diversified so that individual needs of students can be (as far as resources permit) accommodated. Students follow different curricula and, ideally, develop themselves along their respective tracks. In some systems, such a diversification is realized in diverse types of schools. The German tripartite system of Gymnasium, Realschule, and Hauptschule, and the Dutch system of MAVO, HAVO, and VWO are typical examples (Cheng 1990; 1994b). In other systems, the diversification is achieved in diversifying the curriculum. The streaming in France's Baccalauréat (high school diploma) system, which is also imitated in many former French colonies, is an example. There are also systems, such as those in the United States and the United Kingdom, where individualization takes place at the class level within the same school, or even among students in the same class.

Curriculum and examination are only two indications of the individual-collective interplay in education, but they are the most visible at the macro level. Cultural values infiltrate all aspects of a student's educational life (Cheng 1990). For example, Stevenson and Stigler (1992), in *The Learning Gap*, highlight the different emphases in the effort-ability dichotomy among Chinese/Japanese and American societies. The former tend to emphasize effort over innate ability, whereas the latter reflect the opposite. The cultural explanation of this difference is that in East Asian societies, collective and uniform learning expectations require students to strive according to expectations that are not individual-specific, whereas in the West, individual abilities are the basis of expectations for students.

The collective tendency in East Asian culture is also related to the characteristics of classes in schools, the implementation of discipline, and the emphasis on "moral education" and on human relations in general. More recently, there also have been culture-based discussions about the modes of learning (e.g., rote learning), the meaning of learning, and the styles of learning in East Asian systems. Similar studies about other cultures such as the Islamic and Indian cultures are rare, and the study of Western culture is almost absent—quite understandably, because the main thrust of cross-cultural studies is still in the West, and the Western base culture is often presumed rather than studied.

EDUCATION AND VALUES

Education is a means of socialization. From LeVine's (1982, 1984) three concepts of socialization, there could be two interpretations of this statement. First, education reflects the values of a particular culture. Second, education transmits cultural values to the younger generation.

The first interpretation is anthropological and "neutral." That is, inevitably, independent of human intentions, education operates within the framework of values specific to the particular culture. As such, the human agents who work in the education system may or may not be conscious of the value framework, and most of the time may have taken it for granted. Policymakers in education are often even less conscious of such a value framework.

The second interpretation is both anthropological and political. It involves human intentions. On the one hand, education transmits cultural values directly, independent of a social purpose. On the other hand, however, policies of the particular system may involve interventions which intentionally transmit the values of the culture. In this latter case, the values developed as a result of this intervention may or may not be consistent with the conventional values of the culture.

It is the last dimension which gives room for the thematic question of this chapter: Can values be engineered? Since education is not totally a natural reflection of cultural values, and it indeed involves intentional intervention, then it is legitimate to ask: Can education transmit values that are not consistent with the conventional cultural values? If the answer is yes, then another question follows: Can culture be changed by way of intentional and effective intervention through education?

VALUES AND CULTURAL CHANGE

Does culture change? Can culture be changed? When people refer to culture, they implicitly assume a stable set of values that is not easily modified by short-term economic or political changes. This does not mean, however, that culture does not change. Obviously, artifacts, rituals, and ceremonies are modified over time. Behavioral norms change as well, but they do so at a slower pace. Shared values are transformed over a longer period, and such change takes place only when there are rather abrupt shifts in political and socioeconomic systems. Basic assumptions remains constant for a much longer time, often over centuries.

It is change at the values level (and deeper) that concerns us in this discussion. There is very little discussion about value change in the literature. Substantial change in social values is often observable over a longer time span than the lifetime of any researcher; however, the abrupt changes in China and the former Soviet Union may shed some light on this discussion. I will concentrate on China with which I am more familiar.

There have been two major societal changes in China over the past three decades. The first was the Proletariat Cultural Revolution, which started in 1966. The net effect of the Cultural Revolution was an almost complete removal of economic elements from social life. Starting from revolutions in education and all forms of art, the Cultural Revolution successfully changed all symbols and rituals of the "old" society, with a reversion of social orders (the oppressed majority oppressing the minority of oppressors), and an overhaul of basic assumptions such as that about the self. The change was intentional and achieved through forceful policies and vigorous social campaigns. For ten years, the nation lived under an ideology interrelated with a consistent value system.

The second change was the open economic policy, which started in 1978 after the collapse of the Cultural Revolution, when most of the values of the Cultural Revolution were reversed. Economic elements were reintroduced into the nation's life. Incentives for individuals to work hard were reestablished and competition was once again encouraged. The change is still proceeding, but the trend toward a more market-oriented society is unmistakable.

The test question is: How did the culture change? And why? There do not seem to be clear answers. The Cultural Revolution, as indicated by the name, aimed at fundamental cultural change. It was seemingly quite successful at the high times of the revolution. For example, there was virtually a total collectivism over the entire nation for ten years; the overhaul in values was caused unambiguously by policy interventions from the state.

However, at the collapse of the Cultural Revolution, the conventional values relapsed almost immediately. Not only were the values installed during the Cultural Revolution reversed, but those established during the 17 previous years of socialism were challenged. Traditional cultural values soon took over the romance of revolutionary ideals. The reversion of values in this period has been supported by policy interventions that accelerate the process of change, but most of the manifested policies have been endorsements of changes already taking place; policy changes have lagged behind changes in reality.

Strong state intervention did change cultural values for a while, but traditional culture seems to have won in the long run. One may argue that the Cultural Revolution is atypical of a social change because it was forced by strong state intervention. However, it does serve to illustrate the possibility of dramatic cultural change and the role of policy intervention in such a change.

VALUES AND POLICY INTERVENTION

What conclusion can we draw from the case of China? Theoretically, in relation to policy intent, there could be three modes of policy intervention for values transmission: those reinforcing the existing values, those unintentionally going against existing values, and those intending to modify values.

Under normal circumstances, policies reinforce existing values. Anthropologists would argue that policymakers live in a culture that shapes their values. The policies cannot move very far from the values shared by members of their society. Even modern theories of decision making emphasize the notion of "diffusion"(Weiss 1982), which could be seen as the influence of values on the policymaking process.

However, this does not mean that policymakers as free individuals always abide by existing cultural values, or are conscious of the cultural dimensions of the policies they make. President Clinton's emphasis on "character education" in his State of the Union address (January 1997) is an example. The recent introduction of neighborhood participation in basic education in many major cities in China is another. Here, the desire for equity has prevailed over traditional values of competition and tolerance for hierarchies. Elsewhere, I have also argued that the emergence of career guidance as a curriculum component in China has given rise to an emphasis on individuals and individual choice (Cheng 1993). Prompted by pragmatic needs of the emerging job market, the trend might undermine not only the socialist norms of national needs, but also the traditional collectivist conception of individuals (Cheng 1994a). Value changes may take place beyond policy intentions.

There have also been deliberate policies to modify the existing values in the society. Again, within the same China, which still sees itself as socialist, there are policies intended to change the relations between individuals and the state. An example is the recent introduction of student fees (to be implemented nationwide in 1997) and the abolition of state assignment of jobs (to be implemented by 2000). Such policies drastically change the nature of higher education from a national undertaking to a personal endeavor, hence affecting the individual-collective value balance for a whole generation of intellectuals (Cheng 1997b). The entire notion of higher education is being changed from a state enterprise to individual investments.

In Hong Kong, education policies have long followed Western philosophies of education. Although this occurred with no deliberate intention of changing the culture, these policies have fundamentally changed educators' basic assumptions in regard to values concerning individuals and innate abilities. Such a change has taken place notwithstanding the traditional values maintained among the populace. There has been a constant struggle to reconcile Western values implicit in the educational system and the values held by parents and employers. In a way, the entire culture of Hong Kong has been shaped by the struggle between conflicting values (King 1996).

CONCLUSION

Then can values be engineered? In the West, the "East Asian miracles" have tempted many to think of borrowing from the East Asian culture. Clinton's call for character education is but one oblique reflection of such a tendency.

Values, as a matter of culture, change only as a result of fundamental social changes and over a long period of time. Few policies can cause such fundamental changes and most policies are short-lived. However, this does not mean that policies have no role to play in value change. Although it may be difficult for policies to initiate value changes, policies may facilitate those occurring as a result of more fundamental causes. Fundamental changes, however, are beyond the realm of government policies. Hence, while it would be invalid to conclude that values cannot be engineered, such a purpose would require long-term persistent effort and high sensitivity to cultural values. Neither virtue is possessed by most current political leaders.

REFERENCES

Cheng, K. M. 1990. "The Culture of Schooling in East Asia." In *Handbook of Educational Ideas and Practices,* ed. N. Entwistle, 163–173. London: Routledge.

———. 1993. "Reflection of the Market Sector in a Planned Economy: Emergence of Career Guidance in Shanghai." In *Curriculum Changes for Chinese Communities in Southeast Asia: Challenges of the 21st Century,* ed. C. C. Lam, H. W. Wong, and Y. W. Fung, 165–168. Hong Kong: The Chinese University of Hong Kong .

———. 1994. "Young Adults in a Changing Socialist Economy: Post Compulsory Education in China." *Comparative Education,* 30(1):63–73.

———. 1994b. "Quality of Education as Perceived in the Chinese Culture." In *Quality of Education in the Context of Culture in Developing Countries,* ed. T. Takala, 67–84. Tampere: Tampere University Press.

———. 1997a. "Quality Assurance in Education: The East Asian Perspective." In *Educational Dilemmas: Debate and Diversity, Vol 4: Quality in Education,* ed. K. Watson, S. Modgil, and C. Modgil, 399–412. London: Cassell.

———. 1997. "Beyond the Political Narratives: Review of a Decade's Reform in China's Education." Talk at Teachers College, Columbia University, February 20, 1997.

Cheng, K. M., and Wong, K. C. 1996. "School Effectiveness in East Asia: Concepts, Origins and Implications." *Journal of Educational Administration,* 34(5):32–49.

Cleverly, J. 1991. *The Schooling of China,* 2nd ed. North Sydney: Allen and Unwin.

Fei, Hsiao-tung, Xiangtu zhongguo (Earth-bound China). [1947] 1985. Reprint, Hong Kong: Joint Publishers. (In Chinese)

Hofstede, G. 1980. *Culture's Consequences: International Differences in Work-Related Values.* Beverly Hills, CA: Sage.

———. 1991. *Cultures and Organizations: Software of the Mind.* London: McGraw-Hill.

Hsu, F. L. K. 1985. "The Self in Cross-Cultural Perspective." In *Culture and Self: Asian and Western Perspective.* ed. A. J. Marsella, G. Devos, and F. L. K. Hsu, 24–55. New York: Tavistock.

Kim, U. 1994. "Individualism and Collectivism: Conceptual Clarification and Elaboration." In *Individualism and Collectivitism: Theory, Method and Applications,* ed. U. Kim, H. C. Triandis, G. Kbgitgibasi, S. C. Choi, and G. Yoon, 19–40. Thousand Oaks, CA: Sage.

King, A. Y. C. 1996. "The Transformation of Confucianism in the Post-Confucian Era: The Emergence of Rationalistic Traditionalism in Hong Kong." In *Confucian Traditions in East Asian Modernity,* ed. W. M. Yu. Cambridge, MA: Harvard University Press.

LeVine, R. 1982. *Culture, Behavior and Personality,* 2nd ed. New York: Aldine.

———. 1984 "Properties of Culture: An Ethnographic View." In *Culture Theory: Essays on Mind, Self and Emotion,* ed. R. A. Shweder and R. A. LeVine, 67–87. Cambridge, MA: Cambridge University Press.

Schein, E. H. 1992. *Organizational Culture and Leadership.* San Francisco: Jossey-Bass.

Solomon, R. H. 1971. *Mao's Revolution and the Chinese Political Culture.* Berkeley: University of California Press.

Stevenson, H. W., and J. W. Stigler. 1992. *The Learning Gap: Why Our Schools Are Failing and What We Can Learn From Japanese and Chinese Education.* New York: Summit Books.

Triandis, H. C. 1989. "The Self and Social Behavior in Differing Cultural Contexts," *Psychological Review,* 98:506–20.

Weiss, C. H. 1982. "Policy Research in the Context of Diffuse Decision-Making." In *Social Science Research and Public Policy-Making: A Reappraisal,* ed. D. B. P. Kallen, G. B. Kosse, H. C. Wagenaar, J. J. J. Kloprogge, and M. Vorbeck. Windsor: NFER-Nelson.

NOTES

CHAPTER TWO: ARE ASIAN VALUES DIFFERENT?

1. For several differing views see Peter L. Berger and Hsin-Huang Michael Hsiao, eds., in *Search of an East Asian Development Model* (New Brunswick, NJ: Transaction Books, 1988) and Tu Wei-ming, ed., *The Triadic Chord: Confucian Ethics, Industrial East Asia: and Max Weber, Proceedings of the 1987 Singapore Conference on Confucian Ethics and the Modernization of Industrial East Asia* (Singapore: Institute of East Asian Philosophies, 1991). A powerful statement of the Asian position appears in Fareed Zakaria, "A Conversation with Lee Kuan Yew," *Foreign Affairs,* March/April 1994, 73(2):109–126. Perhaps the most controversial contemporary argument arose over Samuel P. Huntington, *The Clash of Civilizations and the Remaking of World Order* (New York: Simon and Schuster, 1996). This book takes an empirical approach, reporting on institutional and behavioral expressions of value preferences in Asia.

2. An early, and still interesting, reconception of regionalism in terms of cultural affinities is Bruce M. Russett, *International Regions and the International System, A Study in Political Ecology* (Chicago, IL: Rand McNally, 1967).

3. Harold D. Lasswell and Myres S. MacDougall, *Jurisprudence for a Free Society, Studies in Law, Science and Policy* (New Haven, CT: New Haven Press, 1992). Abraham Maslow, *Motivation and Personality* (New York: Harper's, 1954). Papers by Heffron, Inkeles, and Hayhoe in this collection present alternative interpretations, which also seem useful for purposes of analysis and comparison.

4. One antecedent of the idea was Jane Addams in *Democracy and Social Ethics,* (New York, Macmillan 1902). It was brought back to life by James S. Coleman's "Social Capital in the Creation of Human Capital," *American Journal of Sociology,* Vol. 94, Supplement S95-S120, 1988. Its current reincarnation in the public's attention may be credited to Robert D. Putnam's *Making Democracy Work: Civic Traditions in Modern Italy* (Princeton, NJ: University Press, 1993), and his "The Prosperous Community, Social Capital and Public Life," *The American Prospect,* Vol. 13, Spring, 1993. These interpretations tend to regard social capital as an independent variable, and then to look for the consequences of its presence or absence. The PBRC study treats it as a dependent variable, as a partial product of efforts by governments and other value-creating organizations to develop or strengthen it. An advocacy position for that approach is taken by Glenn C. Loury, "The Social Capital Deficit," *The New Democrat,* May/June, 1995, and by Cornelia Butler Flora, "Social Capital and Sustainability: Agriculture and Communities in the Plains and Corn Belt," Journal Paper No. J 16309, *Iowa Agriculture and Home Economic Experiment Station,* Project No. 3281, 1995, reprinted in *Sustainable Agriculture Newsletter,* Fall, 1995. Current research is under way at the Institute for Development Research, Boston University School of Management, by L. David Brown and Darcy Ashman under the title "Participation, Social Capital and Intersectoral Problem-Solving: African and Asian Cases." *World Development,* 1996, 24:9, 1467–1479.

5. Contemporary scholarship focuses on the positive uses of social capital, but its exploitation for evil purposes remains a constant problem in human development. The NSDAP was a source of social capital for Hitler's Germany, just as religious fundamentalism has encouraged excesses against human dignity throughout Africa and the Middle East, as well as in parts of Asia.

6. Over the next five years, the Pacific Basin Research Center will explore a variety of influences on the formation of social capital in Asia and the Pacific.

7. New York, United Nations, 1993.

8. For convenience's sake, the mnemonic device, PEWBSARD, uses one letter rather light-heartedly to stand for each value: P standing for Power, E for Enlightenment, W for Wealth, B for Well-Being, S for Skill, A for Affection, R for Respect, and D for rectituDe. The most recent treatment of these values is Harold D. Lasswell and Myres S. McDougal, op. cit. See also Henry F. Dobyns, Paul L. Doughty, and Harold D. Lasswell, eds., *Peasants, Power and Applied Social Change: Vicos as a Model* (Beverly Hills and London: Sage, 1971); Harold D. Lasswell and Allan R. Holmberg, "Toward a General Theory of Directed Value Accumulation and Institutional Development," in Ralph Braibanti, ed., *Political and Administrative Development* (Durham, NC: Duke University Press, 1969), 354–399 and Harold Lasswell, Daniel Lerner, and John D. Montgomery, *Values and Development, Appraising Asian Experience* (Cambridge, MA: MIT Press, 1976).

9. The most comprehensive survey of rights as values is Myres S. McDougal, Harold D. Lasswell, and Lung-chu Che, *Human Rights and World Public Order* (New Haven, CT: Yale University Press, 1980). Taking the further step of analyzing human responses in search of values, Nussbaum and Sen consider the capacity to pursue such categories of preference and proposes to seek indicators of them as "evaluation space." See Martha Nussbaum and Amartya Sen, eds., *The Quality of Life* (Oxford: Clarendon Press, 1993).

10. See A. Kaplan, "Content Analysis and the Theory of Signs," *Philosophy of Science* 10, 230–247; Harold D. Lasswell, "Describing the Contents of Communications," in B. L. Smith, H. D. Lasswell, and R. D. Casey, *Propaganda, Communication, and Public Opinion* (Princeton: Princeton University Press, 1946); and Harold D. Lasswell, Nathan Leites et al., *Language of Politics* (New York: Stewart, 1949). The use of content analysis for the study of group and national values appears in several excellent studies of "cognitive codes." Ole Holsti, "The Belief System and National Images: A Case Study," *Journal of Conflict Resolution* 6(3); Roger Cobb, "The Beliefs Systems Perspective: An Assessment of a Framework," *Journal of Politics* 35, (Feb. 1973.)

11. Human Rights, Status of International Instruments: Chart of Ratifications as at 31 December 1994 (New York and Geneva: United Nations, ST/HR/5, Sales No. E87.14.2, 1995).

12. For an excellent description of these differences, see Amitav Acharya, *Human Rights in Southeast Asia: Dilemmas for Foreign Policy* (Toronto: University of Toronto-York University Joint Centre for Asia Pacific Studies, Eastern Asia Policy Papers 11, 1995).

13. Basic data taken from Annual Survey of Freedom Country Scores, 1972–73 to 1995–96, (New York: Freedom House, 1997). Minghong Lu, a fellow at the Pacific Basin Research Center, has made further calculations based on these reports.

14. *Human Rights: Positive Policies in Asia and the Pacific* (forthcoming).

15. Donald Emmerson, "Do Asian Values Exist?" He concludes that the World Values Survey confirms that Asia affords a "somewhat higher priority to order and a somewhat lower one to participation and freedom," based on a comparison between China, India, Japan, and South Korea, and 18 Western countries. Conference Report on "Cultural Sources of Human Rights in East Asia," *Human Rights Dialogue* 5 (June 1996): 3.

CHAPTER THREE: DIFFUSION OF VALUES AND THE PACIFIC BASIN

1. See, for example, Alex Inkeles, *National Character: A Psycho-Social Perspective* (New Brunswick, NJ: Transaction, 1996).

2. The work of David McClelland, Gabriel Almond, Alex Inkeles, Sidney Verba, Seymour Martin Lipset, and other scholars in cross-national research all attests to such differences.

3. Koreans emphasize the differences between themselves and the Japanese: See for example James Fallows, *Looking at the Sun: The Rise of the New East Asian Economic System* (New York: Pantheon, 1994) 77–8.

4. See, for example, Gary G. Hamilton, "Overseas Chinese Capitalism," in Tu Wei-ming, 1996. See footnote 6 for full reference.

5. Englewood Cliffs, NJ: Prentice-Hall, 1970.

6. See, for example, Tu Wei-ming, ed., *The Triadic Chord: Confucian Ethics, Industrial East Asia, and Max Weber,* (Singapore: Institute of East Asian Philosophies, 1991); Tu Wei-ming, ed., *Confucian Traditions in East Asian Modernity: Moral Education and Economic Culture in Japan and the Four Mini-Dragons* (Cambridge, MA: Harvard University Press, 1996).

7. Harold W. Stevenson and James W. Stigler, *The Learning Gap: Why Our Schools Are Failing and What We Can Learn from Japanese and Chinese Education* (New York: Summit Books, 1992).

8. "Cultural Explanations: The Man in the Baghdad Cafe," *The Economist,* November 9–15, 1996, 23–26.

9. Tu Wei-ming, ed., *The Triadic Chord: Confucian Ethics, Industrial East Asia and Max Weber,* op. cit., 53–4.

10. Max Weber, *The Religion of China.* (Glencoe, IL: The Free Press, 1951) 151, quoted in Wolfgang Schluchter, "World Adjustment: Max Weber on Confucianism and Taoism," in Tu Wei-ming, ibid., 1991, 27.

11. Gary G. Hamilton and Kao Cheng-shu, "Max Weber and the Analysis of East Asian Industrialization," in Tu Wei-ming, ibid., 109–10, quoting from Max Weber, *The Religion of China,* op. cit., 248.

12. Ambrose Y. C. King, "The Transformation of Confucianism in the Post-Confucian Era: The Emergence of Rationalistic Traditionalism in Hong Kong," in Tu Wei-ming, ibid., 205.

13. Theodore de Bary, "Neo-Confucianism in East Asia," in Tu Wei-ming, ibid., 152.

14. Koh Byong-ik, "Confucianism in Contemporary Korea," in Tu Wei-ming, ibid., 190–193.

15. Kim Kwong-ok, "The Reproduction of Confucian Culture in Contemporary Korea," in Tu Wei-ming, 1996, op. cit., 213.

16. Ibid., 220, 221, 222.

17. Ambrose Y. C. King, op. cit., 207.

18. Ibid., 208.

19. Hwang Kwang-kuo, "Dao and the Transformative Power of Confucianism: A Theory of East Asian Modernisation," in Tu Wei-ming, 1991, op. cit., 241, 255.

20. *The Economist*, November 9–15, "Cultural Explanations: The Man in the Baghdad Cafe."

21. John Wong, op. cit. 281. Tu Wei-ming, *Confucian Ethics Today: the Singapore Challenge*, (Singapore: Federal Publications, 1984).

22. Wong, op. cit., 290, 291

23. Ibid.

24. Amartya Sen, "Human Rights and Asian Values." *The New Republic*, July 14 & 25, 1997: 39–40.

25. John D. Montgomery, "Are Asian Values Different?" in this volume.

26. On the relations between affluence and democracy, see the work of Seymour Martin Lipset: "A Comparative Analysis of the Social Requisites of Democracy," *International Social Science Journal*, 45(2):155–176; and "Social Requisites of Democracy Revisited," *American Sociological Review*, 59(1):1–22.

CHAPTER FOUR: CONTINUITY AND CHANGE IN POPULAR VALUES ON THE PACIFIC RIM

1. Presented as the keynote address at the conference on "Diffusion of Core Values Through Formal and Informal Education in Asia and the Pacific," jointly sponsored by the Pacific Basin Research Center, Soka University of America and the University of Hong Kong, January 12–14, 1997.

2. This branch of the Amazon is called the Rio Negro.

3. Of the studies we have relied on most heavily, the goal of having data for at least two points in time was met in two instances. For Taiwan, a survey taken in 1963 could be compared with one completed in 1991, as reported in Robert M. Marsh, *The Great Transformation: Social Change in Taipei, Taiwan. Since the 1960s* (Armonk, NY: M. E. Sharpe, 1996). For Japan we have surveys using the same questions asked every five years from 1953 through 1993, as reported in Chikio Hayashi and Tatsuzo Suzuki, *Beyond Japanese Social Values* (Tokyo: Institute of Statistical Mathematics, 1990) 63–118, supplemented by Research Committee on the Study of the Japanese National Character, *A Study of the Japanese National Character: The Ninth Nationwide Survey* (in Japanese), *Research Report No. 75, General Series*, (Tokyo: Institute of Statistical Mathematics, 1993).

4. In the sources we rely on heavily, differentiation by age is strongly emphasized in the report on Shanghai and that for Hong Kong. On Shanghai see Godwin C. Chu and Yu, Yanan, *The Great Wall in Ruins: Communication and Cultural Change in China* (Albany: State University of New York Press, 1993). On Hong Kong see Lau, Siu-Kai, and Kuan, Hsin-Chi, *The Ethos of the Hong Kong Chinese* (Hong Kong: Chinese University of Hong Kong, 1988).

5. Whyte used this method of sampling for his study of marriage and family patterns in Chengdu as reported in Martin K. Whyte, "From Arranged Marriages to Love Marriages in Urban China," in Chin-Chin Yi, ed., *Family Formation and Dissolution: Perspectives from East and West* (Taipei: Academica Sinica, 1995). The same technique was used in collecting samples in Baoding as reported in Whyte, "The Persistence of Family Obligations in Baoding," unpublished, 1996.

6. Whyte, ibid., (1966). The proportion of the adult offspring, as against the proportion of their elderly parents, *disagreeing* with the idea that obligations to their children should come ahead of obligations to parents, was: elders 50 percent, their adult children 65 percent. In judging whether obligations to one's career should come ahead of obligations to parents, the proportions *disagreeing* were: elders 23 percent vs. 49 percent among their adult children. That the elders would respond thus, seemingly contrary to their interest, can be explained by assuming they absorbed this ideology under Communist influence, an influence much diluted for their adult children who spent more of their formative years in the post-Mao atmosphere.

7. A more cynical, although not necessarily contradictory, interpretation of the phenomenon is offered by Godkin, who is quoted by Marsh as seeing the increase of extended kin gathering for ancestor worship as "the deliberate, conscious, social construction of tradition." (Marsh, op. cit., p. 139). Marsh notes that religious behavior at temples and other manifestations of folk religion declined in Taiwan between the 1960s and the 1970s, but since the 1980s has been reviving. He believes the cause, curiously enough, to be modernization. Precisely because social change has been so rapid, he suggests, the Taiwanese need some "return to their roots."

8. The question number is 5.1d. The other alternatives offered were: repaying moral indebtedness *(on-gaeshi)*; respecting individual rights; and respecting freedom.

9. Details of question wording and descriptive statistics will be found in Hayashi and Suzuki, op. cit., and Research Committee, op. cit. For a full-scale application of this approach to defining the basic ethos of the population of the United States see Inkeles, "National Character Revisited," *The Tocqueville Review,* Spring 1991.

10. Presumably this response is derived from the Confucian tradition which placed such heavy emphasis on test performance as a criterion for holding office. This question, numbered 5.1c-1, was first used in 1963, when 75 percent said they would hire the person with the higher score rather than the relative. Over time, support for this view did fall some, with only 67 percent still taking the same position in 1993.

11. The question number is 5.6. The more demanding boss who nevertheless looks out for you was selected by 85 percent in 1953 and 40 years later, in 1993, by a similarly overwhelming majority of 82 percent.

12. The question number was 5.6b, and it was first asked in 1973, when 74 percent chose the firm with the family-like atmosphere. By 1993 the preference for this type of firm over one with higher wages had decreased somewhat to 65 percent.

13. The question was number 9.3. Chosen by 79 percent in 1953, the popularity of the Japanese garden increased until it accounted for 90 percent of all the votes in 1973.

14. Thomas A. Metzger, "Hong Kong's Oswald Spengler: H. K. H. Woo (Hu Kuo-heng) and Chinese Resistance to Convergence with the West," *American Journal of Chinese Studies,* in press. Support for Metzger's assumption about the long-term continuity of this pattern of thought will be found in Lee, Leo Ou-Fan, "In Search of Modernity: Some Reflection on a New Mode of Consciousness in Twentieth Century Chinese History and Literature," in Paul A. Cohen and Merle Goldman, eds., *Ideas Across Cultures: Essays on Chinese Thought in Honor of Benjamin I. Schwartz,* Council on East Asian Studies, (Cambridge, MA: Harvard University Press, 1990).

15. Such adaptations are, of course, not peculiar to Asia. One may well ask how much of the original meaning of the Fourth of July remains for the millions of Americans who stream to beaches, or gather their families for backyard barbecues, without a mention or thought of the significance of the date as a celebration of the founding of their nation. One may equally wonder how many of those who at Easter time roll eggs and dress as bunnies have in mind the significance of the day as celebrating the resurrection of Jesus.

16. The question was number 4.10.

17. Chu and Ju, op. cit., Chapter 8, especially Table 8.10.

18. This value set the standard of behavior for women, including obedience to father before a woman got married and to the husband after marriage, while among the virtues it stressed morality, proper language and manners, and diligent work.

19. "The way of the golden mean" is part of Confucian ethics. It counsels avoiding extremes and encourages moderation in all things. The principle of "differentiation between men and women" holds that because men and women are different they should be treated differently. The value called "discretion for self-preservation" urges avoiding the false and sinful, but at the same time it urges one to avoid getting in trouble. For a fuller account of the meaning of these values and others in the set of eight tested, see Chu and Ju, op. cit., 222–244.

20. The proportion voting to "discard" the rejected values, is the percent among the young followed by the percent among the old: "way of the golden mean"—62/68; "three obediences and four virtues"—64/87; "discretion for self-preservation"—51/76. See Chu and Ju, op. cit., Table 10.1.

21. The question was identified by the number 2.4.

22. This was, of course, least true of the largest entity, namely Communist China.

23. See Inkeles and Smith, *Becoming Modern: Individual Change in Six Developing Counties,* (Cambridge, MA: Harvard University Press, 1974); Inkeles, *Exploring Individual Modernity,* (New York: Columbia University Press, 1983).

24. See Inkeles, Broaded, and Cao, "Causes and Consequences of Individual Modernity in China," *The China Journal* 37 (January 1997), 31–59.

25. For evidence that the qualities which define the modern individual are basically the same in women as in men, and that the experiences which contribute to making women more modern are very similar to those which produce modern attitudes and behavior in men, see: Broaded, Montgomery, Cao, and Inkeles, "Women, Men, and Construction of Individual Modernity Scales in China," *Cross-Cultural Research* 28(3):251–286, and Inkeles, Broaded, and Cao, "Causes and Consequences of Individual Modernity in China," *The China Journal* 28(37):31–59.

26. The zero order correlation of years of urban experience and the OM score for both ease Pakistan and India was .23, significant at the .001 level. Taking into account years of factory experience brought the figure to a nonsignificant .07 for East Pakistan, but in India it remained at the highly significant level of .21. Controlling for mass-media exposure brought the correlelation down to .18 in East Pakistan, but raised it to .29 in India, in both cases still significant at .001. (Inkeles and Smith 1974, Table 15.2).

27. This effect was more apparent in 1963 when the contrast between the countryside and the city was still sharp. In 1963 the regression weight for urban exposure was .17 and for occupational status .16, both statistically significant at better than .05. Although Marsh did not present a strictly comparable regression for 1991, the data he did report suggests that the effect of urban exposure, while still positive, has slipped below the level of statistical significance. (Marsh, op. cit., Table 12-3).

28. The interaction of exposure to the media—which in the case of the Shanghai sample after all meant the official Communist sources—and of exposure to Western influences, on the other hand, is quite complex, and warrants being looked at issue by issue before any general conclusions, if any, can be reached.

29. On Taiwan, for example, occupational status was correlated with education at .58 and with household income at .48 in the 1963 sample and in the 1991 sample the respecive coefficients wer .55 and .37. See Marsh, op. cit, Table 3.3.

CHAPTER SIX: MEASURING IMPACTS OF SOCIAL VALUE AND CHANGE

1. The author would like to thank Mandy Au and Leung Shuk Kwan for their assistance in searching resource materials and the literature for the completion of this article, and Mark Constas and the editors for their critical comments. However, mistakes and shortcomings in this article remain the responsibility of the author.

CHAPTER SEVEN: PROMOTING HUMAN RIGHTS IN EAST ASIAN VALUES: BASIC EDUCATION'S ROLE

1. The author thanks James Williams for his extensive and helpful comments on this paper. (The author is appreciative of the support provided by the Pacific Basin Research Center and the encouragement of its remarkable director, Professor John Montgomery.)

2. In 1992, educators from around the world met to determine a strategy for "Education for All." Basic education was equated with nine years of formal education or its equivalent.

3. With appropriate socialization and preparation to enter a labor force, Japanese and Taiwanese school-children would become effective instruments of Japan's national goals.

4. In "Open Programs" in many schools in the U.S., the students in the same class negotiate with the teacher for an individualized program of study. Accordingly, they are taught and assessed individually.